The Sound of Our Town

The Sound

Brett Milano

# of Our Town

A History of Boston Rock and Roll

Commonwealth Editions ■ *Beverly, Massachusetts*

*To Marlene Silva, my partner, muse, and
permanent nightclub crush*

Library of Congress Cataloging-in-Publication Data
Milano, Brett.
  The Sound of our town : a history of Boston rock and roll / Brett
Milano.
     p. cm.
  Includes index.
  ISBN 978-1-933212-30-2 (alk. paper)
  1. Rock music—Massachusetts—Boston—History and criticism.
  2. Rock groups—Massachusetts—Boston—History. I. Title.
  ML3534.3.M55 2007   2007014924

Cover design by John Barnett / 4 Eyes Design
Interior design by Joyce C. Weston
Cover photo courtesy of Willie Alexander
Printed in the United States.

Commonwealth Editions is an imprint of Memoirs Unlimited, Inc.,
266 Cabot Street, Beverly, Massachusetts 01915.
Visit us on the Web at www.commonwealtheditions.com.

Contents

Introduction

"One-two-three-four-five-six!" So begins the countdown to the Modern Lovers' "Roadrunner," one of Boston's great rock anthems. Though originally recorded in 1971, and later by Jonathan Richman, the band's leader, in 1976, it's still a song that every new Boston band is expected to know, if not actually play. Freewheeling and off center as the city at its best, the words strike a chord with a new crop of college students every year: "I fell in love with the modern world, I got my radio on. . . . Here we go down Route 128!"

I was nowhere near Boston when I first heard that song; and Richman managed to convince me that Route "128 down by the power-lines!" was a really romantic place (this is what they call poetic license). I hit town for graduate studies in September 1980, and I knew I was in a music town when I dumped a few hundred into a checking account at That's My Bank in Kenmore Square and saw a familiar tall figure wearing shades across the room: in town less than an hour and I'd already spotted Ric Ocasek of the Cars.

Across the street stood the Rat, a place I'd heard about when an album called *Live at the Rat* showed up at my college radio station. In broad daylight it didn't look much like the "subterranean den of iniquity" that the announcer Oedipus had promised on the record, but I saw that soon enough. I'd like to say that I saw the heavens open when I first visited the place, but all I saw that night was a pre-fame Joan Jett doing a pretty good set. Still, the place had a way of drawing you in—maybe it was the barbeque sauce. I've lost count of the moments, celebrations and crises alike, that were resolved with one more rendition of Lyres' "Don't Give It Up Now."

Boston's rock scene quite literally began in the shadow of its Puritan heritage, and in some ways we've been kicking against it ever since. Boston was never an industry hub to match Los Angeles or New York, and we don't have quite the history of the southern music capitals. Still, we've beaten the odds often enough: in the seventies with the J. Geils Band, Boston, the Cars, and Aerosmith; in the eighties with the Pixies, 'Til Tuesday, and Aerosmith; in the nineties with Buffalo Tom, the Lemonheads, and Aerosmith; and in the new millennium with the Dresden Dolls, Godsmack, Aerosmith, and a few players to be named later.

Still, Boston is more than the sum of its superstars. Local music fans are a passionate lot, and everyone knows about that one band above all others that should have made it big. The one band that played the life-changing set in front of fifty people, that band whose album just didn't do justice to their earthshaking live show. The only problem is getting two people to agree on which band that was. Suffice it to say that there are hundreds of Boston acts that have taken turns being the greatest unknown band in the world, at least for one night.

Beyond that, there's a certain sensibility that unites Boston's famous bands with the nonfamous ones. "We love our eccentrics here," Oedipus told me recently. "Look at all the people who did make it and it's a pretty eccentric group." It also takes a certain dogged determination to aim for greatness here, knowing that the odds of making it aren't in your favor. Eileen Rose, a local songwriter whose work is full of dark beauty, was thinking this over recently. "You can be the greatest band in the world here all by yourself," she told me. "Rock and roll was born of repression and oppression. There's enough of that Yankee conservatism here to fuel a lot of music."

Any survey representing fifty years of Boston music is bound to be hopelessly incomplete. What I've tried to do here is give a feel for each of the eras, let the musicians tell their stories, and nod to everyone who makes the sound of our town the beautiful mess that it is.

As a local hero, Willie Alexander, once sang, you might "see an old friend or run from a ghost on Mass. Ave." There seem to be a lot of ghosts around lately: you can't go to the Rat or revisit the freak scene at the Tea Party. You won't see Dylan hanging out at Club Passim, you won't find Mark Sandman hanging out in Central Square.

Yet somehow, the scene keeps regenerating. Given the present climate, few cities are able to sustain a grassroots scene driven by clubs, small-label CDs, and college radio; yet this one does. It's not the same modern world, but you can still fall in love with it. Get the radio on, here we go down Route 128.

The Beginning

(1955–1960)

The G-Clefs, the Tune Weavers, the Sophomores: Ka-Ding Dong

Boston rock and roll was born a few blocks away from a Puritan meet-inghouse. In fact, John Eliot Square in Roxbury has at least three his-torical distinctions: in 1632 the Puritans established First Church, still the center of the quiet town square. In 1775 William Dawes began his ride, in conjunction with Paul Revere's, from the same spot. And a mere 180 years later, when something called rock and roll was starting in 1955, a group of neighborhood kids who called themselves the G-Clefs rehearsed their harmonies in the nearby corridors and on street corners.

One of the four brothers who anchored the G-Clefs, Arnold "Ilan-ga" Scott, still lives in that neighborhood, with a fifth-story window looking down on the streets where they used to practice. "This is it. You're standing in the place where it all started," he notes with a the-atrical wave of the hand. But Eliot Square doesn't look like any kind of rock-and-roll ground zero, for Boston or anywhere else. A few blocks away are Malcolm X Boulevard and the Roxbury Community Col-lege, but the only sign of music in Eliot Square comes when a car drives by with some hip-hop blasting from the speakers. As we look out the picture window on this quiet winter afternoon, there's nobody walking on the streets, much less singing on the corner. There are some cars parked in front of the community center, church, and grade school, but the town square is so quiet that the Puritans would probably still recognize it.

Ilanga's house is decorated in muted reds and whites, with some Tchaikovsky sheet music sitting on an upright piano—part of an *Urban Nutcracker* production he's lately been working on with neighborhood youth. A performer since his teens, he's rail-thin, his features delicate and still somewhat youthful. The opera and theater posters on the walls attest to his refined taste and to his decades working in dance and theater. His CD collection is large enough to fill only one shelf; jazz from a college station is on the radio. Nowhere is there any sign of Little Richard, Chuck Berry, or any of the other rock-and-roll greats that his group, the G-Clefs, once shared the stage with.

Yet this is indeed the part of town that produced Boston's first significant rock-and-roll disc: the G-Clefs' "Ka-Ding Dong," which went to number twenty-four on the national charts in 1956. It was a modest hit and a modest start to Boston's rock-and-roll history. Certain records from this era—Little Richard's "Tutti Frutti," Chuck Berry's "Maybellene," Elvis's "Hound Dog"—sounded like musical and cultural explosions from the get-go. "Ka-Ding Dong" wasn't quite as momentous, but it did pack a kick. Echoed drums, cowbell, and a hyperactive guitar solo, topped off by a singer who delivered the nonsense syllables with a knowing wink, as if good taste wouldn't let him say what he was really thinking when his baby called his name. Like many of the best early rock records, it's the sound of teenage hormones running wild. Not a bad start for a city's rock history.

Boston can't claim the exotic backdrop that other musically strong cities can boast. There was no equivalent of New Orleans' Storyville, where whorehouse piano players laid down the jazz and rhythm foundations that would slink their way into rock and roll. Nor did it have a blues mecca like Memphis's Beale Street, where the lines between rhythm and blues and early rock were blurred. Boston didn't even invent the distinctively East Coast sound of doo-wop (as street-corner harmony singing became known), which emanated mainly from New York. What Boston did have was a high concentration of working musicians and an ability to absorb new sounds as soon as they came along.

Appropriately, Boston rock and roll started with a group that wasn't, strictly speaking, that much of a rock-and-roll group. The G-Clefs were more properly a vocal group, one that took as many hints from the

Mills Brothers' traditional pop harmonies as it did from Little Richard's brand of wild abandon. They're also a uniquely long-running band, with no personnel changes since Ilanga replaced Joe Jordan in 1957 (as of 2007, all five members of the fifties lineup—brothers Ilanga, Chris, Ted, and Tim Scott, and Ray Gibson—were still together), that tried on different sounds over the years, but their initial run of singles was enough to evince a multiple personality. On "Ka-Ding Dong" (and its even more eloquent follow-up, "Zing Zang Zoo") they're firmly grounded in lively R&B and jump blues. Yet their second big hit, 1961's "I Understand (Just How You Feel)," was the most wholesome of pop ballads.

The doo-wop era may well have been the only time that Boston's rock and roll ever lived up to the city's refined New England stereotype. Along with "Ka-Ding Dong," the area's biggest fifties hit was "Happy, Happy Birthday Baby" by a Revere-based group, the Tune Weavers. With a melting lead vocal by the late Margo Sylvia, it's a sad slow dance: the singer breaks into tears at her ex-boyfriend's party, even announcing, "Hope I didn't spoil your birthday," on the way out. It's teenage masochism at its finest, but hardly the stuff of parental nightmares.

Likewise, the Sophomores' "Cool Cool Baby"—another Boston doo-wop record that made small waves regionally—is lively and bright but wholesome at the core, its tune bearing a strong resemblance to Bill Haley's novelty hit "See You Later, Alligator." A fellow Roxbury group strongly influenced by white pop, the Sophomores took their inspiration (and adapted their name) from the Four Freshman, the polished midwestern group that inspired the Beach Boys a few years later. Since they didn't have a major national hit, the Sophomores are the underdogs of Boston doo-wop, thus highly rated by critics and aficionados. "No bragging intended, but we were good," points out one of the group's members, Rolle Clements. "We weren't your typical rock-and-roll group, since we came in from the pop side. Nobody was thinking of getting famous; we just sang on street corners to have some fun."

A doo-wopper's territory didn't have to be a street corner, though; it could be a storefront, an alley, or anywhere else with good acoustics and room for an audience. "Franklin Field in Dorchester was always a good spot, because you could fit a lot of kids," recalls Harvey Robbins, who sang in the Roxbury group the Interludes and today promotes revival concerts under the Doo-Wop Hall of Fame banner. "Also, the

G&G, a delicatessen on Blue Hill Avenue where a lot of the Jewish kids would congregate." Robbins sang in the integrated Zorros before joining the all-white Interludes and recalls that black and white kids were in it for the same reason: to express themselves, to stand out in a crowd, and, above all, to meet girls. "We had our own bathing suits, gold ones with 'Interludes' monogrammed in italics. They made us look pretty cool when we walked down the beach."

For early rockers, crossing over from black to white audiences was part of the game: the Memphis producer Sam Phillips famously deduced that he had a white singer with a black sound after Elvis Presley walked in the door. And the Motown impresario Berry Gordy Jr. conquered the world with a roster of black acts that were sharp and polished enough to be unthreatening for white ears (and funky enough for more enlightened tastes). Boston's doo-woppers were a clear pointer to the Motown approach, sounding as close to racially neutral as an early rock act could get. Few other acts would record singles as diverse as the G-Clefs' "All My Trials" and "There Never Was a Dog Like Lad"—the first a traditional gospel-blues song, the second a rather cornball canine ballad—or would even want to.

In short, groups like the G-Clefs and Sophomores found themselves pretty much immune to any racial divisions that sprang up in their often-tense neighborhood. To hear Ilanga describe it, the harsher side of Roxbury—which saw a wave of riots in the wake of Martin Luther King's 1968 assassination and today sees numerous hysterical news stories on gang violence—just didn't exist yet in the calm setting of 1956.

> Yes, there was much racial tension in the fifties, but music was something that brought kids together. In our community there were white and black vocal groups and there was competition but no real rivalry; we all did record hops together. We didn't have televisions, so we socialized on street corners—it was all about getting out of the house and hanging with your clique. That's where the vocal groups emerged—you'd walk down the alleyways where the acoustics were good, and hear five people scatting in the corner. It wasn't until we started touring that we even realized what racism was. Sometimes the curtain would open and the faces would drop when they saw that the G-Clefs were black. Sometimes they'd promote us without a photograph.

It's not that late-fifties Boston didn't have its share of gang battles or James Dean types; it's just that they didn't overlap much with the doo-wop community, and that local rivalries weren't usually based on race. "That *Blackboard Jungle* lifestyle was very real," recalls Harvey Robbins. "One day I was walking down the street, my buddy Lenny pulls up and tells me to get into his car. I look around the backseat, and it's full of guns, chains, brass knuckles. And Lenny says, 'Pick something you're gonna use—we're battling the Quincy Rats because they were looking at our girls.' And I was sitting there terrified, saying, 'Well, maybe they had a reason!' I only got out with my life because the Quincy Rats didn't show up." On the other hand, he never saw a rumble between black and white. "I swear that I grew up with no awareness of color. Our janitor at Roxbury Memorial High was a black guy married to a white woman; no problem. The G-Clefs had us sing in their rehearsal room once; I was only intimidated because they were older and more successful. But they told us we were great."

Indeed, the G-Clefs' musical story is a bit like Elvis Presley's in reverse: Elvis copped a lot of his vocal style from the Baptist church services he snuck into as a boy in Memphis. But the G-Clefs worked out their harmonies in a different environment, at an integrated Catholic church. "We came out of the choir in St. Richard's in Roxbury, an interracial choir," Ilanga recalls. "Integrated choirs weren't so rare at the time; that would happen later. Our neighborhood had a lot of Italian and Irish. We sang the hymns in Latin; the four of us brothers—Ray wasn't a Catholic but he lived next door to us. His acute ear heard that sophisticated sound against the R&B. You can hear the sophistication in our voices that we took from there: We'd say KUH-ding-dong, while other people would say KAH-ding-dong."

Inflections aside, the group's roots in an integrated neighborhood made it a quintessentially New England melting-pot. "We were always dressed so clean, so Bostonian. And our manner of speaking was the same way; we didn't really have the black inflection. Our producer, Jack Gold, had a vision of us from the start. He saw us as a more sophisticated black group. We thought we were going to sing R&B, but his idea was for us to sound more like the white groups, like the Tokens or Bill Haley & the Comets. He saw that we had a distinctive sound, and it wasn't necessarily a black sound."

Even in 1956, national success looked like something that Boston kids could aim for. The jazz clubs made the music business seem accessible; their parents were able to see the likes of Duke Ellington and Sarah Vaughan in the flesh. And Jack Gold was among the budding entrepreneurs who were starting to launch talent in town. After an unproductive session with an early G-Clefs lineup, Gold got a talent-scouting position with a new label, Pilgrim Records, based on Huntington Avenue in Boston. (One of his first signings, the Dee-Jay Quartet, included the singer Joe Smith, who would be running Warner Bros. Records in the sixties.) "Ka-Ding Dong," cowritten by Joe Jordan (the original member whom Ilanga replaced), came from the group's first Pilgrim session and was released in July 1956.

The following December the group passed the acid test by appearing in the legendary DJ Allen Freed's Christmas show at Harlem's famed Apollo Theater—where the famous hook would pull you offstage if you weren't cutting it. "We were dressed well, we knew what our routine was to be, so we got out there and did it. Sounds easy, but we were petrified when we heard the people screaming. But once you hit the stage you transcend the fear: here we are, hurled onstage from the projects, so what do we do? Well, we knew how to sing. So that's what we did." It's what they'd do in different settings for decades to come, initially sharing tour buses with the likes of the Everly Brothers and Paul Anka, then moving on to Vegas in the seventies. In between they even played for the late-sixties hippie crowds, recording some music to match. (Their period single "I Shall Sing" wasn't far from the Afro-funk of the Chambers Brothers and War.) "That was us being a vocal group, knowing that we'd have to revamp for a different audience to succeed. 'What's this gig about? Okay, we'll do it.'"

From the start the G-Clefs were known as "a well-behaved group of kids," and old traditions die hard; Boston's first rock group is still a well-respected outfit that works with underprivileged kids and does annual shows during the Christmas season. "Our friends and family used to cheer for us and make us feel like we were stars. So in our eyes we were always famous, even before we left Roxbury. Our audience was always the people in our community, people we knew from grade school and family. So you get the spotlights and the hit records, but your community keeps you grounded. It wasn't like growing up in the Jackson family." He gets wistful while looking once more out the window, pondering how the neighborhood has changed. "It used to be a different world. What makes it nice is when I walk the streets and see people who've lived here for a while. They realize what was here."

Gene Maltais: Gangwar!

But rock-and-roll decadence has a way of coming out of the woodwork. Even while the G-Clefs were doing their community proud, a more depraved brand of rock and roll was just under the radar. As inner-city Boston was alight with elegant harmonies and smooth dance steps, one guy in the respectable town of Concord, New Hampshire, was coming up with this:

Splash of blood and thunder—Man, are we gonna fight!
The Sharks have got us under, and man, that just ain't right!
Jackets of black leather, pipes and hobnail boots,
Gonna be stormy weather, and there'll be blood on their suits . . .
We're gonna rumble, gonna roar,
Gonna storm up and start this gangwar!

Parents across New England would have shuddered if they'd known that a song like Gene Maltais's "Gangwar" was even being written, much less pressed to vinyl. This, after all, was the era when a national hit like Link Wray's "Rumble" (an instrumental, no less) was banned from many radio stations simply because of its title. Fortunately, they didn't have to find out about "Gangwar": along with Maltais's other recordings, the disc was not a hit and didn't draw much notice—at least not until decades later, when the crazed record collectors who love primitive rock and roll dug the records up and reissued them on compact disc. But the very existence of a record like "Gangwar" is proof that the sound of rockabilly—the hopped-up style that grew out of country music in the South—had gotten as far as New England. Along with "Gangwar," Maltais's handful of singles included the spooky and sexy "Raging Sea" and the self-explanatory "Lovemaking"—both testament to the darker teenage passions lurking behind the respectable surface of the Boston area in the Ozzie and Harriet era.

Boston and New Hampshire's rockabilly scene was strictly small time. No major stars or national hits came out of the circuit, but the ascent of Elvis meant that anyone who looked or sounded vaguely like him could make a small wave; a slap bass and a ducktail haircut could get you at least an opening slot on a larger rock-and-roll show. New

Gene Maltais after hitting Nashville. (Courtesy Jack Warner)

England's rockabilly records by the likes of Maltais, Sonny Lane & the Downbeats, and the Satellites have been championed by collectors over the years; an early-nineties CD series called *The Raging Teens* brought some of them to light. Even today there are bands in Boston that play that style much as it was played a half century ago. One of the best, the Raging Teens, even took its name from those discs.

At this point, there was a clear stylistic division between black and white rockers: the former did doo-wop, the latter patterned themselves after Elvis. And though there wasn't much hostility between the two camps, there wasn't a lot of blending, either. "I remember seeing the Genies, a black group who had a small hit with 'Who's That Knocking,' " recalls Jack Warner, a longtime collector who put *The Raging Teens* compilations together. "The audience was mainly white, and at one point the group started dancing with the girls in the audience. And I thought, Hmm, this is different. It was an unusual thing that we could accept. I think the kids were seeing more mixing at those shows than they were used to in their suburban schools; it was one of the first chances they had to get together. And you realized that was what they were probably afraid of in the South."

Meanwhile, the white kids who emulated Elvis at least had a good chance of getting a date. "It was a different version of being the big man on campus, a way of elevating your status a little," Warner notes. Thanks in part to the sheer audacity of his records, Gene Maltais is the best known of the lot, and his story is no ordinary rock-and-roll saga: even in 1956, it was rare for a suburban nobody to hitchhike his way to Nashville and have a record contract three days later.

Still, when the man himself is tracked down—at his current home in Florida, where he's "enjoying life and going to the beach every day"—it's hard to separate the myth from the reality. To hear him tell it, Maltais was always one step away from rock stardom, and he would have gotten there if not for his near-obsessive dislike of contracts— even today he swears he's never put his name on any business agreement, claiming, "My father told me never to sign anything I didn't understand"—and his habit of mouthing off to potential employers and music legends alike.

It's true enough, however, that he essentially talked and pushed his way into a recording contract during the early days of rock and roll. And it wasn't every late-fifties youth who responded to compliments about his singing by deciding to hitchhike his way from New Hampshire to Nashville. "It was summertime and it was boring," he says by way of explanation. "We didn't have any drugs and cocaine back then; the most that could happen was you worked out of town as a lifeguard. I used to hang out at the Puritan Restaurant in Concord, just dropping a nickel in the jukebox and singing along. People started telling me, 'You're pretty good, you ought to make a record,' so that's what I went out to do. I just went to the highway and stuck my thumb out."

Since this was a kinder and gentler era, aspiring rock stars were still allowed to barge into publishing and label offices and sing a few bars. So Maltais hit Music Row armed with "Crazy Baby," an upbeat rock tune, and "The Raging Sea," which he thought would be a perfect ballad for Elvis. Unfortunately, not everyone in Nashville was going to respond well to a kid with a ducktail, a guitar, a couple of unpolished songs, and an attitude. "I got thrown out of everybody's office. A lot of them said I sucked. Actually," he corrects himself, "they said I was terrible, because back in those days suck wasn't invented!"

After three days of frustration, he knocked on one last door, where he met a friendly secretary who was willing to give him a shot. "I'm there crying to her, 'I got these songs and nobody wants to hear them.' So she pushes a button and says, 'Webb, you want to come out here for a minute?'" This was the great honky-tonk singer Webb Pierce, who nodded his head and passed Maltais over to a talent scout from Decca, the label he recorded for. "This guy, Paul Cohen, comes in and hears me and he says, 'I like it, let's cut the kid.' That made me pretty scared. I thought it meant they were going to cut me with a knife."

Mighty relieved when he realized they meant cutting a record, Maltais received fifty dollars for a nice hotel room, spent a buck to stay at the YMCA, and pocketed the rest. The recording session wound up featuring a handful of major names: Owen Bradley (who did landmark sessions with Patsy Cline) handled the production, the singer and producer extraordinaire Anita Kerr helped with arrangements, and the top-flight session player Hank Garland played guitar. The result was a cool, rockin' platter that Elvis's fans would have related to. Maltais says he enjoyed cutting "Crazy Baby," but things got less comfortable when he realized they also needed a B-side—on which they tried to turn him into more of a sensitive teen idol. "Paul Cohen wanted a ballad, so I did one I hadn't really finished writing, 'Deep River Blues.' He was looking for a cross of Johnny Ray and Chuck Berry, which would have been a new style. So they had me singing it, crying it, all this crap; and after seven takes I'm about ready for the graveyard. Finally Anita Kerr handed me this black stuff she took out of a Coca-Cola machine. It was Karo syrup, and it kept my voice from breaking down."

That session was enough to burn him out on Nashville. So instead of sticking around for his record to get released, he continued his cross-country adventures. In Pennsylvania he talked himself into the office of the rock pioneers Bill Haley & the Comets. "In those days you could walk into any place if you knew what to tell them. So I told them I had a record coming out, that I was stranded, and that I wanted to write them a song. So they paid me twenty-five dollars, but I never bothered to write the song."

In New York he met up with the Sharks, the real-life street gang that inspired "Gangwar." "They were cool guys so I decided to write a song about them. That's where I saw the chains and the hobnail boots. It wasn't supposed to be progang or proviolence; there was a verse at the end that said, 'No more gangwar, no way we're gonna do this stuff.' But I just forgot to put that verse on the record." And back in New Hampshire he issued that song on his own label, and he had his first, unsuccessful experience with payola. "This radio DJ said he'd play my song for fifty dollars. And I'm thinking, great—that must mean they're going to play my song and give me fifty dollars besides."

During his short stint as an aspiring rock-and-roll star, Maltais managed a few scrapes with industry bigwigs. A rehearsal for Ted Mack's *Amateur Hour* (the *American Idol* of its day) didn't quite go as planned. "He said I was terrible, so I told him to go F himself and walked out." He met the singing star Connie Francis in Nashville, but he declined to work with her because he didn't approve of her boyfriend, the late Bobby Darin. "She kept telling me how much she was falling in love with this guy, and I wound up hating the guy just because of what I was hearing her say about him." And before leaving Nashville, he got on the wrong side of another country star: "Paul Cohen played me this record by Mel Tillis, telling me he was sure it would be a hit. I said it was the worst song I ever heard in my life. Then Mel Tillis turns around, all crazy and out of breath. And I'm saying, 'Calm down, will ya? It's only a song, for Chrissakes.' That was my problem, I always told people exactly what I was thinking."

Realizing he wasn't cut out for mainstream success, he traveled a bit more before joining the police force back in Manchester, New Hampshire. Meanwhile, that "Crazy Baby" 45 that young Gene had made during his trip to Nashville did indeed wind up coming out—but alas, Decca threw its promotional money behind another, more commercial singer it had just signed. "They told me, 'We got good news and bad news. We're putting your record out but we're not going to promote it.' The problem was that they had just signed this guy out of Texas. The guy meant nothing to me. Buddy somebody." As fate would have it, Buddy Holly made a more substantial contribution to rock-and-roll history. But Gene Maltais was the first of the gifted eccentrics who'd move Boston's sound for decades to come.

The Surf Era to the British Invasion

(1961–1966)

Arnie Ginsburg: Woo Woo

Gather rooound, everybody!
Cos you're about to hear,
The show that's gonna make you smile from ear to ear.
It's Arnie Ginsburg on the Night Train show!

He plays the old and new,
The swinging and the blue,
He plays all the records especially for you.
It's Arnie Ginsburg on the Night Train show!

So come on Arnie . . . Let's goo—oo—o!

The late fifties and early sixties are a time forever associated with surf, fast cars, and AM radio. In Boston we at least had the AM radio—and if you were around town at the time, you knew the above jingle by heart. For the full effect you'd have to imagine it sung by a quartet of pretty crude rock-and-roll voices, complete with thick South Boston accent ("He plays all da rekkids . . ."), and Arnie adding his sound effects—train whistles, slide whistles, hooters, and whatever else he could get his hands on—after every line. Appearing seven nights a week on WMEX-AM, Arnie "Woo Woo" Ginsburg (the nickname came from his trademark sound effects) was Boston's favorite rock-and-roll DJ—and in this era, that made you more famous than many of the performers. The show carried clear across the state, so kids in the suburbs, towns, and cities got their nightly fix from the same place.

Boston in the early sixties wasn't quite the Los Angeles of *American Graffiti*—there was no place to surf, since there is no surf in Boston Harbor, and, besides, it's too cold ten months of the year. And our cruising possibilities were strictly limited: we had no Sunset Strip or Hollywood Boulevard. But some experiences were universal: you could still cruise to the beach; it just meant going to Revere or Nantasket. The latter seaside town was home to the Surf Ballroom, one of the first local spots to provide a steady home for live rock. And you could get the drive-in experience at unlikely places like the Adventure Car Hop on Route 1 in Saugus.

Cruise down Route 1 these days—strip malls, chain restaurants, car dealerships, plastic cows (much like middle America, in fact, except maybe for the plastic cows)—and you wouldn't believe it ever had a teenage hangout. But the Adventure Car Hop had a hip image, decent burgers, and attractive waitresses—everything you'd really need on a summer night in 1961 or 1962. The hip image stemmed from a handful of promotions the drive-in did on Ginsburg's show. When the Twist was the craze, it offered a Twist Burger, topped with twisted onion rings. For a time you could get a Beatle wig with every burger; once it even gave away a "Chinese back scratcher," one of those long sticks with the fake hand at the end. ("Confucius say, man who have itch on back needs back scratcher," said the ads. Yes, this was a less culturally sensitive era.)

But their biggest hit was probably the Ginsburger, a two-for-one hamburger that was served on a 45-rpm record—a current chart hit, no less. And, yes, there was a napkin between the burger and the vinyl, to prevent grease from getting in the grooves. There was a second Adventure on Route 9 in Natick, but the promo stunts, complete with occasional live broadcasts, made the Saugus one the place to be. It was like going to a drive-in movie: you'd pull up to the window and give your order, then hang out in your car while girls in cheerleader-type outfits brought the burgers. "Cars were pretty cheap back then, so kids would get their license, buy an old car, and take it somewhere like that," recalls Arnie Ginsburg, now retired and living in Maine. "I heard about kids who'd make their parents drive seventy-five miles just to have a burger in Saugus. It was a fun place to hang out, take your date, meet your friends, and get a little indigestion."

Both nationally and locally, the late fifties and early sixties—between the dawn of doo-wop and the start of the British Invasion—are remembered as a dead time for rock and roll, a period that saw Buddy Holly die in a plane crash, Elvis get drafted, and a bunch of teen idols take over. But history tends to sell this era short. Yes, it gave rock some growing pains but it also produced a ton of great music, from the Beach Boys and the Everly Brothers, to Dion and the Four Seasons, to the first stirrings of Motown. Boston was starting to heat up as well: long before the Beatles took hold, Boston had its first great, self-contained rock-and-roll band in the Rockin' Ramrods, and its first homegrown rock star in the Revere native Freddy "Boom Boom" Cannon. One of Boston's most enduring hits came in 1962, when Bobby "Boris" Pickett, a Somerville native, turned his Boris Karloff imitation, a good beat, and a few horror-movie jokes into the number one song "The Monster Mash"—which is still guaranteed to get airplay every Halloween.

Arnie Ginsburg wasn't the only major DJ Boston produced in this era—Joe Smith had a successful run on WBOS before becoming a hotshot record executive—but in many ways he was the perfect voice for Boston. Neither slick nor overly goofy, he came across like an affable older-brother type who'd tell some corny jokes to get your attention but then bend your ear about a great record he'd just discovered. Smith was heavier on R&B records, but Ginsburg went for the more youthful rock-and-roll sounds. A quickie film from the era, *Disk-o-Tek Holiday,* shows Arnie in his element at the radio studio—but instead of being an exotic hipster like Wolfman Jack in *American Graffiti,* he's there with his pullover sweater and horn-rims, a Buddy Holly of the airwaves. "I compared myself to Ed Sullivan, the most unlikely person for the job," he says. "My voice was weird, and I didn't change my name—at the time, anyone with a name like Arnie Ginsburg who wanted to get on the radio would probably have changed it to some Anglo-Saxon name."

Arnie started his show on WBOS in 1956, when some thought that rock and roll was still a passing fad. His show was on from nine to midnight, and it evolved from some of the less hip programming WBOS was doing. "It came out of Doris Day and Perry Como; we were a Top-40 station. At that time I was one of the few people in Boston playing Elvis heavily." Moving to WMEX in 1959, he worked from a studio on Brookline Avenue near Fenway Park—the perfect place to snag kids off the street to sing along with the jingles and commercials. "Sometimes I'd take the mike out into the street. The show was allowed to be ad-libbed, so I could use the audience to do part of the commercial. I really loved rock and roll, so I would get every new record that came out. You could tell in the first ten seconds whether a record was a hit. One city I always kept an eye on was Cleveland. To me we were very similar because they had a mix with Irish, Jewish, and black populations like Boston does. So a lot of hits came out of those two cities."

Plenty of national hits were broken on Ginsburg's show, including an English record years in advance of the Beatles. "When the English groups were starting out, I saw a title on their chart: 'Does Your Chewing Gum Lose Its Flavor (on the Bedpost Overnight).' I had a telephone call from England on the air, and we were talking about that song title; I was sure it was a joke. But they sent it over a few days later and I put it on the air." That record, by a U.K. favorite, Lonnie Donegan, went on to the U.S. Top Ten. Another on-air stunt involving a new record had an unexpected outcome: a minor West Coast hit, "Louie Louie" by the Kingsmen, made its way to Boston—and with the off-key singer, out-of-tune band, and blown cue after the instrumental break, it struck Arnie as one of the worst records he'd ever heard. So he of course played it on his show that night. "Next day I come in, and we're getting all these calls from record stores—'What's this Louie Louie?' It very quickly became the number one song. I'd played it as a joke, but the more I heard it the more I liked it."

During his heyday, Ginsburg managed to be everywhere at once; on Friday and Saturday nights he'd be hosting record hops at the same time he was on the air (through the miracle of prerecording—his shows were live Monday through Thursday). Record hops could happen anywhere—at high school gyms, town halls, church basements. Sometimes there'd be a famous DJ to spin (Ginsburg did a monthly one at Somerville

High); sometimes a local band would be there, usually one that specialized in covers of whatever was on the charts.

Going to the Surf in Nantasket was more of a night out, a longer drive to see bigger names in a bigger venue. The crowds there were usually well dressed—the guys in jackets, the girls in full-skirted dresses—and the setting was a classic, cavernous dance hall, complete with a gold curtain behind the stage, a relic from the big-band era. Owned by the South Shore's prominent Spence family, the Surf was a no-alcohol teen hangout; the door opened at seven and you'd be out by midnight. Ginsburg's weekly record hops were a favorite social attraction; the bands would often be local cover bands, and teens went mainly for the party and the chance to meet girls or guys from other schools.

Some musical history was made at these hops as well. In 1963 the Surf was, appropriately enough, the second stop on the Beach Boys' first East Coast tour. (The first was a matinee the same day at the Music Hall downtown, where the group played in tandem with a fashion show from one of the local department stores.) Ginsburg recalls it was the biggest crowd his hops ever drew—Roy Orbison, who played there around the time "Oh, Pretty Woman" was charting, was a close second.

A favorite style at the time was surf instrumentals—fast, flashy tunes whose skittering guitars and wailing saxes suggested the thrill of catching a wave. Few realized at the time that the inventor of this quintessentially Californian sound, the guitarist Dick Dale, had strong Boston roots. Born Richard Monsour to a Lebanese father and Polish mother, Dale was a Quincy boy who moved west at seventeen. The surf guitar sound was in part adapted from the Middle Eastern music he'd grown up with.

The Rockin' Ramrods, Freddy Cannon: Where the Action Is

One regular band at those hops was the Newton-based Rockin' Ramrods, arguably the first notable self-contained band (as opposed to the all-vocal doo-wop groups) in Boston's history. Even on the small handful of records they made, the sheer mania of the sound is strong enough to mark them as a precursor to punk and garage rock. But what you're really hearing is the sound of a band with professional chops that honed its skills playing for hundreds of teenage audiences with short attention spans. The Ramrods began like hundreds of frat bands across the county, doing mainly surf instrumentals. It was the record-hop circuit and ballrooms like the Surf that taught the Ramrods to give the kids what they wanted: when spy movies were the rage, they did a priceless novelty single called "Don't Fool with Fu Manchu," a "Louie Louie" rip-off with more of that sixties political incorrectness ("He'll slip poison in your fortune cookie!"). By the time the Beatles hit, the Ramrods were well-oiled and ready to take on the Mersey-beat sound. The group even lasted into the psychedelic era, making some records they're less proud of.

"We were just suburban kids, borrowing the guitar player's mom's car so we could get to gigs," recalls their drummer, Jesse Henderson. "For me personally, I was enthralled with the drums; I used to hang around drum shops when I was a kid. I wasn't in it to meet girls. That came with the territory and it was fine, cool. But I really just wanted to play." The more they played the teenage circuit, the more raucous their sound got. "We probably weren't even that good—no, we were okay, and I took pride in the drum parts. But there was a certain energy back then that people remember. We got a lot of the records we were listening to—after the Beatles happened we wasted no time in saying, 'Okay, we're songwriters. And we're growing our hair.'" The Fu Manchu record was made for a long-forgotten spy movie. "None of us were pleased about that one, but they told us we'd make a million dollars if we recorded it."

After Ginsburg had them open for the Rolling Stones at Boston Garden in 1965, the Ramrods continued with the Stones for an East Coast tour. "I think we were just in awe of it all. I remember us looking at each other and going, 'Jeepers, they're not as tall as they look on their albums.' We talked to them a lot on the airplane, but Mick and Keith mainly kept to themselves. Brian Jones was always eager for conversation, though. It was all pretty bare bones. We'd take a regular passenger bus, go to the venue, and play, then sleep back at the hotel."

Now a longtime studio engineer, Henderson remembers mainly how technically slipshod those sixties tours were. "I've got to tell you one thing about those tours: there was no sound reinforcement like there is today. Maybe there was one speaker in the middle of the arena with the scoreboard, and one or two mikes hanging down onstage. And so much screaming you could barely hear a thing you were playing. We kept looking at each other and cracking up. There were screaming girls even for us; I think it was just what they did—peer pressure." In fact,

Henderson's fondest memory of that tour has nothing to do with the Stones. "Patti LaBelle & the Bluebelles were on that tour, and Cindy Birdsong [later a Supreme] was with them. I was pretty sweet on Cindy; she was just a knockout."

Despite their frat-rock roots, the Ramrods had their greatest success in the early part of the British Invasion. They were savvy enough to record a couple of Lennon-McCartney songs, including one ("I'll Be on My Way") that the Beatles hadn't released themselves. The closest thing they had to a national hit, the original "Bright Lit Blue Skies," had a melodic and very English sound, a bit like the Yardbirds, though Henderson says it was really inspired by a Motown soul record. "If you listen to that, it's basically 'Heatwave' by Martha & the Vandellas. We did a lot of things like that. Another record we had, 'She Lied,' was our rip-off of the Dave Clark Five. We wrote that in the car on the way to the studio, just so we could walk in and say, 'Okay, here's a ditty.'" The producer of that single was Freddy Cannon, who released it on his Bon Bon label and often used the Ramrods as his live backup band.

Freddy Cannon—a nice Italian boy from Revere, born Frederico Picariello—made the record-hop circuit as well. Like Arnie Ginsburg, he was less an Elvis type than a teenage everyman whose appeal lay partly in the sheer enthusiasm he put across. And he also had a thing for trademark sounds: the more *whooo's!* he inserted into a record, the better a song it was going to be. According to the late rock historian Cub Koda, those *whooo's!* were the idea of his producers, Bob Crewe and Frank Slay, who needed a way to fill in the holes on one of his first records—but if it works, it works. (Crewe also scored his share of hits with the Four Seasons.) According to some of his contemporaries, Cannon became Boston's first rock star in part because he worked harder than anyone else.

He also made some important friends early in his career. Once Crewe and Slay were in his court, Cannon spent more time in Philadelphia, where he hooked up with Dick Clark, who both put Cannon on *American Bandstand* and had him sing the theme for his next major TV show (the mid-sixties weekday happening *Where the Action Is*). "He was very driven, with a good attitude," Arnie Ginsburg recalls. "If something wasn't going well, he'd come out and make the best of it." "He was a happy guy, man," adds Jesse Henderson. "You could tell he was having fun. After he moved to Philadelphia, his mother, Annette, used to come to see us at the Surf, and lo and behold, we found out that she wanted to manage us."

Cannon's mom also wrote the original version of a song that got reworked into his first hit, "Tallahassee Lassie"—a prototype for the raucous, party-starting records that would make his career. But though he recorded the song "Boston Is My Home" on his first album, most of his hits—"Okefenokee," "Chattanooga Shoe Shine Boy," "Way Down Yonder in New Orleans" (an update of the old Al Jolson number)—celebrated other locales. Most famously of all, his hit "Palisades Park" became the unofficial theme song of one of New Jersey's most famous amusement spots. The author of that tune never wrote or recorded another hit song, but he soon became famous in another line of work: Chuck Barris became the game-show impresario and Gong Show mastermind. Cannon's hits would get revived over the years; the Beach Boys did "Tallahassee Lassie" and the Ramones covered "Palisades Park."

But Freddy Cannon's greatest record doesn't get played as often now. A hit in 1963, "Abigail Beecher" lays out every high school guy's fantasy: having the hippest woman in town as your history teacher. As Freddy notes to a suitably hormone-driven beat, she's a smart lady who knows how to rock: "She knows her history from A to Z, she can teach the Monkey and the Watusi!" No wonder the history class just keeps getting bigger, especially after Abigail shows up at a PTA meeting driving an XKE, carrying a surfboard, and wearing blue sunglasses.

"Abigail Beecher" was the first example of a type who'd turn up in many Boston songs through the years: the intellectual, slightly mysterious rock-and-roll woman. Every era would have its Abigail; the Cars and the Modern Lovers would write songs about women like her. Before long she'd be picking up a guitar herself.

Enter the Fab Four

On February 9, 1964, *The Ed Sullivan Show* featured a couple of bad comics, the cast of *Oliver!,* a trapeze act, and the Beatles. The world changed, and not because of the trapeze act. Garage doors around the country started opening the next morning, as Beatles-inspired kids set up instruments, learned three chords, and proceeded to rock.

The Beatles' invasion didn't single-handedly create the sixties scene in Boston, but it did help to speed things along. By 1963 there were already coffeehouses at Boston University where young combos were finding their sound, and frat houses where anyone who could pull off "Louie Louie" had a guaranteed gig. Kenmore Square already had the Rathskeller, the same place that became a punk hotbed in the late seventies. Even prep schools turned out their share of rock-and-roll bands: it was nothing unusual for prep school kids to pick up guitars between stints with the debate club or the football team. Typical of the era were the Electras, a band out of St. Paul's School in Concord, New Hampshire. Inspired by the Ventures and other instrumental surf combos of the day, they made a small career of playing campus mixers and even released an album. The Electras' musical career never amounted to much, but their bass player—a gangly lad named John Kerry—had some success in a different line of work.

If you grew up in the sixties, you were just as likely to discover rock and roll in a wholesome spot like a church hall, a community center, or one of the many large ballrooms that sprang up mainly around beach and resort areas—the Surf Ballroom on Nantasket Beach and the Broad Cove Teen Haven in Hingham, to name two. Rock wasn't yet the stuff of smoky nightclubs and packed arenas; it was a show that your parents could drop you off to see in broad daylight. A popular local band would be able to jam a thousand kids into one of these clubs on a Saturday afternoon. In this context, the music didn't have to be artistic or staggeringly original; it just needed to have a good beat and be easy to dance to.

Thus, playing nothing but cover songs—other people's hits—wasn't the taboo that it became in more serious eras of rock. This was also the heyday of that long-forgotten mid-sixties ritual, the battle of the bands. If you wanted to blow your school rivals off the stage, it didn't hurt to play a song that everybody already knew. "It wasn't like the seventies, when people started making their own personal statements," notes Erik Lindgren, a musician who's reissued many lost sixties tapes on his Arf Arf label. "You were a dance band, a functional rock band—'Hey, we're having a party, let's get someone to play.' Even if you made your own record, you'd do that in the studio and do the covers when you went out to play."

The British Invasion hit Boston harder and faster than it did most American cities. Other cities were into different sounds. Seattle was still taking a cue from Little Richard and other early rockers. Detroit had its soul music, with the Motown label already up and running. And Los Angeles had Dick Dale, the Beach Boys and other surf-related acts to emulate. But after the Fab Four hit, the vast majority of Boston bands immediately started evincing a Beatles (and later, a Rolling Stones and Animals and Who) influence. Credit geographical proximity, or Boston's enduring intellectualism. "People in Iowa don't have the kind of intellectual stimulation that they had here," Lindgren notes. "Boston had more sophisticated songwriting, more experimenting with chords. And you had more cases where guy loses girl and writes a moody, minor-key ballad. You had the college students, they were searching. And whatever trend was going on in England, the New England kids worshipped it."

What the Beatles or the Stones provided was a powerful double kick: a sound that the kids immediately fell in love with, and a reminder of how easy it was to get started. "There was such a buzz in my school the week of that *Ed Sullivan Show*," recalled Brad Delp, later the singer of the platinum-selling band Boston. "I got a guitar that week, and so did a lot of my friends who are still playing. Before that all we had was Little League, and I knew I wasn't going anywhere with that."

Of course, not everyone who tried to sound like the Beatles came anywhere close. And no roundup of New England teen groups would be complete without a mention of the most inept—and in some eccentric quarters, the most loved—of them all. The Shaggs were three sisters, Dorothy (Dot), Helen, and Betty Wiggin, from Fremont, New Hampshire, who simply weren't cut out to be musicians. They didn't look like pop stars, either: one of the few Shaggs' photos shows all three sisters looking rather plain in scraggly red hair and Sunday dresses. Yet their father apparently strong-armed them into going for it. He paid for their instruments, drilled them during rehearsals (not too well, by all recorded evidence), and, one fateful day, drove them to Revere, where they recorded an album dubbed *Philosophy of the World*—both starting and wrapping up the whole thing on March 9, 1969. What they came up with truly boggles the mind: nobody else who's ever tried to sound like a normal pop group has failed so spectacularly. The drums and bass wander around without getting close to an actual rhythm; the sense of melody is either bizarre or nonexistent; vocals barely stay on the wrong key, let alone the right one. Even the early Beatles sound they were attempting was a few years out of date by then.

By any reasonable standard it's terrible; and yet somehow it's also wonderful. Dot's strangely accented voice sounds more like a wizened Appalachian woman's than a New England teenager's. The attempted tunes are quite haunting, and the lyrics—all offhand musings on boyfriends, parents, and pets—are unusually warm-hearted, even for the sixties. Though it had no effect whatsoever at the time of its release, its legend seems to have grown by the year. The maverick composer Frank Zappa famously remarked that the Shaggs were better than the Beatles. (He made that statement on Boston's WBCN, one of the few stations that kept the album around.) The girls' air of mystery added to their allure: not many outside their hometown ever saw them perform, and after their gigs at the Fremont Town Hall and a nearby nursing home dried up, the sisters went back to small-town obscurity—at least for a while.

In early 1999 (thirty years after its original release) *Philosophy of the World* was reissued on the multinational RCA Records label. Though it wasn't quite Shaggs-mania, there was a lengthy *New Yorker* article in the wake of the CD's release, soon followed by the optioning of film rights to the Wiggenses' story and a one-off reunion performance at New York City's Bowery Ballroom, the last at the behest of their fellow cult heroes NRBQ (whose leader, Terry Adams, is a longtime fan). Adams recently commented, "You can tell Dot, Helen, and Betty came from a great family—it comes through in their loving, unique music. The Shaggs are genuine originals, unaffected, honest, and true." And though Adams's ardent admiration of the sisters' music is clear, his support has been longer and stronger than almost anyone else's. He gave *Philosophy of the World* its first reissue on his band's Red Rooster label in 1980, followed that with an archival collection of studio recordings and rehearsal tapes call *Shaggs' Own Thing* in 1982, and saw to it that both LPs together made it to compact disc in 1988.

Oddly, the mid-sixties is the only era when Boston didn't produce any major national successes. Between Freddy Cannon's pre-Beatles hits and the late-sixties rise of the J. Geils Band, Boston made almost no dents in the national charts. The nearest national commotion came out of Newport, Rhode Island, where a family group called the Cowsills became teen idols. The first album's cover photo of the group stretched out on its Newport lawn hung on many a teenager's bedroom wall. Originally a Beatles-inspired group of four brothers, the

Cowsills expanded their lineup and changed their image with the addition of their mom and their eight-year-old sister, Susan. Clean-cut and fresh-faced they may have been, and wholesome enough to make commercials for the American Dairy Association. But the Cowsills' harmony-driven hits (the biggest were "The Rain, the Park and Other Things" and the theme from the then-controversial musical *Hair*) had a subversive element of free love and flower power. In 1971 some television producers would base *The Partridge Family* on a slicker version of the Cowsills' sound and image.

One Boston combo that nearly made it nationwide was Teddy & the Pandas, whose two local hits ("Once upon a Time" and "We Can't Go on This Way") earned the group national tours with the Beach Boys and Gene Pitney. But the closest Massachusetts came to a sixties hit was one underground classic by the Barbarians, who asked the musical question on every Beatles-era parent's mind: "Are You a Boy (Or Are You a Girl?)." A truly motley crew, the Barbarians were a long-haired, antisocial-looking bunch with the crowning touch of a one-handed drummer: Victor "Moulty" Moulton had lost his left hand in a fireworks accident at fourteen; he managed to play pretty well with a drumstick fitted into his hook. Few would have guessed that these tough-looking guys hailed from Provincetown, the Portuguese fishing village turned artist's colony at the tip of Cape Cod. Provincetown has been associated for many years with a strongly gay culture—it's a shame that none of the town's drag-queen performers have thought to revive the Barbarians' greatest hit.

Boston did produce one timeless anthem—sort of. The Standells' "Dirty Water" will forever be known as Boston's theme song and as one of the great sixties garage records to boot. The only problem is that it wasn't a Boston record. The group that sang, "Oh Boston, you're my home!" was really from Los Angeles, and their writer and producer, Ed Cobb, was a Texan who wrote the song in honor of his Boston-born girlfriend. There have been a few true Boston "Dirty Waters" since then: the Lines got some early-eighties airplay with a metal version, and Peter Wolf sang it with Bruce Springsteen during a 2002 encore at the Fleet Center (since renamed TDBanknorth Garden). For the most part, though, playing "Dirty Water" in Boston is like playing "New York, New York" in New York City—so obvious that relatively few people do it.

The Remains, the Lost: Don't Look Back

Boston during the sixties is best remembered for two of the city's greatest near misses: the Remains and the Lost. Both were signed to big national record labels (Epic and Capitol, respectively); and both had front men (the Remains' Barry Tashian, the Lost's Willie Alexander) who went on to careers still active today. Tellingly, both bands currently have more music in print than they ever released while together. The Remains got as far as *The Ed Sullivan Show* and seemed to have everything it took for the big time—good looks, sharp suits, killer songs, and legendary live shows. Everything, that is, except that all-important hit single.

Why they never got one remains a mystery, though it may be for the same reason the Remains would inspire young punks for decades to come: their best records were just too wild to be commercial. Listen to the Remains' greatest non-hit, "Don't Look Back," and you're hearing raging post-teenage hormones in all their glory: Tashian testifies like a manic preacher, the band races each other to the next riff, and there are wild screams in the background. This was just the sound you got from a mix of raw talent, Beatles and sixties soul influences, and a whole lot of abandon.

Nowadays you'd call the Remains a garage band, but that term didn't exist in 1965. "It is a good description of how bands like us came together and practiced, though," Barry Tashian says today. "We started playing together at Boston University, so we thought we'd make some extra money by carrying our gear across the street. That was when the Rathskeller opened up its space downstairs—a stage made of boards on crates, picnic tables, a jukebox, a few beer signs. It really seemed huge back then. We bought some speakers, these huge metal horns that were meant for public address systems or football games. They must have been horribly high-ended, but they cut."

It was a life-changing trip to England that caused Tashian to form the band. Spending the summer of 1963 as a traveling student, he wound up in London and had the quintessential sixties rock experience. "I went down to a club called the Café des Artistes on Earl's Court Road. Saw a band play and can't even remember their name, but I had my mind blown. They were doing Eddie Cochran songs, [Muddy Waters's] 'Got My Mojo Working,' songs like that. I had this vision

The Remains in New York, 1966. (Courtesy Barry Tashian)

where all the guys onstage were having a conversation with their instruments, all playing to a central focal point. I saw this blue light—there were blue lights on the stage and I was sitting toward the edge of the stage facing a chair. It was very dramatic, kind of a visionary experience for me, and it's the real reason I started the Remains."

Drawing his bandmates (Vern Miller on bass, Bill Briggs on piano, and Chip Damiani on drums) from bands playing Boston University, Tashian went to work. Rocking in the mid-sixties meant a lot of college and fraternity gigs, playing with crummy equipment, and occasionally schlepping your own gear. But it also meant that the good bands could stand out in a hurry, since there was so little competition at the time. Within a year of Tashian's fateful trip to England, the Remains had picked up management and a record deal; they signed with Epic Records, whose sister label, Columbia, recorded Bob Dylan and Johnny Cash. They played *The Ed Sullivan Show* in December 1965, after Sullivan himself caught their show at Trude Heller's club in New York City. It also didn't hurt that one of Tashian's BU friends was Don Law Jr., whose father was a producer at Columbia Records. Helping the Remains get signed was the first of many smart career moves Law would make.

Yet in Tashian's view, the essence of the Remains was in those early club and frat house shows; to some extent the rest was downhill. "That's what it was all about for us. Having that feeling of teamwork and being aware of each other, not just looking out at the audience and playing your parts. Looking at each other and being able to communicate, that was the magic. The fraternity party was one of the things that got us going. It gave us the idea that the wilder you could be, the better. We'd always try to work everything up to a climax—some were better than others, but every song had to have one. We'd take a song like 'Got My Mojo Working' and turn it into an instrumental jam that could go on however long, depending on the night. We were having a ball."

Making records was a little more problematic. "Hey, we didn't know anything about making a hit record. Maybe we tried to do too much, putting too much energy into it, instead of focusing on a simple commercial idea that people could get their heads around. The energy you hear on 'Don't Look Back'—that was simple frustration with how badly we wanted to have a hit record. We just figured we could do it if we put the right enthusiasm in." The Sullivan show is a much less pleasant memory than the frat houses. "I see it now and we really weren't that bad. But when we did it, it was scary. We had no television experience and didn't know how to act. They wouldn't let us play loud, and they put our amps twenty-five feet away from us and surrounded them with these baffles, so you couldn't hear anything. It wasn't a great experience."

Nor was the Remains' most celebrated gig, on August 29, 1966, when they played a show that went down in music history. The show at Candlestick Park in San Francisco found them on the verge of breaking up, having realized that the hit single wasn't going to happen. A recent change of drummer had taken away some of the live magic, and they were once again in a situation where they couldn't hear much of what they were playing. As it turns out, the night wasn't a great one for the headlining band either: the Beatles topped this bill on the last concert (barring one London rooftop show three years later) that they'd ever play.

It even felt a little ominous if you were onstage. "I mostly remember it being dark and foggy," recalls Tashian. "They had the floodlights on in the stadium, and somehow I have the image of turning around and seeing the lights and the fog on the San Francisco waters. It was windy and cold, and the stage was a long way from the stands. I had a feeling that the music was getting blown out to sea. We did maybe twenty shows on that tour and we wanted to go out on as high a note as possible, but we didn't have the same groove without Chip, our original drummer. I just have this sense of darkness about that last date." The Beatles would rally in a big way to make *Sgt. Pepper,* but that 1966 tour—which began with a near arrest in Manila and included a U.S. boycott after John Lennon's comment that he was "more popular than Jesus"—may have been their lowest moment. For Tashian, the start of the psychedelic era was his cue to get out of rock and roll altogether.

After the British Invasion, virtually every scene in the country had its own Beatles and its own Rolling Stones, the former a wholesome band with a more polished sound, the latter the bad boys with a raunchier sound and sexier image. The Remains and the Lost were the Beatles and Stones of Boston, but it's hard to say which was which. The Remains sounded like outlaws, but they were actually pros who wore suits onstage, rehearsed themselves to a fine polish, and lived relatively clean lives. On the other hand, the Lost really were the boys your parents wouldn't like, the ones who got themselves fired from a Catholic Youth Organization dance when the priest caught them smuggling in alcoholic beverages. A handful of producers tried to corral them in the studio and failed. So why are their surviving tapes full of chiming guitars, sweet harmonies, and even the occasional harpsichord? Their single "Everybody Knows"—a hit in the Boston area and as far away as Puerto Rico, though not much in between—has a gentle folk-rock sound; yet Willie Alexander sings with a knowing, punkish sneer. Just chalk it up to the mid-sixties, when you'd find the young innocents and the juvenile delinquents at the same dances, maybe even in the same band.

From the start, members of the Lost were wiser and more cynical than most of the teenagers who saw the Beatles on *Ed Sullivan.* Alexander was studying art at Goddard College in Vermont when he saw the Rolling Stones on *The Mike Douglas Show,* and he knew music well enough to know where the Stones were coming from. "I said, 'They're just playing Chuck Berry. Hey, I can do that!' At the time I fancied myself a jazz drummer and a painter. The Rolling Stones gave me the idea that you can become your own painting. I don't know if we thought that our

A gig flyer from Where It's At. (Courtesy Willie Alexander)

music was high art, but we definitely thought of ourselves as artists."

Alexander now lives on a quiet residential street on the North Shore, but his attic testifies to four decades in rock and roll: one wall is fully covered with bumper stickers, seemingly drawn from every club and radio station that's ever existed in the Boston area. His collection of framed concert posters goes back to 1965, when the Lost and the Ronettes played at the long-gone Kenmore Square hotspot Where It's

Courtesy Willie Alexander

At. And that beat-up electric piano that he's played in too many bands to count is still plugged in and ready for action. If the Boston scene has a single godfather, Willie Alexander is it. He was around to ride the sixties with the Lost, surf the punk wave with the Boom Boom Band, and become more eclectic in the decades since, as his music took on shades of Beat poetry and free jazz. Most recently, he's rocking again with the reunited Boom Booms, and after forty years in the game—the past twenty of which he's spent stone-cold sober—he still sports traces of the elegantly wasted look he wore as a teen.

But as he notes, both the bands and the audiences in 1965 were more likely to be wasted for real. The circuit at the time was likely to include high school rec rooms and church dances during the day and clubs serving alcohol at night—not that the former were necessarily any more wholesome than the latter. "We weren't supposed to be drinking in the teen environments, but it's not like the teens weren't all loaded and wanting to punch each other out. We had to hide under the stages between sets, far more at the teen clubs than the adult ones. We got to be huge in Worcester and we'd get mobbed there. The girls liked us, so they'd throw beads. Then the guys would get pissed off, so they'd throw beer bottles."

Listen to the Lost's surviving tapes and you hear a band hungry to try everything: There's raw R&B, sophisticated ballads, glimmers of psychedelia, all evincing the freewheeling spirit of the time. But as was true of most sixties bands, the real action happened onstage. On a good night, they could let fly with a blues jam. On a bad night, there was always "Louie Louie"—the one song that no frat house band could survive without. "You could play all your originals and you'd get such-and-such a response. Then you play 'Louie Louie' and they mob the dance floor; you're kings. But we put lights in our bass drum and if we were good boys and the club owner liked us, we would turn off the overhead lights and do the Rolling Stones instrumental '2120 South Michigan Avenue.' Our version was twenty minutes long, with harmonica solos making boat noises."

That may be why the band's records never quite took off, but it's more likely because the producers of the day didn't know what to do with a raw rock band. "I couldn't even shake maracas in the studio, because the engineers couldn't handle it. We couldn't do what we did live, and they'd bring material to us to record. Some of it was pretty

A 1965 music trade magazine ad from *Cash Box*. (Courtesy Willie Alexander)

painful." Still, their modest success allowed them to open up for now-legendary bands—which, as the Remains found out on the Beatles tour, could be a mixed blessing. When they opened for the Beach Boys, they got a receptive crowd, a hundred bucks, and a steak dinner, and the added perk of hanging out with the group's drummer, Dennis Wilson.

At the other extreme was a Brandeis University show with Diana Ross and the Supremes. "The opener was supposed to be Blood, Sweat & Tears; but they canceled out and we got called in instead. So we're up there, rocking out and standing our guard, but kids were getting up and filing out because they wanted to see this other band. That soured me on college gigs for a while."

As the Lost's career stretched into 1967, the gigs got more free-wheeling and the life got less innocent. "We were just out for adventure; and we weren't alone in that. There were gigs where I would fall offstage; I remember one where I fell into some large woman. A happy landing, as it were." Alexander also had the habit of forgetting to eat; he missed the band's Capitol audition because he was in the hospital with acute malnutrition. "I remember one show at the Tea Party where we get onstage and one of the guys turns to me and says, 'I forget how to play, man.' Put it this way: when we were first recording for Capitol, someone was shooting up in the stall. That wasn't quite the marketing incentive they were looking for." Meanwhile, the band's sex appeal didn't go unnoticed, and not just by women in Boston: playing the Scene club in Times Square in New York, they spotted Tennessee Williams among the admirers. "Words like groupies weren't even part of the vocabulary then; but they were there."

Musical rules were changing as well. Bands were moving out of the youth centers and into free-form spots like the Boston Tea Party that would become the stuff of legend. Choreographed shows were going out; spur-of-the-moment happenings were coming in. As Alexander recalls, "Those teen clubs where you had to dress like little soldiers were gone; now there was a big joint in every city where the kids could just rock out. They didn't have to wear neckties anymore."

The Tea Party and the Bosstown Sound

(1967–1970)

The Psychedelic Era: The Red Sox Are Winning

> See, when you are ready to live . . . ask me, and I'll help you, get
> some money, and take the train, hours later, zap . . . into the hallu-
> cination of life, wrapping itself around you, so don't protest . . .
> don't sing a green beret song and please don't scream, you
> wouldn't get past the doors. . . . Just walk in and open your
> brains . . . and relax, they don't hurt you there. . . . They just touch
> you inside with music.
>
> > —Penny Henes of *New England Teen Scene*,
> > reviewing the Hallucinations

What happened in Boston, and the culture at large, toward the end of
the sixties isn't likely to happen again anytime soon. The civil rights and
anti–Vietnam War movements were both well under way, and because
of the new psychedelic influence on pop culture, the dance parties of a
year or two before were looking like a bygone civilization.

History may paint the late sixties as a psychedelic free-for-all—

which it was, but you have to keep in mind that many of the kids who created that counterculture saw the possibility of losing their lives in Vietnam. In Harvard Square alone, you had at least three cultures feeding into each other. There was the square itself, which had attracted enough hippies and freaks to become a miniature Haight-Ashbury. There was the folk hangout Club 47, where the social activism of post-Dylan folk was feeding into the music. And there was Harvard University, which had become a hotbed of antiwar activism. On April 9, 1969, more than three hundred Harvard students seized the administration building in an antiwar protest, throwing out three deans and locking themselves in. They were later forcibly removed from the building.

And then there was the acid. What happened in Boston around 1967 wasn't much different from what happened in San Francisco and to varying extents in most American cities. But Boston—and specifically Harvard—was where LSD and related substances had quietly entered the culture seven years earlier, through research done by a psychology lecturer, Timothy Leary. Initially, Leary saw the drug as a means of treating alcoholism and reforming convicted criminals. By 1960 Leary had begun working with graduate students at Harvard Divinity School on experiments to determine if psilocybin and, later, LSD could induce a profound religious state (yes, they could). Both Leary and his associate, Richard Alpert, later known as Baba Ram Dass, were dismissed from Harvard in May 1963—though contrary to legend, only Alpert was fired for giving drugs to students. Leary's official reason for dismissal was absenting himself from the university without permission.

Nonetheless, anyone who got near a campus by the end of the sixties would encounter the fruits of Leary and Alpert's labors. As early as 1964 the effects of LSD were felt as far away as Goddard College in Vermont, where Ted Myers, a future Lost and Ultimate Spinach member, was studying psychology. "My friend Steve was in the science lab there, and one day he found a vial labeled mescaline sulfate—just a vial sitting in the lab; we never found out how it got there. And it was absolutely pure, the real stuff, something you wouldn't see very often again. We'd been reading Aldous Huxley's *Doors of Perception,* so we knew what the stuff was. We knew we had to have a straight man with us in case we started thinking we could fly. As soon as we felt it coming on, we went on a motorcycle ride through the woods. That experience changed everything."

By 1967–68 the psychedelic consciousness seemed to be everywhere. Suddenly there were a club called the Psychedelic Supermarket,
a chain of clothes stores called the Freeque Boutique, even pizza parlors
called Sgt. Pepper's and the Yellow Submarine. "You could walk down
the street and see who was psychedelicized and who wasn't," Myers
says. "Clothes became more colorful. Wild patterns, looser-fitting shirts
than the ones we used to wear after we first saw the Beatles. People
started wearing those funny glasses with the little square frames that
would perch at the end of your nose."

As word of the carnival atmosphere got around the Northeast, the
number of musicians headed to Boston increased. One short-time visitor was Van Morrison, who lived in a street-level Cambridge apartment,
on Green Street behind Central Square, during 1968. Morrison, his
wife, and her son were all crammed into the tiny space. As Peter Wolf
wrote in *Rolling Stone,* "They were flat-out broke. The place was bleak
and barren, with little more than a mattress on the floor, a refrigerator,
an acoustic guitar and a reel-to-reel tape recorder. They had no phone
and little food." Morrison met Wolf before a Howlin' Wolf show at the
Tea Party; the two became fast friends and Morrison even appeared as a
guest on Wolf's late-night radio show on WBCN. The poverty was
short-lived, however: while in town, Morrison began writing *Astral
Weeks,* the album that would recreate his career.

Another drifter who briefly hung around Harvard Square was the
late Gram Parsons, a gifted California singer who was on a mission to
convert rockers to country music. Among the first to fall into his orbit
was Barry Tashian, recently out of the Remains. "Gram did have something about him that I didn't understand at the time, but time has
shown that he was a very wealthy young man, and a very troubled one.
That I think gave his music a lot of meaning—he wrote out of pain,
and his emotions were very connected to his music. But I didn't know
that at the time; all I knew was that he had tremendous musical taste,
knew a million country songs, and was great fun to play with. And here
I was after the Beatles tour, a burnt-out rock musician at twenty-two.
Then to hear country songs like 'Six Days on the Road' and 'Truck
Driving Man'—to hear those same three chords used in so marvelous a
way—I started falling for it right away." Tashian's country conversion
was for real; he wound up touring with both Parsons and his protégée,
Emmylou Harris; he then cut a string of acoustic albums with his wife,

Holly. Parsons went back to LA to join the Byrds and the Flying Burri-
to Brothers, and he remains an influence on both rock and country
music to this day.

Others came to town and stayed. The guitarist JJ Rassler grew up
bored and music-starved in Philadelphia, and he noticed that Boston
bands kept appearing in his life. "First I saw the Rockin' Ramrods open
for the Stones. The next year I saw the Remains open for the Beatles.
So I think, Okay, what's going on in here?" Armed with a guitar and
little else, Rassler—who's been a Boston fixture ever since, with bands
including DMZ, the Odds, and the Downbeat 5—took a plane east in
1968. "I was carrying a knapsack with hashish in it. And on the plane I
asked people, 'Okay, so where does someone like me go?' They told me
it was Harvard Square."

His first sighting of the place didn't disappoint. "I thought I was
dreaming. Philadelphia had been very stiff, working class, the music
very soul-oriented. But Harvard Square was like Disneyland—the all-
around openness of being free. I had heard that people could smoke
joints in pizza parlors, so of course I went and tried it. And I got away
with it. Once we were smoking pot on Cambridge Common; a cop
came over and nobody even flinched. He finally said, 'Look guys, I've
got to bust you just because you saw me looking and you didn't even
put it away.'"

The Square offered plenty of chances to indulge oneself musically
as well, whether it was larger shows at the Harvard Stadium (site of
Janis Joplin's last local appearance), Sunday afternoon "be-ins" on Cambridge Common, or the new breed of folksingers who were checking
into Club 47. One fixture at the club was the Jim Kweskin Jug Band,
whose mix of folk-blues, old-time camp, and gonzo humor was easily
weird enough for the hippies. There was a member of the Jug Band
who particularly caught Rassler's eye. "Maria D'Amato became a
heartthrob of mine. She was as close to a combination of Carnaby
Street and [the Brazilian chanteuse] Astrid Gilberto as I could imagine." Then a Cambridge resident, D'Amato later scored a hit single,
"Midnight at the Oasis," under her married name, Maria Muldaur.

Others remember the atmosphere as far less idyllic, especially after
word of the Kent State shootings got around in May 1970. "The mood
got ugly after that, changing a peace movement into a violent and rev-
olutionary movement," recalls a former WBCN-FM staffer, David

Bieber. "It felt like our own version of the Days of Rage. For a while the only people making money in Harvard Square were the people replacing broken glass in the bank windows."

But the rock musicians weren't alone in their antiwar stance—or, for that matter, in their crushes on Maria Muldaur. As the folksinger Chris Smither points out, there was a lot of common ground between the Harvard Square hippies and the folkies who packed into Club 47, the basement room that survives today as Club Passim. "My impression was that the folk and rock scenes were pretty much the same culture; no antagonism there. Most of the rock people were singer-songwriters, too; they just decided to do it with electric guitars. So I felt perfectly comfortable hanging out with J. Geils and people like that."

Smither remembers Club 47 as "an extremely romantic place," and it didn't look much different from the Passim of today; though the stage was in a different position (at the left wall parallel to the street, so only the backs of the performers were visible from outside). The main difference was the cloud of smoke that usually hung over the place; so it was more like a Greenwich Village coffeehouse than the health food and hot chocolate hangout it is today. It held only about 150 people, but it nevertheless booked blues legends such as Muddy Waters and Howlin' Wolf—no wonder the budding rock guitarists were in the crowd. Smither played Club 47 only once himself—in June 1966, when his friend Eric von Schmidt coaxed him onstage—but he was among the many who had their worldview shaped there. Other folk clubs were equally active at the time—Jacks, up Mass. Ave. toward Central Square, was one of Bonnie Raitt's favorite hangouts (and would later be the site of the Pixies' first show). But Club 47's position in the heart of Harvard Square put it closer to the cultural battle zone—not to mention the literal battle zone when the antiwar riots erupted.

"I remember going to the Square that night to see what the commotion was, and having to turn right around because of all the tear gas. The whole Square was just a cloud of smoke at one point," Smither recalls. He mentions that one famous singer he knew was among those throwing bricks through bank windows. "We were young and absolutely certain that we were going to change the world. It wasn't something you necessarily talked about onstage; it was just understood. You made your statement by what you wore, what you were, and what you looked like. I had my hair down to my ass, wore bellbottoms, smoked a lot of dope, and played guitar. Someone asked if I was a hippie and I'd say, 'What else do you think I look like?'"

The most puzzling and polarizing figure to emerge from the Cambridge folk world was undoubtedly the late Mel Lyman. Often photographed in lumberjack shirts and sporting a short-haired, all-American look, Lyman had a David Lynch sort of affect, so normal it was a little unsettling. As histories would have it, Lyman was either a benevolent spiritual leader who founded a community that survives to this day, or a borderline-dangerous, drug-driven messiah. In any case, Lyman took his personal mission well outside the confines of the music realm; he freaked out the straight world as few banjo players ever have.

A transplant from California and Oregon, Lyman came to Boston in the early sixties and participated in some of Timothy Leary's early acid studies. After two years with the Jim Kweskin Jug Band, Lyman gained his first true notoriety by taking the stage at the close of the 1965 Newport Folk Festival, just after Bob Dylan had caused shock waves with his first-ever electric set. As the crowds filed out, Lyman played a ten-minute, solo harmonica version of the hymn "Rock of Ages"—a gesture that was interpreted either as a strike back for traditional folk or as a way of turning the day back over to God. Soon afterward, he played a string of solo gigs at the Orleans coffeehouse on Charles Street; these would turn into churchlike meetings as Lyman stopped playing music and discussed happiness and fulfillment with the audience. A writer from *Boston After Dark,* an alternative weekly, reported, "His gentleness, honesty and warmth pervade the Orleans; the audience becomes noticeably kinder by the end of the evening." In his first book, *The Autobiography of a World Savior,* Lyman wrote that he came "from the planet of pure being, same place Christ came from."

It's not quite true that Lyman claimed to be God—but then, he never claimed he wasn't. Interviewed in the *Avatar*—an underground magazine that covered all manner of drugs, sex, religion, and astrology and became an outlet for Lyman and his followers—he said, "A lot of people send me letters saying, well if you're God I'm gonna be God too, man. That's all right. I arouse SOMETHING. At least someone wanted to be part of what I said I was part of, or wanted to be what I said I was." Lyman's following grew to include musicians, writers, and actors. (Kweskin went from being Lyman's boss to being his disciple; the music critic and *Crawdaddy!* magazine founder Paul Williams and the actor Mark Frechette, star of the Antonioni film *Zabriskie Point,* were also in his corner.) In 1968 Lyman and his "family"—whose membership hovered around one hundred—had taken up residence in the Fort Hill neighborhood of Roxbury. Though the members objected to words such as "cult" and "commune," there were elements of both. The members worked cooperatively repairing houses and landscaping grounds, replacing the hippie lifestyle with a strong work ethic; and all were ferociously devoted to Lyman. As Chris Smither put it, "All I knew was that they were far too interested in one guy to be of any interest to me."

Some detected a darker undercurrent in the group's workings. A 1971 album on Warner Bros., *Jim Kweskin's America* (which Lyman produced under an alias), is one of the spookiest folk records ever made; it turns familiar ballads into funeral dirges. Lyman's writings certainly took on a harsher edge: in an oft-quoted manifesto for the *Avatar* he wrote, "I am going to burn down the world / I am going to tear down everything that can not stand alone / I am going to shove hope up your ass / I am going to turn ideals to shit. . . . And then maybe someone will be able / to see something as it really is / Watch Out." The *Avatar* itself was nearly shut down in 1968, after Lyman published a centerfold blow-up of four familiar, four-letter Anglo-Saxon words; the case was thrown out of Cambridge court and the magazine continued until 1971. Late that year *Rolling Stone* published a lengthy piece, much disputed by family members, that implied excessive drug use, mind control, megalomania, and threats of violence; the story equated Lyman's family with Charles Manson's. Kweskin was quoted as saying (granted, to a reporter he wasn't getting along with), "The Manson Family preached peace and love and went around killing people. We don't preach peace and love. And we haven't killed anybody—yet."

But the threat never materialized. Lyman was reported to have died in 1978, at forty, of natural causes—yet details remain unclear and some believe that he simply went underground. And the Fort Hill family carried on and prospered, even went mainstream; in recent years some of Lyman's devotees were reported to be still living in Roxbury. A glossy, family-produced art and philosophy magazine, *U and I,* made its debut in 1985. By 1986 their holdings included eight houses in Boston and three on Martha's Vineyard, a loft in Manhattan, and a farm in Kansas of several hundred acres. And *People* magazine reported that "the Lyman clan now stands as perhaps the most durable—and financially success-ful—of any commune to come out of the Aquarian '60s." Another piece in the *Los Angeles Times* testified to the family's rehabilitation: "Once-Notorious '60s Commune Evolves into Respectability."

A different confluence of music and politics became especially clear when James Brown was booked to play Boston Garden on April 5, 1968, one night after Dr. Martin Luther King was shot. The King assas-sination caused long-simmering racial tensions to erupt in a number of cities; Washington, D.C., and Chicago both saw riots and fatalities. Boston, with thirty arrests and no fatalities, got off relatively easy, though Roxbury saw an immediate wave of rioting and looting after the news broke. A sense of anger and betrayal went through the black community; youth groups went from door to door demanding that store owners close their shops; and stores in Roxbury were pasted with flyers reading, "This store is closed until further notice in honor of Dr. Martin Luther King, the fallen martyr of the black revolution."

Officials at Boston Garden initially panicked and canceled the Brown concert, fearing more violence—until they realized what might happen if a few thousand of his fans showed up that night and found out there'd be no show. Mayor Kevin White came up with a workable, if expensive, solution: the city would pay James Brown's $60,000 guar-antee, but the local public TV station, WGBH, would also broadcast the show and citizens were encouraged to stay home and watch. As it was, only a few thousand made it to the Garden that night, though many more watched the telecast.

Brown didn't make any specific topical references during his show (that would come four months later, when he recorded his first politi-cal single, "Say It Loud—I'm Black and I'm Proud"); but the tightly wound atmosphere is hard to miss on the surviving audiotapes. One of his hits, "I Got the Feeling"—on any other night, a good-natured funk workout—sounds more urgent as he addresses the crowd: "Have you got the feeling? Then stand up now and be counted!" Some of the au-dience rushed the stage a few songs later, causing Brown to stop the show and spend a few minutes calming them down: "I'll be all right, I'll be fine. We're all black up here, let us finish the show. Let's represent our own selves. I can't finish the show if I can't get respect from my own people. Now are we together or aren't we?" It's got to be the only recorded instance of James Brown getting rattled onstage.

The effects of the King riots would be felt in city policy for decades to come; the city's racial divides would grow more extreme, at their worst being expressed by white riots over the city's busing experiments in the mid-seventies. The Garden show was a small moment of catharsis, a moment during which black and white crowds—who were probably both holed up in their living rooms watching James Brown—were more together than they probably realized. And somewhere in the WGBH vaults sits a videotape of one of the most intense performances that Brown ever gave.

This sense of cultural upheaval, and the attendant dead seriousness, carried into all aspects of the local music world. A new breed of music press was appearing, with the launch of the weekly *Boston After Dark* (later to become the *Boston Phoenix*) and the shorter-lived magazines *Fusion* and *Crawdaddy!* Rather than being focused on pop culture and celebrity, as it is today, music criticism in the early days had a more intellectual bent that took personal and political context into account.

This trend would extend well into the seventies, when Jon Landau wrote his oft-quoted Bruce Springsteen piece—which solidified his friendship with Springsteen and led to his becoming his manager—for the *Real Paper* (another alternative weekly) on May 22, 1974. The most famous line from this piece is actually a misquote: Landau didn't write, "I have seen the future of rock'n'roll, and its name is Bruce Springsteen." Rather, two-thirds into a long think piece in which he pondered his relation to music as he turned the ripe age of twenty-seven, Landau wrote, "Last Thursday, at the Harvard Square Theater, I saw my rock 'n' roll past flash before my eyes. And I saw something else: I saw rock and roll future and its name is Bruce Springsteen." A subtle difference, but the true quote sounds less like ad copy and more like the sociopolitical discourse of the rock press in its early heyday.

The most celebrated Boston club from this era, the Boston Tea Party, didn't serve alcohol. It didn't have to. After all, other forms of mind alteration were easily available, and that way and you could walk through the Tea Party's front doors with no booze on your breath. ("Get off before you get in" was a favorite saying at the time.) With its unusually high ceiling, the bare-walled space had an almost churchlike feel; this mystic mood was enhanced by the swirling light show and the pot smoke that inevitably hung over the place. The balcony in the rear was usually abandoned, the crowds preferring to get closer to the band.

Courtesy Paul Lovell

Snacks and sodas were available; the rest was up to you. "What's totally foreign to the current scene is that you were able to bring your own," recalls Rick Harte, who'd become one of Boston's leading early-eighties record producers. "We used to show up with bottles of Almaden or Mateus; that seemed to be the normal thing at the time. So was vomiting before the band even got on."

You could also pick up something of an altered state just by walking in the door: the Tea Party wasn't a bar or a theater or even a nightclub per se—just a cavernous, wide-open space (unlike New York's more famous Fillmore East, which had seats). This space was more conducive to free-form dancing on the floor and free-form playing onstage. The original Tea Party on Berkeley Street (the venue later moved to Lansdowne Street, where Avalon stands now) had been an underground movie theater and, before that, a synagogue. The Lost headlined the Tea Party's opening night on January 20, 1967, only a month before they broke up. "It was a lot less sanitized than a mid-sixties club like Where It's At, where they wouldn't even let you smoke onstage," Ted Myers recalls. "It seems there was less rowdiness; people were listening to the music more, while they were spinning around on that big open floor."

Behind the scenes, however, the Tea Party was anything but a makeshift hippie operation. Its owner and manager, respectively Ray Riepen and Don Law, were among the first business giants to come out of Boston music. According to Fred Goodman, in the book *The Mansion on the Hill,* the two made an odd match: both were sharp and ambitious, but Riepen saw the big picture, while Law was "extraordinarily disciplined," a man who knew how to make great concepts translate into business success. One initial payoff was that Law was able to bring the right up-and-coming bands into the club that Riepen had started, putting together the formative shows that went down in local history.

Despite its name, the Tea Party proved quite open to the British; and its proximity to the United Kingdom made Boston the first stop for some major tours. Thus, Led Zeppelin made its American debut there on January 23, 1969; the pre–pop star version of Fleetwood Mac played a blues-soaked weekend, February 5–7, 1970, that became a great live album when the tapes were dug up many years later. Bands were usually booked for a full weekend, so the serious fans would catch the Thursday show and then spread the word; David Bieber recalls seeing Elton John play a Thursday for about fifty people. Yet the story was as much about that communal vibe as it was about the individual bands. "I don't remember seeing anyone get hassled. There was an inherent trust in seeing like-minded people, having the comfort zone to run around in." The one downside to this utopian vibe was that concerts didn't exactly run like clockwork. If the headliner was a free-spirited band like Sly & the Family Stone, the time on your ticket had very little to do with the time they'd actually show up. "I always thought there were two great moments," Bieber says. "One was when you got into the club; the other was when you finally got out."

Farther down Commonwealth Avenue, past Kenmore Square—near the current site of Boston University's School for Public Communication—stood the Psychedelic Supermarket, another ballroom–type space that wasn't even that psychedelic. "It was the low-end version of a place like the Tea Party. Just a downstairs funk palace; you've been in a million of 'em," recalls the keyboardist Tom Swift, who played the club with his Tom Swift Electric Band (including the guitarist Billy Squier, who next joined the Sidewinders, then Piper, and subsequently went on to solo fame in the eighties). Swift later became a mainstay of the R&B band Duke & the Drivers. "There was some Day-Glo evidence in the Psychedelic Supermarket, some black-light evidence, but it was really just a cavernous room, it looked like the ground floor of a parking garage. It was a good room for the times, a good place to get your chops. We opened for everybody, but I especially remember the Moody Blues. We played maybe twenty minutes, but they were great gentlemen and stood there watching for our whole set."

And the Supermarket could indeed look psychedelic if you were in the right state of consciousness. A future punk rocker, Steve Cataldo, then leading the band Front Page Review, has more colorful memories. "It seemed like they let the people who worked there go wild with the design—'Psychedelicize this, boys!' So they really Day-Gloed it. In fact, it was pretty tough to see anything because there were so many poles. But they turned on the purple lights and it got pretty gone. You could be stoned or tripping and nobody would bother you." Cataldo's early band also played regularly at the Unicorn, a basement coffeehouse near the Prudential Center.

Along with concert halls, rock radio was being absorbed into the counterculture. AM radio, with its all-hits formats and fast-talking DJs, was giving way to a new style of FM radio. Boston took the leap on March 15, 1968, when the classical station WBCN-FM (whose initials stand for Boston Concert Network) switched to a rock format. It was Ray Riepen who divined the emerging trend for free-form FM radio, and he found a struggling station that needed all the fresh blood it could get. The original crop of WBCN DJs were voracious music fans with strong political opinions, wide-ranging tastes, and an urge to change the world. The last trait is no exaggeration: in its early days WBCN billed itself as "the American Revolution"; one slogan was "Ugly radio is dead"—both a slam at traditional, entertainment-based AM frequencies and a nod to the counterculture hero Frank Zappa, who had inscribed "Kill Ugly Radio" on an early album cover.

If one thing distinguished WBCN (and its free-form radio brethren throughout the country) from modern commercial radio, it was the eagerness to do things that station owners, advertisers, and record labels wouldn't like. Advertisers were refused on philosophical grounds. ("If they knew our audience, they'd realize our listeners would rather have bad apartments and sizable record collections instead of the advertisers' values, which are the reverse," Sam Kopper, the production manager, told *Boston Magazine* in 1970.) And entire albums were aired before they were even released: during September 1969 WBCN got hold of the Beatles' forthcoming album *Get Back* and played it from start to finish. As it turned out, the album never came out at all—the Beatles reworked it and released it as *Let It Be,* and WBCN's broadcast is still the source of bootleg tapes of the original version.

Abbie Hoffman, one of the Chicago Seven defendants, Bill Baird, an early birth control advocate, and the son of an imprisoned runner-up in South Vietnam's presidential election were all interviewed on-air during prime time. Listeners were briefed on how to send ninety-cent telegrams to public officials. And the jazz great Rahsaan Roland Kirk

A WBCN airplay chart from mid-1981. (Courtesy Asa Brebner)

came into the studio and expounded at length on race relations. For all
that, early WBCN wasn't quite as far removed from the classic AM
radio model as it liked to think. Many of its on-air personalities—most
notably the J. Geils Band's singer Peter Wolf—did hip-talking DJ patter
with the best of them. And WBCN's DJs did spin some of the same hit
singles and oldies that were heard on the rest of the dial: they just felt
free to segue from those into Muddy Waters, Miles Davis, the Philadelphia Orchestra, and anything else that appealed that day. It was a jumble
of weird and familiar elements, flowing together with psychedelic
logic, a perfect soundtrack for Boston at the time.

Not surprisingly, it took a bunch of hippies with folk-scene connections to make the one record that best reflects the late-sixties
Boston zeitgeist: Earth Opera's "The Red Sox Are Winning," a wildly
noncommercial record that anyone who listened to WBCN in 1969
would remember. The members of Earth Opera were only temporary
Bostonians, and the two leaders later had Grateful Dead connections:
the singer-guitarist Peter Rowan and the mandolinist David Grisman
both recorded with Jerry Garcia and became celebrated acoustic players
in their own right. Earth Opera was their attempt at a rock band, and a
trippy band it was. Cramming an album's worth of ideas into a three-
minute single, "Red Sox" captures the altered state that was Boston in
the late sixties. The musical setting changes every few bars, from ironic
cocktail jazz to an old-timey foxtrot, and parts are sung through a
megaphone, as if some twenties crooner is looking in on the chaos.
Things get linear only during the chorus, when Rowan sounds like
he's speaking from a dream: "No summer this year in the days of the
war. But the Red Sox are winning." In other words, normal everyday
life is still going on somewhere, just not on this planet.

Ultimate Spinach, Orpheus, and "Bosstown": The Clown Died in Marvin Gardens

Boston circa 1968 is remembered mainly for a movement that didn't
move. Just when the psychedelic era was in full swing, and loose FM
radio playlists were making all kinds of musical experimentation possible, MGM Records launched a marketing campaign known as the
Boston or Bosstown Sound. The label's reps had begun coming to
town the year before, apparently ready to sign anyone who looked
vaguely freaky. A whopping fourteen Boston bands recorded for the

label, though most of the attention went to the first three: Orpheus, Ultimate Spinach, and Beacon Street Union. The unspoken strategy was that Boston would replace San Francisco as America's happening mecca for underground music.

It didn't, however, and Bosstown Sound became one of the more spectacular flops of its era—in fact, Orpheus's "Can't Find the Time" was the closest thing to a hit to come from more than a dozen albums. The music was pitched straight at the hippie culture, which distrusted anything that smacked of corporate hype—and the idea of setting up one musical city as a rival to another was hype in a nutshell. So was a cover story, "The Selling of a New Sound," that ran in the *Wall Street Journal* in January 1968, before hardly anyone had heard any of the albums. Even a term like *Bosstown* harked back to the goofiness of AM radio, hardly what the ultraserious Woodstock-era audience was after. "The sound heard round the world: Boston!" read one of MGM's ads. "Where the new thing is making everything else seem like yesterday. Where a new definition of love is helping to write the words and music for 1968." Not surprisingly, *Rolling Stone* magazine—then strongly associated with the San Francisco scene—was among the first to call bull.

The real problem was that, to put it charitably, the music wasn't always the best that Boston had to offer, or the most representative. The label's producer, Alan Lorber, who oversaw most of the Bosstown records, was into experimenting with orchestration; combine a heavy-handed producer with psychedelically inclined bands and the result is truly over the top. "It just sounded like everybody wanted to sound like the West Coast bands, and not even the best ones," sneers Willie Alexander. "A lot of those bands reminded me of Country Joe & the Fish." Notably absent from any of the MGM releases was Boston's longtime love for rhythm and blues; harder bands like Peter Wolf's blues-rocking Hallucinations were missing.

Also passed over was a band known as the Crow, especially unusual for the time as a white band with a black singer. "It was a pretty heady band," the singer told me in 1999. "We did some recording, but I'll never let anybody hear it. They made me do Aretha Franklin songs— they sound fine but I sound like a Munchkin. They named it the Crow in my honor, because I was the only black one. And my mother thought it was a bad-luck name; she thought I should leave because they were going nowhere. I'm not superstitious, but we really did go nowhere." The singer, however, did go somewhere—specifically to Germany, where she made some enormously popular disco records. Her name is Donna Summer.

But MGM did make a play in late 1968 for the newly formed J. Geils Band, which by then had Wolf up front. It was the Geils band's first offer, and they came close to signing. "The deal they offered us wasn't much different from the one we took with Atlantic—something ridiculous like $25,000 to make six albums," Geils recalls. "But it sounded good when we were lucky to make $600 at a gig. It was finally Peter who said, 'This just doesn't feel right, it doesn't ring true.' So we passed." As a result, the Geils Band lost a chance to play at Woodstock: their manager, Ray Paret, had a slot for one of his bands, but it went to the one who took the MGM deal. Playing at Woodstock, however—early on Friday evening, before the big crowds showed up—didn't do much good for Quill, the MGM band who did get the slot. Also playing at Woodstock was the former Remains drummer N. D. Smart, who was in the original lineup of the guitarist Leslie West's group Mountain.

"A lot of us were pretty upset at the hype," says Ted Myers, who went from the Lost to the Bosstown-associated Ultimate Spinach, about MGM's strategy. "We didn't want to be part of it; since lots of people were ridiculing it as being phony—a blatant attempt by a record company to exploit the idea of the San Francisco sound. It was going to look transparent to anybody who had any brains, and it was no wonder we got put down."

"Because San Francisco was so happening at the time, there were a bunch of New York producers who wanted to find something like it on the East Coast," notes Orpheus's leader, Bruce Arnold. "They knew they wouldn't find it in Hartford or New Haven. And New York wasn't going to do it because New York was associated with having millions of people, not with colleges or youth culture. But the idea of a college town with a young population, plus the ragtag bunch of kids you had in Cambridge—it all started looking good. Cambridge was looking like Berkeley to them."

Arnold says that MGM's producers, Alan Lorber and Wes Farrell, sent reps to local music stores looking for bands. "They went into stores like Wurlitzer's [the downtown instrument outlet] and other places where people bought music, asking if people knew any bands. That's how they found us. Harry Sandler was working at Wurlitzer's, and he told me he'd set the deal up for us if he could be the drummer—so that's how he joined the band. We auditioned for Alan Lorber in a warehouse in town; he probably had auditioned several bands that day." Since his band was the most successful of the lot, Arnold's memories of the era are a little friendlier. "Personally, I couldn't object to being part of a huge, professional promotional campaign. The MGM people were ambitious to exploit the Boston scene, and I would have been a fool to say, 'Don't include me in that.' But the fact of the matter is, we could have stood on our own."

Heard today, the Bosstown records have a certain period charm. A song like the Ultimate Spinach's "Ballad of the Hip Death Goddess"— with its sitar, finger cymbals, and weighty spoken intro ("See the glazed eyes! Touch the dead skin! Feel the cold lips, and know the warmth of the hip death goddess!")—just wouldn't be attempted today, at least not without irony. But the camp factor is outweighed by the overwhelming melancholy; you'd get the impression that Boston bands spent the late sixties waiting for Prozac to be invented. Earnest vocals and haunting minor-key tunes are the rule; the Beacon Street Union's magnum opus, "The Clown Died in Marvin Gardens," meshes images of doom, acid, and Monopoly. And the aptly named Head Game gave one of their songs this less-than-promising start: "Shackled by the ways of love within the house of rain / The madrigal of whispering, they say you offer pain." It is most definitely not "Louie Louie."

A few surviving mid-sixties bands, including Teddy & the Pandas on the Tower label, were encouraged against their better judgment to go psychedelic. The most reluctant was the former surf combo the Rockin' Ramrods. After a few hitless years they linked up with Lorber, who convinced them not only to retool their sound but to change their name as well. "I remember the conversation: 'You can't call yourselves the Ramrods anymore,'" the drummer Jesse Henderson recalls. "So they came up with this spacey psychedelic name for us: Puff. Next thing I knew, we were at this fur shop in the Village buying our fur outfits—nice, huh?" Puff's album was one of the least successful of the batch.

Many of the musicians lived to fight another day: Beacon Street Union's leader, John Lincoln Wright, would swear off rock, take up country, form the traditionalist Sour Mash Boys, and remain a local fixture for decades to come. Later Ultimate Spinach lineups featured the

The Chameleon Church with their drummer, Chevy Chase, third from left. (Courtesy Willie Alexander)

guitarist Jeff "Skunk" Baxter, later to attain fame as a Steely Dan member and a Doobie Brother. But the most unlikely face ever to show up in a Boston band was the future comedy star Chevy Chase, who played drums for Chameleon Church, the band Ted Myers fronted after his stints with the Lost and Ultimate Spinach. In photos from that era, Chase looks ultraserious in his pageboy haircut and Nehru jacket; you can practically imagine him taking a pratfall and revealing the whole thing as a put-on. But no, Chameleon Church's one album sounds at least as earnest as anything else from the era; its wispy, Donovan-like sound provides a vehicle for Myers's acid-inspired musings on universal love. And the drumming? Serviceable enough and confined mostly to simple hand percussion, but it's not hard to understand why Chase went into another line of work.

"He was a funny, good-looking guy who was dead set on becoming a drummer and kept pestering me to form a band," Myers recalls of Chase. The two met because of Myers's friendship with the comedy group Channel One, where Chase was starting his onstage career. "Frankly, I was never that enthusiastic about his drumming," Myers admits. "But he had a lot going for him, great looks and personality. We did a lot of funny things onstage that bore no resemblance to the way our album sounded. Chevy had one bit where he'd be the front man, come up and sing nonsense lyrics to a James Brown riff that we'd play." The band also got involved with Channel One and contributed to some of its off-Broadway shows. "We appeared in one routine as a band that played in the nude, backing up an overdressed lead singer; a little fat guy with glasses in psychedelic regalia.

Orpheus was the odd band out in this psychedelic party. Just freaky enough to please audiences of the day, it was really a pop group writing emotive three-minute songs. The sound was close to West Coast "sunshine pop" (think the Association or the Mamas & the Papas) but with a few dark New England clouds. "Can't Find the Time" may be their one moment of pure inspiration, but one great single is a respectable legacy—especially since this one has been revived as recently as 2000, when Hootie & the Blowfish recorded it. "I wrote it to be a hit," Bruce Arnold says. "It's a timeless sound, everybody can go 'ba-ba-ba-ba-da-da' along with it. I would hear it on the radio and be overjoyed. I remember playing that song at the Hatch Shell on the Esplanade; it was the Fourth of July and there were maybe twenty thousand people there. The acoustics were so good that I could hear people singing along, and I was incredibly gratified."

The late sixties proved to be a friendly time for musicians with grand designs and ambitions. This was, after all, the era when Leonard Bernstein sang the Beach Boys' praises. Arnold wanted Orpheus to be one of those visionary classical-pop fusions; so the heavy orchestrations that sank other Bosstown Sound albums were a more natural fit for Orpheus. "My whole experience of the late sixties was more a musical one than anything else. The people I associated with were the ones who introduced me to Satie, Debussy, and Fauré; those had a tremendous effect on my life. I felt that we were on the search for the new American music."

With those ambitions in mind, Orpheus styled themselves as chamber musicians, even going so far as to insist the houselights be turned on during some of their shows. Credit the loose atmosphere of the time that they were able to share bills with the heaviest rock acts— Cream, the Who, Janis Joplin—and get away with the chamber gambit. "I just thought that if we were going to get up there and play these difficult compositions, we'd appreciate it if people would listen to them. Sometimes we'd play a date that had been set up as a psychedelic show, where the bands before and after us would have a light show, and we'd insist on not using one. Our guitar player, Jack McKennes, had a very friendly demeanor, so he was able to put people at ease, and that helped a lot. But I always wanted to take it even further. Maybe we could have made it like Elvis in Las Vegas, where it was more intimate and everyone was sitting around him. And suppose we brought some couches in?"

Bosstown Sound ended as ignobly as it began. In early 1969 Mike Curb (later the conservative Republican lieutenant governor of California) took over as the head of MGM Records. One of his first actions was a well-publicized purge from the label of all acts that he deemed to be advocating drugs in their music. Such rock legends as the Velvet Underground and Frank Zappa's Mothers of Invention were among the first to get the axe—ironically enough, Zappa was about the only major sixties figure who never used drugs. Eric Burdon & the Animals, who made no secret of their copious consumption, were somehow allowed to keep their contract, perhaps because they were making more money than the Velvets or Zappa.

Since they were possibly using drugs and definitely not selling huge amounts of records, that meant the Boston bands were among the casualties—even the relatively straitlaced Orpheus (who did make another album on a different label). True, Ultimate Spinach probably wouldn't have kissed the Hip Death Goddess without chemical help. But the purge didn't sit well with Bruce Arnold, whose lyrics were about as innocent as they got in that era. Making matters worse, Orpheus was about to sign a profitable contract with Capitol Records, who dropped the deal when the band appeared on Curb's blacklist. "I was going to meetings and saying, 'Do I look like a heroin addict to you?' And where were these drug lyrics I was supposed to be writing? 'Baby, remember when we turned on to a rainy day'—was that supposed to be it? Or, we had a song called 'I Can Make the Sun Rise.' Maybe they thought I meant that literally."

But MGM did succeed in finding a group that would sell more records with absolutely no drug references. One of the early high-profile signings under Curb's regime was the squeaky-clean Osmond Brothers. The sixties were ending fast.

Dawn of the Superstars

(1970–1976)

Two snapshots of Boston's rock and roll world circa 1971:

One Friday night in April, the future *Boston Phoenix* music editor Jon Garelick is hanging out with some friends in his Boston University dorm, when his roommate runs in raving about something he'd heard outside. It turns out he's just come across a very early hometown show by Aerosmith, before their debut album had come out. "Hey, get out here," he says. "There's a band that thinks they're the Rolling Stones!" Someone asks if they're any good. "Who cares? They think they're the Stones, let's check them out!"

Another weekend around the same time, the young guitarist Lenny Kaye, later to become an important record producer and a key member of Patti Smith's group, looks out his Harvard Square window and sees a bunch of enthusiastic guys packed into a car: it's the J. Geils Band on their way to one of their early gigs. "I'm living in a ground floor apartment, and I hear a car horn beeping. I look out and it's Peter Wolf and the rest of the band, on the way to some college gig. It was just a classic moment—the excitement, the jumping up and down in the car, the sense of destination. I remember looking at that car and thinking, 'This is the very essence of rock and roll.'"

As the seventies started, Boston rock finally started to loosen up and come out to play. The late sixties had been a heavy time for music—

not only in Boston, but in most cities where the music was inseparable from the social and political unrest. But in Boston, you had the added element of classic New England depression. It's there in the Bosstown Sound records, which have barely an upbeat tune among them. It's there in bands like the Remains and the Lost, whose sound was always a bit dark and intense. It's no surprise then, that 1970 would see the national rise of James Taylor, the Martha's Vineyard native who'd become the very model of the achingly sensitive singer-songwriter—initially with songs he wrote while being treated for depression at McLean Psychiatric Hospital in Belmont, Massachusetts. Another Boston-based troubadour who came in on Taylor's wave was the Virginia transplant Jonathan Edwards, whose music had a sunnier sound—but his one national hit, 1971's "Sunshine," opened with this buzz-killing line: "Sunshine go away today, don't feel much like dancing."

The depression is even there in some of the teenage garage-rock records that have come to light on recent compilations of sixties obscurities. Consider "Mary Is Alone" by Dry Ice, a Revere band who had a polished sound somewhere between the Beatles and the Who (its front man would later turn up in the aspiring seventies arena metal band Angel). Dry Ice's stab at hitdom, "Mary" is ostensibly an antidrug song, but it has this downer of a chorus: "Mary is alone and she wants to live / But all she sees is death." It's a lovely song, but you have to wonder: if kids in a teenage rock band during 1966 can't be happy, what hope is there for the rest of us?

The winds were shifting by the early seventies, however, as Boston was about to rediscover a little thing called fun. The J. Geils Band and Aerosmith were soon to take their place as Boston's first two superstar bands; and both bands were something of an antidote to the heaviness of the hippie-Bosstown era. The Geils Band proudly wore their love for vintage rhythm and blues; an early R&B nugget, "Ain't Nothing But a House Party," would be their battle cry for decades to come. And Aerosmith would grow beyond the initial Stones comparisons to stand as one of the definitive American rock-and-roll bands.

Norman Greenbaum: Spirit in the Sky

One advance sign of Boston's lighter mood was the 1970 release of a quirky little record that hit the charts out of nowhere: "Spirit in the Sky" by Norman Greenbaum. Though it wasn't pegged as a Boston record, the artist was indeed an area native who'd been at Boston University before heading to California in the mid-sixties. Despite its gospelish lyric, the song was essentially a good-timey, jug-band tune that got an extra kick from the primitive fuzz guitar and echoed drums. Thirty-five years after its release, the song is still a radio staple and frequently turns up in films and TV commercials; even Elton John recorded it in his early days as a session singer.

"Spirit in the Sky" launched a small wave of Jesus songs on the Top 40 (Ocean's "Put Your Hand in the Hand" and Brewer & Shipley's "One Toke Over the Line" would follow in early 1971), but its creator was in fact a nice Jewish boy from Malden. Like many kids who grew up in the cold Northeast, Greenbaum spent his teenage years dreaming of moving to California. "The weather, the beaches, the surfers, the blonde girls—that's quite an attraction," he says today. As a BU student he did make a few stabs at a music career, playing open mikes in local coffeehouses, notably Café Yana near Fenway Park. "I had a few fans—everybody had one or two. Mine were mostly the people I knew from hanging out. I was a folksinger-songwriter, but I wasn't into sad or depressive songs, or historical ones like Gordon Lightfoot. I was really looking for a television career, but I was deemed a little too racy, a little far-out for the tastes of comedic TV at the time."

Comedy songs initially made Greenbaum's career when he hit Los Angeles. He formed Dr. West's Medicine Show & Junk Band—a quintessential hippie-humor band of the time—and had a small national hit with "The Eggplant That Ate Chicago." When that band ended he made a more serious attempt to write a hit single, and the bolt of lightning struck when he saw the country star Porter Wagoner on TV. "I'm watching him and thinking, Well, that's cool. He dresses in these glitzy, Nudie cowboy country-singer suits [a reference to Nudie Cohn, who designed elaborate suits for the likes of Hank Williams and Elvis]. He's got Dolly Parton in his group; that's pretty cool too. Then he stops and does a religious song; I guess that brought middle America closer to him. Well, I never thought of anything like that. And coming from a Jewish background, I didn't have a clue. So I decided that if I'm going to write a religious song, it has to be about Jesus. More people can relate to that."

Writing the song was easy, but it took another six months to figure out the arrangement. Only after throwing out a folk version, a folk-rock version, and a country version did Greenbaum come up with the fuzztone-guitar version everybody knows. "It was kind of an electric delta blues, and I'd loved that kind of music since the coffeehouse days. I had a friend who was pretty ingenious; he built the custom fuzztone that we used. People thought we must have done something weird, but the only unusual thing besides the custom fuzzbox was that I finger-picked instead of using a pick. Other than that it was just a Telecaster through a Fender tube amp, all pretty straight."

The follow-up single was even more unlikely. Shopping one day with his wife, Greenbaum saw the guy in front of him buying a five-pound ham, and he asked her, "When are you gonna buy me a canned ham?" Then he went home and wrote "Canned Ham," using that question as the opening line. "I mentally reverted back to Dr. West for that one," he notes. But it's never a great commercial strategy to follow a song about Jesus with one about ham; and thus he never scored the necessary chart-busting follow-up. "The main problem with 'Canned Ham' was that people heard it and started wondering if 'Spirit in the Sky' was a put-down. So I was deemed a one-hit wonder." Greenbaum wound up buying a dairy farm in Petaluma, and since his hit-making career proved short-lived, he still hasn't performed "Spirit in the Sky" in Boston—even if a few thousand wedding bands probably have.

The Modern Lovers, the Sidewinders: Come Out and Play

One non-Boston band that looms large in Boston history is the Velvet Underground. Though forever linked with New York City, it played fre-quently at Boston's Tea Party, and the band—in particular its leather-jacketed, street-poet leader, Lou Reed—would become icons of punk rock. Their connection with Boston was nailed down when the group's founding bassist, John Cale, left after two albums in the fall of 1968, and his replacement was a Boston musician, Doug Yule.

The Velvets' story was effectively over when Lou Reed left in 1970; but there was another, more obscure chapter. Two of the remaining members (Yule and the drummer, Maureen Tucker, by then the one original left) attempted to carry on, and they filled the lineup with two more Bostonians: Walter Powers on guitar and Willie Alexander, recent-ly out of the Lost, as the front man. (Alexander had played with Yule in another post-Lost band, the Glass Menagerie.) This Boston Velvets line-up lasted for one European tour and a few U.S. festivals in the fall of

The 1977 Modern Lovers lineup backstage at the Hammersmith
Odeon in London. Clockwise from top left: D. Sharpe, Leroy Radcliffe,
Asa Brebner, and Jonathan Richman. (Courtesy Asa Brebner)

1971, and Alexander recalls the band was largely accepted as the real
thing. "I think people knew the Velvet Underground by reputation,
without having seen them—people seemed to think I was John Cale.
To me it was a ghost band, and the main problem was that I didn't
know any of the songs—ever! I had to beg Doug, 'Hey, give me a clue
on some of these.' So he hands me a little cheat sheet, but at the bottom he'd written, 'Fuck it—Fake it!'"

The Velvets were a prime influence on the Boston band that
formed in 1970 and gave the ultimate kiss-off to Boston's hippie era:
the Modern Lovers. A teenage rock outpouring fronted by a genuine
teenager (at the outset, at least), Jonathan Richman, the Modern Lovers
were everything the Bosstown bands weren't: raw, rough, optimistic,
hungry for romance, and, to quote a lyric, "in love with the modern
world." And it didn't hurt that Richman sprinkled his lyrics with a previously unheard-of amount of local references. "Put down your cigarette and drop out of BU," he sang to a girl who was evidently too chic

to talk to him. "If I were to walk through the Museum of Fine Arts in Boston, first I'd go to the room where they keep the Cézanne," he sang in another lyrical manifesto. "But if I had by my side a girlfriend, then I could look through the paintings, I could look right through them. . . . That's a girlfriend! That's a g-i-r-l-f-r-e-n! . . . That's something that I understand." Okay, so nobody ever gave out points for spelling. But if the late-sixties bands were hung up on making their grown-up statement, Richman's songs stated, quite plainly, what was really on a teenager's (and quite a few grown-ups') mind.

The Modern Lovers were arguably Boston's first great punk-rock band. "They could be terrible, but in a way that made you want to come back and see them again," recalls Aerosmith's bassist, Tom Hamilton. The Modern Lovers also had an anti-hippie attitude that put them right in line with the punks of the later seventies. In another love ballad, "I'm Straight," Richman scolds a girl who wants to go out with "hippie Johnny" instead of him—a dig at the band's original guitarist, John Felice. "I didn't mind, we were friends," Felice says. "The situation in the song was hypothetical—Jonathan was painting with a very broad brush in those days. But I was making no attempt to hide my love affair with mind-altering substances, whereas I think Jonathan smoked pot once in his life, and it made him deathly ill."

The music was equally brash, with the sneering vocals and dirty, distorted organ sound (the Harvard-schooled keyboardist Jerry Harrison would join the landmark band Talking Heads in 1976). Richman's love for the Velvet Underground was reflected in that sound; and John Cale would produce some of the band's demos, a portion of which eventually became their eponymous (and posthumous) debut album. But unlike the Velvets, who exuded downtown cool with their streetwise look and lyrics, the Modern Lovers sounded life-affirming and looked relatively innocent—Richman was often photographed in striped shirts, sporting either a sensitive gaze or a kid-next-door smile. Their signature song, "Roadrunner," belongs on anyone's list of the most exhilarating songs to come out of Boston or anywhere else: "Radio on!" yells the band as Richman sings of cruising down Route 128 past the Stop & Shop, convinced that life couldn't possibly hold anything better.

But if you'd come to Boston in 1971 and asked any insiders who the next band would be to break out of town, they probably would have named the Sidewinders. While Aerosmith and J. Geils respectively

Flyer drawn by Jonathan Richman. Caricatured, left to right, are David Robinson, Ernie Brooks, Richman, John Felice, and Jerry Harrison (Courtesy Willie Alexander)

had the loud rock and R&B bases covered and the Modern Lovers were helping create punk rock, the Sidewinders were waving the flag for catchy tunes and harmonies; and the band boasted a lead singer whose windblown hair and baby face made him a pop star waiting to happen. Playing sixties soul and pop songs along with similarly styled originals, the Sidewinders were the very thing that late-sixties culture had frowned upon: a party band.

Another of Jonathan Richman's flyers. (Courtesy Willie Alexander)

Those who saw the Sidewinders live remember the singer Andy Paley's sex appeal and Eric Rose's hotshot guitar leads. "The chemistry was so great that you could have been seeing Mick Jagger and Keith Richards," remembers Helanie Saad, a longtime scenester who was Paley's girlfriend at the time. "Such a wonderful thing to see on Boston Common, after those years of hippie bands and blues bands." Saad recalls exchanging harsh looks with a blonde who was eyeing Paley during a show, not realizing that she was Robert Kennedy's daughter Kathleen. "Andy had the blond pop-star hair, like a young Leif Garrett, and he had that way of holding the tambourine. So, yeah, he was so

The later Sidewinders lineup with Billy Squier. (Courtesy Willie Alexander)

attractive that I nearly got arrested by the Secret Service over it."

"We were into making people dance" is how Andy Paley, now based in Los Angeles, puts it. "I gotta say, when we started there wasn't much going on that really inspired me. We wanted to be different from everybody else, and we got a good following because we played a lot of mixers. At the time we were coming up, people were still doing long, endless jams and we weren't into that; all the songs we did were really short. What we did had nothing to do with anger and politics; it was all about catchy songs. Somebody wanted to hear a song, we'd give it a try. We'd do 'Harlem Shuffle,' 'Midnight Hour,' all those AM radio songs. We'd play four sets a night, maybe five. It was probably a little bit lighter than what had come before."

The Sidewinders and the Modern Lovers shared a rock-and-roll house at 27 Putnam Avenue in Cambridge, just off Harvard Square and within easy walking distance of Tommy's Lunch and the Orson Welles Cinema—both long-running hangouts for bohemians on a budget. "We'd meet each other after a show, hang out some, and then go to sleep. We were kids living out our rock-and-roll dream."

People like Peter Wolf and Steven Tyler (the respective front men of the J. Geils Band and Aerosmith) would wind up over at the house as well. Paley recalls:

At the time nobody was bigger than anybody else; that would happen in the long run. One time we played a gig with Aerosmith in Revere—a club that seemed to change its name every six months. It would declare bankruptcy, then open under another name. On this night the owner tried to stiff us for a certain amount of money; and Steven and I got together and decided we'd get tough on him. So we walked into the office ready for a fight, and he immediately pulled a gun on us. So we said, "Well, okay." There were five guys in Aerosmith and five in the Sidewinders, and I think everyone went home with twenty bucks that night. Somehow you did these gigs if you wanted to keep playing.

Certainly the world was ready for a band like the Sidewinders—and, indeed, bands like them did make it big, but the Sidewinders didn't happen to be one of them. The new movement of glitter- or glam-rock was just starting up, a movement that bridged sixties-inspired songwriting with the irreverence of late-seventies punk and threw in a lot of good old decadence. The image was wildly sexual, as guys in makeup and ballet outfits would forever redefine the notion of sex appeal; anyone who's seen an early-seventies photo of David Bowie in full regalia can guess at the amount of redefined sexuality going on at the time.

The definitive U.S. band of the genre had to be the New York Dolls, a proudly heterosexual (and as their legend would have it, extremely and actively heterosexual) band that wore more makeup than a roomful of *Glamour* cover girls. Boston was one of the few cities other than New York to pick up on the Dolls, who played the Club in Central Square a few times. Even Aerosmith—as their own legend has it, the most heterosexual band of them all—dabbled in gender-bending via the scarves and boas Steven Tyler wore onstage. Strip away the image and a lot of this music was out-for-kicks rock and roll; but the image was a part of the picture—something to titillate the insiders and offend everyone else.

Squares were duly shocked, but misfit teenagers had something they could take to heart. Critics and insiders also loved the social threat that bands like the Dolls represented. Both the Modern Lovers and the Sidewinders wound up with a foot in both camps: on the Boston mixer circuit, they played to Harvard and BU undergrads on date night. And on trips to New York, they played for Andy Warhol and his crowd at Max's Kansas City. "The Sidewinders weren't a glitter band, but they were very contemporaneous with the Dolls and their sound could've swung that way," figures Lenny Kaye.

The one thing the Sidewinders lacked was a solid album to put them across. By all accounts, their one RCA album (released in 1972, and now nearly impossible to find) didn't do the trick, though many of the tunes sound solid enough. But it does seem a bit reined-in, not quite the endless party that the group was known for. It was Lenny Kaye's first production job, and he's willing to take the rap for its commercial failure, though lack of label promotion and simple bad luck were likely factors as well. "It was pretty conservatively played and mixed by all of us. It was more of a starting point; we recorded some songs afterward that were truly epic. There was one called 'We Can Make a Better World,' which was in that Bruce Springsteen 'Born to Run' mold. But by then the band's lifeline was fading fast."

The Sidewinders soldiered on for a couple more years; and their last lineup featured the one member who did become a rock star: Billy Squier, a Wellesley native, joined in the later days, though only as a guitarist. He'd take the mike in the mid-seventies with the band Piper, then make a trio of platinum and multiplatinum solo albums from 1981 to 1984. The Sidewinders packed it in after a proposed TV series fizzled; the industry mogul Neil Bogart was pitching them as a teen-idol act in the vein of the Monkees and seventies stars the Hudson Brothers.

Yet Paley found his destiny the first time he saw the inside of a recording studio. He went on to a lucrative production career, working with the rock legends Brian Wilson and Jerry Lee Lewis. Before moving behind the boards full-time, however, he made one more stab at a front man's career. Teaming up with his brother Jonathan, he made a Paley Brothers album that came out in early 1978. If the Sidewinders' album was too early for its time, this one was a couple of years too late: the carefree sound didn't fit in with the punk-driven aggression of the late seventies. But the album's greatest non-hit, "Come Out and Play," sums up a lot of what the Sidewinders had been about. Using his best pop-star voice, Paley offers a romantic but hardly innocent invitation to a girlfriend: "I know you've been hurt, I know that you cried; I know that you won't be satisfied, until you come out and play!" Though written a few years later, that song was early-seventies Boston in a nutshell.

Aerosmith: Movin' Out

The Nipmuc Regional High School auditorium in Upton doesn't rate on anybody's list of glorious rock venues. But it's a gig, and a gig is all the band wanted when it made its worldwide debut there on November 6, 1970. There wasn't even a stage, so the band set up in a corner while the kids danced. Not having written any original songs yet, they played a set full of favorite tunes by John Lennon ("Cold Turkey"), the Rolling Stones, and the Yardbirds. The audience was receptive, or at least it danced; and the band celebrated by ripping off a bunch of T-shirts from the phys ed department. And so the career of Aerosmith was under way.

It was gigs like that—plenty of them, in every no-glory venue they could find—that turned Aerosmith into a world-class band. "We thought we were one from the beginning," the bassist Tom Hamilton recalls. "We were probably in denial about how much focus and hard work it was going to take to make it." By the time the band started achieving nationwide success, locals had probably stumbled across a free Aerosmith show or three. "We did a lot of free shows," recalls Joey Kramer, the drummer. "A lot of high schools and hops, country clubs in New Hampshire—the King Ridge ski mountain was a good one. We did high school dances in Littleton, the student union at BU, the Franklin Park Zoo—anything we could to get our name out there." Hamilton recalls that navy bases were also a good bet, since they'd throw a free dinner into the bargain.

Aerosmith during their eighties comeback. Left to right: Tom Hamilton, Joey Kramer, Brad Whitford, Steven Tyler, Joe Perry. (Photo: Paul Robicheau)

Aerosmith is now enshrined as Boston's first superstar band, and after more than thirty-five years they likely hold the record as the longest-running, all-original lineup in rock-and-roll history. But their origins were as humble and as low-budget as anyone else's. High school friends Joe Perry (guitar) and Tom Hamilton (bass) had hung out together in New Hampshire, and they moved to Boston with rock-and-roll dreams. These were partly realized when they recruited Steven Tyler (born Steven Tallarico), a singer and drummer, to join their fledgling band; it was Perry who convinced Tyler he'd be a better front man if he wasn't stuck behind the drums. A pair of onetime Berklee students, the drummer Joey Kramer and the guitarist Brad Whitford (who replaced a short-time member, Ray Tabano), came in to complete a lineup that at first had energy, ambition, and little else to show.

As Hamilton recalls, the out-of-the-way gigs happened because at the start of the seventies there wasn't enough of a club scene for a band playing original songs. Even before they had any originals ("Movin' Out," which would appear on their debut album, was the first of their own songs), Aerosmith had grand designs. So more of their inspiration came from beloved British acts like the Stones, Jeff Beck, and Fleet-

wood Mac than anything happening in Boston. "Even if we were playing schools, we wanted our shows to feel more like a concert than a
club vibe. I had just graduated from high school myself, so I didn't
think of those shows as, My God, we're playing for high school kids.
Long as they had a stage we could play on, we were happy." They even
had a stage backdrop for those early shows, an orange tribal banner that
Tyler had permanently borrowed as a souvenir when he went to the
Woodstock festival in 1969.

Three hundred a month bought them an apartment at 1325 Commonwealth Avenue—a classic rock-and-roll flophouse deep in the heart
of BU territory. Guitars and amps were stacked along the walls ("when
we weren't out losing them," says Kramer), and the five band members
shared the three bedrooms and one bathroom. Their first rehearsal space
was also in the BU area, and much of the day and night was devoted to
music—save for one half hour that was given to a different ritual. As
Kramer recalls, "If we were rehearsing, we'd stop right at 4:15, hitchhike
home, and pile into Brad's room because he was the only one who had
a TV. We'd pile in there, smoke a bone, and watch *The Three Stooges.*
That happened every day, and we're still fans of theirs today."

One enduring mystery about Aerosmith is the source of their band
name. Fans are aware that Kramer came up with it; he's maintained that
Sinclair Lewis' novel *Arrowsmith* was not where he got the idea. Even
the band's box set, *Box of Fire,* claims it was "just a cool sounding word"
that he used to scribble in high school notebooks to kill time. But the
actual source of the word may be more of a surprise. "I had a high
school friend named Patti, and we used to sit up in her bedroom playing records," he says. "We played a lot of the Nazz, and Harry Nilsson—
that Nilsson album, *Aerial Ballet,* was one that we listened to a lot. So
that's where Aerosmith came from; it was a play on [Nilsson's] title and
the word aerial."

Getting evicted from their BU practice space proved to be the first
turning point in the band's career. A friend of the band (the Reddy
Teddy bassist Scott Baerenwald) hooked them up with a new rehearsal
space at Berklee College of Music, where, they were told, the local impresario Frank Connelly (who'd brought the Beatles into town a few
years earlier) sometimes checked out new bands. "One day we were
rehearsing and the lights went down," Hamilton recalls. "We couldn't
see into the hall but we heard someone saying, 'It's all right, now play a

few of your songs.'" They found Connelly's management contracts waiting for them afterward.

Connelly also hooked up their first New York showcase—an open-ing slot for the British band Humble Pie and future star Edgar Winter; there were managers and label reps in the audience. This proved to be both a high and a low point in their early career. "We played forty-five minutes of our songs, and thought we played really well. We come off-stage and [Winter's manager] Steve Paul said we were 'not bad for a baby band'—that was a phrase that bothered us for a while." They would probably have been happier with a phrase from a review of their 1973 debut album that appeared in *Creem* magazine, from tougher-than-thou Detroit: "These guys played my neighborhood and they're still alive, so what are you waiting for?"

Success continued to come in stages, usually when the band was too busy on the road to notice. That first album— recorded at Inter-media Studios on Newbury Street, after the industry legend Clive Davis saw a later New York show and signed them to Columbia—in-cluded a song that everyone in the band thought would be their first hit, "Dream On," Tyler's one piano ballad on the record. And it was a hit—three years after its release. In a rare turn of events, "Dream On" peaked on the charts at number fifty-nine upon its release in 1973, but it didn't really catch on until 1976, by which time the band was two more albums into its career. "We always thought it would be a hit; we had no doubts about anything we were doing," Hamilton recalls. "But after 'Dream On' came out, our manager showed a sheet of responses from all these stations. Whatever we did, we couldn't get it on the radio. And he said, 'Okay, we're not going to make it that way, so you better get back on the road.' The song probably caught on because of all the touring we did."

Aerosmith would tour with many of the major seventies acts, but the first matchup had to be the strangest: they were put on the road with the Mahavishnu Orchestra, the spiritually inclined jazz-rock band fronted by the guitarist John McLaughlin. "We'd do our forty-five min-utes, then McLaughlin would come onstage and ask for a moment of silence," Kramer recalls. "When he couldn't get that moment of silence anymore, he asked us to leave the tour."

Boston audiences would see many of the band's fluctuations in for-tune firsthand. When the initial album failed to take off, they moved into another band house, this one in Brighton's Cleveland Circle, and came up with the material for the classic sophomore album *Get Your Wings*. "We rallied for that one," says Hamilton. "The label told us, 'The next record had better kick some ass,' but we were feeling pretty inspired." Another early peak was a local show at Paul's Mall that WBCN aired live on April 23, 1973. A couple of songs made it onto their official live album, 1978's *Live Bootleg,* but fans have unofficial copies of the whole thing. As Hamilton says, "We could still play [in later years] when we were wiped out. But that show was an example of how in-the-pocket we could be before the drugs took over."

As for the hard times, those came later. Suffice it to say that it's not always easy when a band has both a strong work ethic and an equally strong hedonistic streak. As Hamilton recalls, "When we went into [the studio for] the third album [1975's *Toys in the Attic*], I wanted to buckle down and become a better player, and I wanted to start writing as well. So I applied myself; I'd get out my cocaine and practice all night. We also did speed in the early days—not a lot, but it was great for practicing. So there were times when we used stuff like that to become better at what we did. And that works, until you start getting the money to use it all the time. That *Draw the Line* album [from 1977] was the height of the decrepitude. The title song is still one of our favorites to play. But I hear that record and I hear what drugs were doing to the band." A public, drug-fueled fallout, and an equally public recovery and multi-platinum (and multigenerational) comeback, would follow in the ensuing decades. But for Aerosmith, the seventies were perhaps the wildest part of a long, wild ride.

The J. Geils Band: Ain't Nothing but a House Party

The Catacombs on Boylston Street was a club that lived up to its name. Set in a subbasement near the Arlington T stop, its music room was two floors below ground. The first flight downstairs led to a pool room; the music was another flight below. If you were the day's first band setting up to play, you'd turn on the light and throw something to scare away the cockroaches. In short, it was a perfect place for a gritty R&B band to sweat it out onstage. And if you got there on a typical night in 1968, the band you'd see jamming on Chicago blues standards was a formative version of Boston's first superstar band. Of course, neither you nor the band would have guessed that yet.

Few groups are more closely associated with Boston than the J. Geils
Band, even though it only had one native Bostonian in its lineup. Over
the next decade and a half, the group would play to every kind of tiny
club and stadium-sized audience, release more than a dozen albums,
and ultimately become a fixture on radio and MTV. By the eighties the
band had fans who hadn't even been born in the Catacombs days. But
the marathon, multi-encore live shows remained their calling card.
Even after they'd moved up to the stadiums, a Geils Band show was
never over until everyone in the place was ready to drop.

Before the J. Geils Band that everyone knows—the band with the
spectral, shades-wearing Peter Wolf up front—there was the J. Geils
Blues Band. Like many musicians who hit town in the late sixties,
Geils, a New York native, and his bandmates—Danny Klein on bass and
the harmonica whiz Magic Dick (Klein was born in New York and
raised in New Jersey; Dick was from New London, Connecticut)—fell
in love with the blues and changed their lives accordingly. That meant
dropping out of Worcester Polytechnic, where the three met and began
playing together. They got more education from the nearby Union
Music store, which carried instruments along with the vintage vinyl
they craved. "I remember distinctly, me and Dick used to walk down
there with five bucks in our pocket," Geils recalls. "I'd say to him,
'Okay, you buy this Muddy Waters record, I'll buy this Little Walter, and
we'll swap.' Dick was the kind of guy who could hear the harp playing
on one of those records and learn it in ten minutes—whereas I'd be
learning my B.B. King riffs, but it would take me half a day."

The trio left Worcester in the spring of 1967 and moved into the
first of two band houses, on Waldo Avenue in Inman Square, in Cambridge. The newly formed J. Geils Blues Band started performing soon
afterward, and it found itself part of a new musical environment. Bob
Dylan had done his famous electric performance at the Newport Folk
Festival two summers earlier; as a result, electric music was everywhere
—even in folk clubs like Harvard Square's Club 47 and the Prudential
area's Unicorn, which had been staunchly acoustic before Dylan
dropped his bombshell. "It really was a change of attitude," Geils says.
"The Chicago guys started coming in, electric bands like Muddy Waters and Howlin' Wolf. Whereas if you'd walked into Club 47 with an
electric guitar and an amp in 1964, you'd have either been thrown out
or shot."

The band intersected with Dylan's world early on: the young Chicago blues great Mike Bloomfield, who'd played the electric guitar in Dylan's band at Newport, hit Boston for a show and went looking for the Geils band. He found them at the second band house on Mountfort Street in Boston, where they'd moved in the summer of 1967. Now demolished along with the rest of the buildings on the street, the house was a few blocks away from Fenway Park; band members used to watch Red Sox games on their black-and-white TV and open the window for a live soundtrack.

Geils recalls, "Dick was in his room playing along with a Little Walter record, I was in my room playing B.B. King, and Danny was down the hall playing to an Otis Redding record. Mike Bloomfield knocked on the door and said, 'This sounds like where we live in Chicago. This must be the place!'" Another early brush with greatness came when the bluesman Buddy Guy wrapped up a show at Club 47 and went across town to the Unicorn for a late-night summit. "Someone had told him about us," Geils says. "It's one thing to learn stuff off the records, but another to be standing next to Buddy Guy onstage. What did it sound like? We sucked! But we jammed until three in the morning, and that's how you get better."

If fate hadn't intervened, the Geils Band might have kept on as a traditionally minded blues band. But they were deciding to get rid of their original singer and drummer just as Peter Wolf's band, the Hallucinations, was about to break up. A fellow New York transplant, Wolf had grown up tuned to the sound of street-corner doo-wop. But in Boston he'd already been making a name as a charismatic DJ for WBCN. (He would carry his jive-talking "Woofa-Goofa-Mamma-Toofah" persona onstage.) He brought the band a strong personality and a less reverent approach to R&B. With him came the Hallucinations' drummer, Stephen Jo Bladd, the one native Bostonian.

"That was our step away from folk blues," says Geils. "The other thing Peter and Stephen understood wasn't just the R&B influence, but the idea of a musical show: we'd come on and do a couple instrumentals, then build up to Wolf's entrance. It wasn't as well rehearsed as the James Brown show, but we started coming in from that angle, as opposed to all those bands in flowered shirts who stood there looking like the Grateful Dead—that was exactly what we didn't want to be." The final piece of the picture was Seth Justman—a Washington, D.C.–born

Peter Wolf meets the crowd at a Worcester Centrum show with the J. Geils Band. (Photo: Paul Robicheau)

Boston University student, five years younger than the others—who'd taken to hanging out at the Catacombs shows. "He'd sit down and play the piano, and we struck up a friendship. We gave him an audition and, sure enough, he shows up and starts schlepping this big organ up the stairs. Wolf was immediately suspicious: 'What's that, a piece of your grandmother's furniture?' But we heard him play, and in two minutes flat Stephen was saying, 'Yeah, man!' So he was in."

Thus the classic six-piece lineup was under way—just in time for more drastic changes in the music business. Soon-to-be major players like Don Law were bringing national acts into town, and the concert circuit was growing nationwide. "That all stemmed from Dylan at Newport," Geils says. "It spawned a lot of new promoters and agents who got the vision to get hold of ballrooms and do rock concerts. It happened in a lot of second- and third-level towns across the country that had unused movie theaters." Record labels were likewise thinking big, along the lines of chart success and long-term careers—and the bands most likely to get courted were the ones drawing crowds in those theaters. So it was that an Atlantic Records scout (and blues fan), Mario Medious, showed up at one of their Tea Party shows (incidentally opening for Atlantic's Led Zeppelin) and convinced his boss, Jerry Wexler, to grab the Geils Band before someone else did.

In some ways, the business then was far more innocent than it is now. Bands were allowed years, and multiple albums, to find their audience. That didn't necessarily mean they'd get rich, at least not from the records: Geils says that his band didn't make a dime from any of their albums until well into the eighties. But they did get to keep developing, scoring a few hit singles along the way. "Looking for a Love," from their second album, 1972's *The Morning After,* and the reggae-tinged "Give It to Me," from their fourth album, *Bloodshot* (1973), were the first real breakthroughs. It took nearly a decade before the major hits, "Freeze Frame" and "Centerfold," came along. But by that time the Geils Band had built their name as a live act.

"We did everything ass-backwards," Geils admits. "People would have a hit record, then go on tour and make money. We did the opposite. People would buy our records because they saw us on tour. When we signed with Atlantic, we didn't have a lawyer, an agent, or even a manager." But they learned fast, signing up with the agent Frank Barsalona and a manager, Dee Anthony, two of the music business's emerging big guns. Anthony, who began his career road-managing Tony Bennett in the fifties, was a player with his share of savvy: it was Anthony who told one of his other clients, Peter Frampton, that his studio albums weren't hitting and that he should release a live one instead. The result—*Frampton Comes Alive!*—was at the time one of the biggest-selling albums in history.

Anthony also got the Geils Band out of trouble more than once. Geils recalls a show in the mid-seventies, playing for a shady promoter in Atlantic City. "We made a good amount of money for that show, something like ten thousand dollars up front. Three days later we get a phone call—it turned out that the whole ten grand had been counterfeit. So Dee says, 'Hey, don't worry about it. I'll write you guys a check and we'll put the ten grand into petty cash.' And that's what happened. Over the next three years we spent the counterfeit money on office supplies and passed it all around New York."

The Geils Band opened for Black Sabbath on their first national tour; but soon-to-be bigger names would be opening for Geils before long. "After we started headlining, we had a rule that there was always an opening act. One time fairly early on, we were booked into a fancy hall in Princeton; we pull up and the sign says, 'An Evening with the J. Geils Band.' We pull in and said, 'No, we don't do that. We don't play with an intermission. We do our show and that's it. You have to get us an opener—a folk singer, a comedian, anybody. Just get someone.' Finally someone speaks up and says, 'I know this guy who plays piano and does his own songs, he's pretty good.'" The piano player not only did the show, but he wound up going in a louder direction himself. His name: Billy Joel.

Other shows were less glorious. "Believe me, we played plenty of shows for twenty people, even after we had records out. There was one in Johnson City, Tennessee, that had maybe two dozen people. And Wolf comes to the front of the stage and says, 'All you people, forget your seats, come down front and we're gonna play for you.' It was one of the best shows we ever did. Another night we decided that we were going to outlast the audience; we were going to keep playing until they went home. I think we did eleven encores, practically another whole show. We were pulling songs out of our hats that we didn't even know—'Okay, let's go back and jam a blues!' We finally beat them."

Though the Geils Band's two seventies live albums, *Full House* and *Blow Your Face Out,* didn't reach the commercial heights of *Frampton Comes Alive!* they kept people coming in; by 1977 the lack of a real hit single didn't keep them from headlining Madison Square Garden. A live version of "Must of Got Lost" became an FM radio favorite, as much for Wolf's manic spoken intro ("It's Woofa Goofa with the green teeth!") as for the song itself. "It sounded like he was winging it, but he developed that over time, much like a comedian would," says Geils. "The one on the record was a particularly good one.

"It became clear to us early that we were learning the game, and that the name of the game was making hit records," Geils says. "And we came to realize that we were in show business as much as we were in the music business. I had always wanted to be Miles Davis or Charlie

Parker, but here I am in the same business as Sammy Davis Jr. We didn't necessarily set out to make hits; but we weren't trying to be noncommercial, either. So we tried to keep our edge while we branched out. 'Give It to Me' was reggae, and I'll credit Wolf on that one—he brought a Bob Marley record into rehearsal and said, 'Hey, listen to this, it's a whole different thing.' Later we dabbled in disco, but it was black, R&B–influenced disco. Instead of trying to sound like Muddy Waters or Otis Redding, we were making our own music, and we always said, 'I'll know it when I hear it.'"

After slowly building for more than a decade, the Geils Band finally had its commercial breakthrough just in time for the MTV era. A few factors made it possible. They'd left the Atlantic label in 1977 and signed with EMI, which was more determined to score hits. Justman took a stronger hand in the musical direction, modernizing the sound with synthesizers and massive-sounding drums. He came up with "Centerfold" and, together with Wolf, wrote "Freeze Frame," two of the catchiest songs of the band's career. And the band had a secret weapon in Justman's older brother Paul, a filmmaker who could direct videos. In particular, the "Freeze Frame" video, with the band splashing around in multicolored house paint, did a good job of catching their offbeat sense of humor.

"We saw how things were changing," Geils says. "You'd turn in the album, they'd say, 'That song's a hit, you need a video to go with it.' And we'd say, 'Huh?' But Paul came in and was the liaison with the label. He'd already done a J. Geils Band documentary called *Postcards*—just us hanging out in a bar shooting pool—that never got released, but it exists somewhere. It gave us a leg up to have him around."

But the band's greatest hit turned out to be the original lineup's swan song. Interpersonal tensions, largely between Wolf and Justman, welled up during sessions in the spring of 1983 for the studio follow-up to *Freeze Frame;* suddenly Wolf was out and the band made a brief, unsuccessful attempt to carry on without him. As a result, the Geils Band played its last shows (until a short-lived 1999 reunion) without realizing it. They were booked to play New Year's Eve 1983 at the Worcester Centrum; they added two extra shows because of the demand for tickets. So the story ended barely two miles away from the college that three of its members originally dropped out of—not with a ceremonial farewell, but with one last house party.

James Montgomery, Duke & the Drivers: Schooling Them Dice

Rhythm and blues continued to gain steam, and by the early seventies Boston and Cambridge were home to a hardworking and hard-playing (in both senses of the word) group of blues-schooled musicians who held court at clubs like the Western Front and Cambridge's long-since-shut Candlelight Lounge. And as the bandleader James Montgomery recalls, some of the best moments happened before and after the shows. "You'd be having a beer somewhere and the next thing you know, you'd be sitting next to Bonnie Raitt or Livingston Taylor—it just wasn't that uncommon. Our band had a big orange tour van, and we called it the Club d'Orange. Sometimes the party would be at my house, or at Bonnie's. But we'd throw in a case of beer, drive it around, and pick up people. Nobody had made the big break yet, so it really was about hanging out with a bunch of friends."

Bonnie Raitt, a Los Angeles transplant, was the most successful of the college students who dropped out to play music full-time. After two years at Radcliffe College, she became a fixture on the blues-folk circuit, playing often at Club 47; and the chops she learned opening for legends like Muddy Waters and Sippie Wallace informed the raw, bluesy flavor of her first few albums. Though she did most of her recording in Los Angeles, she and her band would remain visible on the Cambridge scene. Montgomery recalls one show that he and Raitt's bassist—the bearded, eccentric character known as Freebo—threw together at the spur of the moment. "Freebo would call me up and say, 'I'm in town for a couple of days; let's put together a band!' So we booked ourselves into Jacks as Stupid Liver and the Walking Xylophones—even had bowling shirts with the initials WX on them. Bonnie sat in, Peter Wolf did too. We started with fifty people in the place, and by the end they were all crowded around on the street."

Montgomery also came here for college; and it says something that a native of Detroit, no slouch of a music town itself, would feel strongly enough about the Boston scene to relocate. He was gigging regularly long before graduating from Boston University, and by 1973 the James Montgomery Band was one of the most successful bands on the northeast college circuit. Credit partly New England's enduring love for the blues, and Montgomery's bringing in some rock-and-roll instincts: he played blues with a hard-driving rock flavor, an approach he'd picked up in industrial Detroit. And with his elegantly wasted look, changing hair color, and penchant for rings and scarves, he looked like a lost cousin of Aerosmith's Steven Tyler. "I even went through a period where I had reddish hair and twenty or thirty bracelets at once," he laughs. "I think my problem was that I wanted to be a hippie in high school and my mom wouldn't let me."

Though the Montgomery band never hit the big time, their position as a leading northeastern blues act put them in some heady company. They were signed to Capricorn, the southern label best known for its recordings of the Allman Brothers Band, with the legendary producer Tom Dowd behind the boards. (Unfortunately, Montgomery recalls that Dowd worked with him just after his last client, Eric Clapton, had steered him toward a more laid-back approach, so the Montgomery Band's sweaty sound was never quite captured.) Montgomery chose to record his debut album in Philadelphia, and one of his favorite memories is of his all-night craps games with the legendary soul group the O'Jays. "They were more than happy to gamble with us, but they kept hitting us with rules we never heard before. One of our guys would roll snake eyes and they'd say, 'That doesn't win—that loses. That's the Philadelphia rule!'" Montgomery lost some cash but gained a song called "Schooling Them Dice," a live favorite for decades afterward.

Montgomery's reputation as a harmonica player also had its surprise payoffs. One New Year's Eve Mick Jagger, a harmonica aficionado, showed up at a club performance and invited Montgomery to hang out afterward. "We spent the rest of the evening riding around in his limousine with three blondes. It was a very interesting New Year's Eve. Really, it just seemed that everyone in the music industry was behaving the same way in those days. You get invited to spend a few days at Steven Tyler's house and it seems harmless enough, until you wind up firing automatic weapons at four in the morning." Indeed, Montgomery makes no secret that he indulged plenty—until one morning in the late eighties when he decided he'd had enough. He resolved to put the same energy into bodybuilding that he'd once put into cocaine, the result being that his looks came to match his muscular sound.

Montgomery's younger comrades on the early seventies circuit were Duke & the Drivers—a band that played Paul's Mall on Boylston Street in Boston in 1974, on a night when the club set an all-time record for alcohol sales. That remains one of the Drivers' proudest achievements,

proof that they pretty much ruled the party circuit at the time. There
was hardly a bar, frat house, or club that didn't get a visit from this group
of rhythm-and-blues fanatics, who all sported colorful names and stage
personae: Henry "Cadillac Jack" Eaton was a slick figure in shades; the
guitarist Joe "Sam Deluxe" Lilly had the lean and shaggy rock-star look;
Greg "Earthquake" Morton was the tall and hulking bass player; Ando
"Rhinestone Mudflaps" Hixon was the colorful MC sporting a lamé
jacket and pencil-thin moustache. And the band's nominal leader was
the mysterious Duke, a figure that nobody ever saw in the flesh. "I've
still never met him," Morton claims today. "I know as much about the
Duke as you do. All I know is that we're on this journey together."

Like the J. Geils Band—for whom the Drivers would open at the
Boston Garden—they started out playing their own cover versions of
favorite little-known singles. But the Drivers' roots go back to Miami,
where Morton used to hang out at TK Studios—at that time a hotbed
of southern soul (and later the home of disco stars KC and the Sunshine Band). "My life was centered in that studio, finishing high school,
and seeing people like Betty Wright, [the producer] Clarence Reid, and
all the people who played on [Wright's hit] 'Clean Up Woman,'" he recalls. But everyone in the group was a fan and collector, and no one
saw a problem with playing mostly borrowed songs—even if some
clubs did. Jacks, outside Harvard Square, wouldn't have them before
they started writing originals, so the first Drivers shows were at the
Western Front, a hidden-away Cambridgeport club.

Morton picked most of their material, mainly soul nuggets that had
been hits only farther south. Though they wound up writing some of
their own songs, the Drivers never had designs on being the most original band around. "Honoring other people's music was really what we
were all about, and it helped to have someone like Joe on guitar who
could translate it. I was a total record geek." The New Orleans figure
Eddie Bo's "Check Your Bucket" was a favorite live number, as was
"What You Got" by a Philadelphia group, the Soul Brothers Six. The
latter became Duke & the Drivers' one hit single, a bigger hit—and a
more spirited record—than the Philly group's original.

Along with their incessant gigging, they got a boost from the wide-
open state of local radio in the early seventies. Morton was a regular lis-
tener to Little Walter's late-night oldies show on MIT's radio station,
WTBS, which played some of the same records that inspired him to

form the band. And the Drivers became identified with the early WBCN—which was less political by 1973 but still freewheeling enough to play a Boston band before it had a record out. "They played our version of 'Check Your Bucket,' which was never even released. And I'll never forget the time I heard [afternoon DJ] Maxanne Sartori say, 'After two Duke & the Drivers songs, there's nothing better than a third one.' So really, 'BCN made us legends in our own mind. One of my favorite moments was a live broadcast we did from the auditorium at BU, where they had to clear the place because it was rocking so hard. You could feel the energy emanating from the radio; it was a great train wreck."

The dark secret in the Drivers' closet is that most of them hail from upper-class backgrounds; Lilly's family founded the pharmaceutical company that developed Prozac—so in a sense he was going into the family business by playing music that made people feel good. Swift is now a lawyer, Morton a restaurateur. "You can say the band was our way of rebelling, but the truth is that our backgrounds didn't have anything to do with it," Morton insists. "What we were really about was taking great music and honoring it. We learned how to write tunes, but getting up there and doing a song like 'Check Your Bucket' gave me more pleasure than anything else in the world."

Orchestra Luna: You Gotta Have Heart

So the early seventies Boston sound was all about rhythm and blues? Not completely. As always, Boston latched onto a certain sound and then created the antidote. And you would have found the antithesis of R&B if you'd wandered into Jeremiah's—a health food restaurant on Harvard Avenue in Allston—on a typical weekend night in 1974. What you saw onstage might resemble a high school theater pageant if the principal were David Bowie. One production number, about how UFOs are coming to save our planet, found the lanky lead singer testifying in drag. For a glossy finale, the band would put on Red Sox uniforms and do the *Damn Yankees* number "[You've Gotta Have] Heart."

Welcome to the world of Orchestra Luna, the first Boston band of its type—whatever that type was. Certainly, its leader, Rick Berlin (then known as Richard Kinscherf), didn't intend to form a cabaret-jazz-Broadway-rock revue. But as often happened in the seventies, a few modest ideas got wonderfully out of hand. Indeed, Berlin entered the music business purely by accident. He moved to Boston from New

Haven—where he'd been part of Yale University's official singing
group, the Whiffenpoofs—and worked at a group home for delinquent
youth long enough to afford an electric piano. One night he was playing and singing with the windows open in his Somerville apartment,
only to have a guy overhear it, knock on his door, and tell him he
needed a manager. The band was signed to a major label exactly six
months later.

Berlin worked fast during that half year. His visitor was a local in-
sider named Harry Bee, who with his partner, Bruce Patch, had already
gotten the local songwriter Andy Pratt signed to the Epic label. (Pratt's
underground hit, "Avenging Annie," was later recorded by Roger Dal-
trey of the Who, who couldn't match Pratt's unearthly falsetto.) Never
having formed a band before, Berlin called in his sister and some New
Haven friends, recruiting the rest of the players from Berklee. When the
dust cleared, he had a motley crew that included two female singers,
one spoken-word specialist, and a hotshot jazz-rock guitarist, Randy
Roos. Another friend, Barry Keating, arrived from Amherst, where he'd
worked on a musical theater project with the fledgling composer-
director and classical pianist Jim Steinman. Ideas for staging and cos-
tuming were being conceived along with the songs and arrangements.

"Nobody told us what not to do, so we just went and did it," Berlin
recalls. "It was very much that Mickey Rooney–Judy Garland idea of
'Let's put on a show!'—but we weren't anywhere near that slick. It was
all very silly and emotional—I mean, we had the guitar player, bass, and
drummer doing one movement of Beethoven's Seventh Symphony.
And we were doing that at rock clubs!"

That, in fact, was one of the more conventional moments of
Orchestra Luna's show. More typical was the UFO number about a
"society of believers," called "SOB-UFO-USA." During this tune, roadies in white coats would pass literature out to the audience, and Berlin
would appear as the fictional society's president, Edith Overlook. "I really loved Patti Smith at the time, so I figured that if she could do mono-
logues, I'd have Edith do one. It was the only time in my life I've ever
done drag." Another production number, "Doris Dreams," was inspired
by Berlin's time working in a beauty parlor. "It was a fourteen-minute
song that went all over the map—jazz, classical, light opera. The girls
had layers of masks that they'd remove during the song, as Doris came
to realize her own inner beauty."

Not surprisingly, Orchestra Luna played its first gig at the Other Side, a gay- and artist-oriented bar near the Theater District. This was where one could meet whatever Andy Warhol associates happened to be in town, along with, as Berlin puts it, "a parade of drag queens, college kids, and big fat gangsters with their girlfriends and boyfriends. It was a place for people who wanted to experience the Boston underworld—that whole post-Stonewall joie de vivre was there." But the less glorious Jeremiah's—"a little hippie place with natural food and spider plants"—became their home base. Garden-variety rockers seemed to embrace them as well; they even shared bills with James Montgomery more than once. As Berlin admits, the lineup's having two pretty women—the singers Liz Gallagher and Berlin's sister, a Mia Farrow look-alike, Lisa Kinscherf—didn't hurt their chances for straight-male appeal.

"When we played our first gigs, Lisa was still dealing with stage fright—She had this tremulous, fearful quality that she was trying to get over in front of your eyes." Roos's guitar prowess also helped balance the band's exotic tendencies; and when Orchestra Luna played a New York party celebrating Frank Zappa's tenth anniversary in music, Zappa picked up the diminutive Roos and hugged him after the set. "I also had friends that liked to see us when they were tripping," Berlin says. "The players were good and the girls were pretty, and you didn't feel there was a wall between us and the audience."

In an era that gave us Bowie and *The Rocky Horror Picture Show,* a band like Orchestra Luna didn't seem too far-fetched. And it somehow made sense that the coproducer of their one Epic album, Rupert Holmes, was working with Barbra Streisand at the same time. (Holmes was a few years away from writing both the musical *The Mystery of Edwin Drood* and the camp classic "Escape [the Piña Colada Song].") Theatrical rock would find its day when Jim Steinman retooled songs from his Amherst musical into Meat Loaf's "Bat Out of Hell," released three years later. But in 1974 the mainstream wasn't quite ready for Orchestra Luna, and the album disappeared soon after its release. "We were called Epic's 1974 mistake. The guy who signed us got fired, probably for signing us," Berlin laments.

The band splintered soon after, though Berlin formed a second Orchestra Luna (this one featuring the singer Karla DeVito, who'd later record and tour with Meat Loaf), then a guitar-led, non-Broadway rock band called Luna. A string of bands followed in the next two decades—

Berlin Airlift, Rick Berlin: The Movie, and the Shelley Winters Project—before he finally declared himself a solo artist around 2000, by then long established as a well-liked fixture on the scene. Those later projects were all relatively normal, songwriting-based groups. But the theatrics of Orchestra Luna, as well as the sexual ambiguity, would be picked up by bands from Human Sexual Response in the early eighties to the modern cabaret rockers the Dresden Dolls.

Berlin was among the first of Boston's openly gay rockers, but in the glittery seventies scene it was assumed that everyone was experimenting with something. "[The question of sexuality] never came up—the attitude back then was that I'm an artist first and my sexuality is second. Besides, my love affairs have always been with very troubled people, and that's something a lot of people can understand," Berlin remarked.

Boston: More Than a Feeling

By the mid-seventies rock and roll had become big business. Stadium shows were now a full-fledged spectacle, and a million-dollar industry was emerging around them. Don Law, the former Boston Tea Party booking agent, was now taking his place at the forefront. According to Fred Goodman's book *The Mansion on the Hill,* there were seventy-six rock shows at Boston Garden between 1976 and 1980, and Law promoted all but three. Despite its humble origins, the next big Boston band would embody the grandeur of arena rock.

After Aerosmith and the J. Geils Band broke through, it took until 1976 for Boston to produce another superstar band. And when that band happened, it appeared out of virtually nowhere. It's no exaggeration to say that hardly anyone in town had ever heard of a band called Boston: they hadn't been in the big clubs, hadn't been written about, had barely played outside the suburbs. But there it was, a song called "More Than a Feeling" that suddenly turned up on FM radio stations nationwide, fitting in perfectly right next to Fleetwood Mac and the Eagles.

Before the end of that year, the band would be headlining arenas, and all eight songs on the album would be on the radio—in fact, "More Than a Feeling," "Foreplay/Long Time," and "Peace of Mind"—the original album's entire first side—have been there ever since. It was an obviously commercial album but also an obviously good one, with sleek guitar tones that hadn't been heard before, a singer with wall-shaking range, and songs that sounded epic but also hit on a direct, emotional level. Right alongside Fleetwood Mac's *Rumours,* Meat Loaf's *Bat Out of Hell,* and very few others, that first Boston disc became one of the flagship albums of the emerging AOR (album-oriented rock) radio format—no small feat for an album that was conceived mostly during off-hours in a basement in Watertown, Massachusetts.

Boston had everything and nothing to do with the local scene, coming out with no buzz and virtually no fan base. But, in a way, they represented every suburban band with dreams of grandeur. The songs on that first album have all the overstatement of mid-seventies arena rock—the ache of romance, the reach for personal freedom, and the inevitable party song. But Tom Scholz's multilayered guitars and keyboards and Brad Delp's high-registered vocals carry those young-adult urges into something epic. Not for nothing did the album feature the thematically inappropriate, but suitably grandiose, image of a spaceship on the cover.

The story of that first album, and how exactly Boston did it, remains the subject of many myths. Many think that Tom Scholz, the band's leader, was a technical brainiac who shut himself away at MIT for half of the seventies while getting his master's degree in mechanical engineering and dreaming up guitar sounds. It's generally supposed that Boston was a studio creation that had never played a live gig before it was famous. Boston actually recorded a song on that album called "Rock & Roll Band," which recalls playing on the streets in Hyannis, "living on rock and roll music," and having record execs show up at their gigs—a good song, but a completely fictionalized version of their history. In fact, Boston did perform, under its original name of Mother's Milk, mainly in suburban clubs for years. But it was the first band from Boston—and one of the first from anywhere—to get famous entirely because of tapes they had recorded before anyone noticed them.

The story begins more than five years before the debut album came out. And Boston began as the union of two suburban cover bands, both of which were going nowhere fast. The lead singer, Brad Delp, and Fran Sheehan, a bassist, were part of Middle Earth, a collegiate band on the verge of breaking up. "I was with them for about a year, and we had no paying gigs in that time. Guess you'd call them all 'exposure' gigs, because there was no money," recalled Delp, who'd joined the band during a spell at North Shore Community College. "We played strictly up and down the North Shore. The best gig was probably at Endicott College, just because it was an all-women's school and we enjoyed that. For a time we had horn players so we could do Chicago and Blood, Sweat & Tears songs, but we didn't do them very well."

With Middle Earth on its last legs, Delp was advised to check out another cover band, this one playing on Revere Beach and needing a singer. This was Mother's Milk, a trio of Tom Scholz (keyboards), Barry Goudreau (guitar), and Jim Masdea (drums). "The songs I remember them playing were the Grateful Dead's 'Casey Jones' and Booker T. & the M.G.'s' 'Green Onions,' which Tom used the Hammond organ on. I thought their arrangements were pretty impressive, so it seemed worth it to audition for them." Nobody was thinking too hard of originality at this point; Delp figured he got the gig because he could do a good impression of Joe Walsh of the James Gang, a favorite of Scholz's at the time. "He [Walsh] had a pretty whiny voice, but I could do it if I had to. With all my years in cover bands, I'd come to pride myself on being a good mimic."

Yet this late-1970 incarnation of Mother's Milk—Delp, Scholz, Sheehan, Goudreau, and Masdea—was essentially the same band that would be known as Boston a half decade later. (Sib Hashian was the main drummer on Boston's album, but Masdea would rejoin later.) And from the beginning, they were doing early versions of what would become famous Boston songs. When he joined the band, Delp was given a tape of what were then its only two originals. One was "Television Politician" (which Boston never recorded but still played after hitting arenas), and the other was an early version of the debut's "Hitch a Ride," then called "San Francisco Day."

Not long afterward a song called "90 Days" appeared; after many rewrites this would become "More Than a Feeling." As Delp recalled, "The original lyric was '90 days since you've been gone'—that eventually turned into 'Woke up this morning and the sun was gone'; but the melody was there from the start. The difference was that the '90 Days' version didn't have that big 'More than a feeling' chorus yet." Many fans assume that the chorus of "More Than a Feeling" was borrowed from "Louie Louie"—and yes, the two songs do have similar chords—but Delp revealed the truth: it was actually borrowed from a favorite James Gang song, "Tend My Garden," which Mother's Milk used to cover. Eventually, Mother's Milk would even have a theme song of sorts: "Mother's Milkshake" was a rocker with the chorus "Shaking, shaking, rattle that money that you've been making." After a change of title and chorus lyric, this would become the well-known Boston song "Smokin'."

Were all these future hits played to club audiences who didn't realize what they were hearing? Yes, but not very often and not to very large crowds. "We were a pretty obscure band," Delp admitted. "We weren't like Aerosmith, a band people knew because they'd played at every high school before they got signed. We did UMass and Boston University, but even after we started writing songs our set was still about half covers. I don't remember us having any real following."

So Boston's studio-bound lifestyle was partly a matter of necessity. But it didn't hurt that the guitarist, keyboardist, and main songwriter Scholz was indeed a gearhead who graduated from MIT and then began working for Polaroid during the Mother's Milk days. As soon as funds allowed, he started working on tapes, calling in Delp to sing and the others to play some parts. Those eight songs on the first Boston album would get re-recorded countless times, with different arrangements and on different equipment. "Nothing ever gets thrown away; it's always filed away for later," Delp said. "Even now, when we work on a record, I hear little pieces of songs that didn't get used years ago." The first recordings were done in Scholz's basement in Watertown; then he invested in a Scully twelve-track machine and moved it to the Poor Farm, a music club in Maynard. "The poor farm was exactly where we thought we were heading," said Delp. "But at that point we at least had a nice console. Tom struck a deal with the club and moved his twelve-track in; in exchange we were able to record there and use their mixing console. Some of those recordings were pretty good; and quite a few of them wound up on the first record."

Not only were those future hits rejected by every record label in the book; they were even rejected by Epic/CBS—the label that eventually released the album. "We got all the form letters back; and they'd have the boxes checked off—usually it was 'needs work' or 'not what we're looking for at this time.' We kept sending our demo tapes out even though we had no connections. We got to CBS by going to New York with a CBS record, looking the address up on the album cover, and going around to leave the tape there. It came back, like all the others."

It would be another few years before a tape reached the right ears.

During that time there were more uneventful gigs, more tweaking of
the studio tapes, and less money—Delp even quit the band for a year,
when a short-lived management team insisted he quit his day job. "I
got married in 1973, and at that time the band wasn't paying the rent.
Finally Tom gave me a call and asked if I'd sing on one last set of
demos; he said I wouldn't have to quit my job. So we went to the Poor
Farm one more time, re-recording what we had done earlier. And Tom
said, 'Look, we're not getting anywhere. If we don't get any positive response to these, I'm just going to find some band I can join and just
play organ.'"

That, of course, was when the planets aligned. Their eventual manager, Charlie McKenzie, didn't even play their demo tape himself; he
heard it playing in somebody else's office. McKenzie passed the tape on
to a friend, Paul Ahern—a high-powered promo man who had strong
radio connections; he'd helped make hits of Fleetwood Mac and the
Eagles. Both heavy hitters now set their sights on Mother's Milk, as the
band was still called. Record execs came to Boston to hear the band,
and a show in Aerosmith's rehearsal space clinched the deal. "I personally didn't think we went over very well at all," recalled Delp. "There
was just a smattering of people in the room. You'd finish one song and
that would be it; they'd just look at you. But I'd say we got signed on
the strength of the demo. You know how the record business is—when
someone like Paul Ahern is working the demo, and he's known as the
guy who broke Fleetwood Mac's single, it means a lot more than Tom
trying to knock on record company doors."

The actual making of Boston's album is also something of a mystery.
The producer John Boylan's name is on it; but fans tend to assume it's the
same music that Scholz and the band recorded over the obscure years. In
fact, the band pulled a fast one on the label: Epic thought Scholz's home
tapes sounded good, but also thought the world wasn't ready for a homemade album; so they insisted the band re-record the whole thing with
Boylan in the studio. Scholz agreed—but instead he went home to Watertown and did the re-recording there, playing most of the instruments himself. The rest of the band went to LA with Boylan, but most of
those sessions were devoted to vocals. Delp did most of his vocals in
LA, though "Something about You" kept the original demo vocal.

Even at the eleventh hour, songs were still being reworked. "Fore-
play," an instrumental that lacked a good ending (it originally ended

with an explosion), finally became the long intro to "Long Time"; the two songs have been surgically joined ever since. The one song Delp wrote on the album, its finale, "Let Me Take You Home Tonight," was the only one done completely in LA, and it's the only song on the record that all five members played on. When Scholz finally went to Los Angeles, he added keyboards to that song, brought in his tapes, and the final album was pieced together.

The one thing nobody seemed to like was the name Mother's Milk. (It probably didn't help that a band called Mother's Finest was already signed to CBS.) So it was that a band still unknown in Boston wound up becoming the city's namesake. Said Delp, "I think it was John Boylan who suggested calling ourselves that, and my first reaction was, 'That's horrible. It's a cliché.' But he said, 'You hear the name all the time because you're from here; but it suggests something for people elsewhere.' When you think about it, there could have been a big backlash. We weren't well known yet like Aerosmith was, so who were we to call ourselves Boston?"

Instead, there was a backlash of a different sort. The punk and new-wave revolution happened within a year of Boston's debut, and battle lines were drawn. For the kids who were listening to Elvis Costello, the Ramones, and the Clash, nothing looked more suspect than a band as proudly grandiose as Boston—especially if they had management associations with California millionaires like Fleetwood Mac and the Eagles. Even while radio was embracing Boston, the new-wavers were deriding them as one of the first corporate rock bands. When the second Boston album, *Don't Look Back,* came out in 1978, the new-wave magazine *Trouser Press* gave it one of the most savage reviews in history: "Anybody who buys this album is an asshole."

In fact, Boston had more in common with the new-wavers than the latter wanted to admit: the punk/new-wave credo of "DIY" (do it yourself) applied handily to the first five years of Boston's career. True, you'd never compare a snarling song like Elvis Costello's "Less Than Zero" to Boston's ornately produced "Long Time," but both artists shared strong Beatles roots. "People like Patti Smith and Elvis Costello were just coming up, and we flew in the face of that," Delp admitted. "But you know, I loved Elvis Costello then and still do—I think [Costello's 1989 album] *Spike* may be my favorite record of anything, even including the Beatles. I heard him on the radio when he was first coming up, and someone asked about Boston, because they knew how he'd respond. He said we were as exciting as a plate of tripe. Maybe I wasn't too thrilled about that."

But the sweaty clubs where new-wave bands played and the sleek seventies rock arenas were different universes, at least for the time being (Costello, the Clash, and others would make it to the sleek arenas by the early eighties). And with radio support and a hit album, Boston went straight to the latter circuit. The success of the debut took them right into the venues where the seventies album-rock luminaries were playing. They started out opening for Black Sabbath, who, despite their sword-and-sorcery image, turned out to be a nice bunch of guys. "They were very secure about sound checks, so they told us to take all the time we wanted," Delp remarked. Others were less accommodating: during a triple bill with the headliner Jeff Beck and Heart, a small dispute occurred between the respective managements of Heart and Boston over who should play first; the argument hinged on whether the former's "Magic Man" or the latter's "More Than a Feeling" was a bigger hit.

Yet Boston's entry into the big leagues was pretty much painless. As Delp remembered it:

> The record had been out for two weeks before we hit the arenas, so people already knew the songs. And of course, these were the same songs that nobody paid any attention to before the record was out. Our first arena show was in Tulsa, opening for Sabbath, and of course I was a little nervous. But we come out, open with "Rock & Roll Band," and because it's been all over the radio, people are already singing along with it. That made everything much easier. Later, when we started headlining, we had Sammy Hagar [later to become Van Halen's lead singer] as an opening act. Here's a guy that's already been around for years, he comes onstage, and people are yelling "Boston!" at him. We were lucky in that we never had to deal with that kind of thing.

As the years went on, Boston—which came to include only Scholz and Delp from the original lineup, plus a revolving cast of supporting players—would maintain a career whose workings got more eccentric as it went along. After the relatively lukewarm reception of the second album—which took a mere two years to write and record—Scholz would conclude that he hadn't been enough of a perfectionist on that one. Thus, work on the third album stretched on for eight years, during which time he was hit with a lawsuit by Epic when he failed to meet their deadline. When *Third Stage* finally appeared in 1986, each track carried a list of the years it had been worked on. The instrumental "A New Life" was started in 1982 and not finished until 1985—and it's thirty-six seconds long. The more epic "Hollyann" was recorded in 1980, 1981, 1982, and 1984–85. If you're wondering how a single song can take so long, just imagine that you've spent years fine-tuning every element of a particular piece, making sure that every guitar tone and vocal overdub is exactly right. Then you decide that a new bridge absolutely has to be inserted after the second chorus.

In later years the band would sell fewer records, but it would still produce them like epics (and take, on average, eight years per album). And Scholz was still shut away in the studio dreaming up guitar sounds, seemingly oblivious to the rest of the music world. When Nirvana paid the ultimate compliment of ripping off the chords to "More Than a Feeling" for the generational anthem "Smells Like Teen Spirit," Scholz would insist he never heard Nirvana's song.

But that's Boston in a nutshell. They've always reached for the heavens, and when they tour they still seem to exist in that seventies' world of larger-than-life arena rock. Even in 2002 their latest album, *Corporate America,* had a spaceship on the cover. "Arena rock has taken on a bad connotation, but we never did anything that we didn't personally believe in," Delp pointed out. "People can say it's commercial, or that they think a song is too simplistic. But one thing I'd never attribute to us is being calculated or pandering."

It was a sad day for Boston—the band and the city—when Brad Delp died suddenly at his Atkinson, New Hampshire, home on March 9, 2007. Known as the friendliest of rock stars, Delp never lost his mighty vocal range. He was set to play Johnny D's in Somerville that night with Beatlejuice, the tribute band he'd fronted over the past decade whenever Boston wasn't on tour. Some found it odd that a well-known singer would join such a band—after all, Boston outsold even the Beatles at one point—but Delp was a confirmed Beatlemaniac who could do good vocal impersonations of all four. Closing most of their shows with "All You Need Is Love," Delp would flash the peace sign at the crowd, wearing his sixties roots proudly.

The Years of the Rat

(1977–1980)

Thundertrain, Reddy Teddy, Willie Alexander: Hit Her wid de Axe

But once again, Boston was working at both extremes. While Boston the band was bringing rock grandeur to the arenas, a rougher brand of rock was making its way through the clubs. Rock-and-roll history says that punk rock broke through in 1977, but in Boston it had already been bubbling up for a few years, at least since the Modern Lovers played in Harvard Square. By the mid-seventies Boston already had a handful of bands who weren't quite punk but a little too raw to fit in anywhere else: there were the Kids (later the Real Kids), Reddy Teddy (whose leader, Matthew MacKenzie, looked like a star in the making), Fox Pass, Third Rail, and Thundertrain. But by now the club scene had dried up for bands playing original songs, the main obstacle at the time.

Some bands found a way around that. "We'd learn two Led Zeppelin songs, play those first and then do our own material all night," recalls Mach Bell of Thundertrain. "The clubs would get upset, I'd get pissed off, and sometimes we'd get thrown out—but those shows could be the really good ones." Indeed, Bell was a regular force of nature onstage. "A lot of the underlying feelings we wanted to bring out were the same ones the punks had, anger and frustration. And we loved bands like the New York Dolls, and the British group Slade. That was

An ad for Reddy Teddy's first single. (Courtesy Willie Alexander)

our problem—We patterned ourselves after bands that had flopped in America! We also liked Aerosmith but wouldn't admit it—to us, Aerosmith were like the guy who sits across from you at a party and likes the same girl you do."

Thundertrain also made an inadvertent bit of rock history. Given the chance to open for the future arena stars Van Halen in Connecticut, they sent VH management a copy of their single, a song well known in Boston at the time: "Hot for Teacher!" A few years later, Bell bought Van Halen's latest album and saw that they too were "Hot for Teacher" —they wrote a different song, but with the same title and idea. "I can't say they stole our song, but we did send it to them," Bell points out. "Though I should mention that our guitar player, Steven Silva, who wrote that song, took it from a pulp-fiction book he got at a yard sale."

Another punk godfather was a man who'd been through a couple of small careers already: Willie Alexander. After his brief stint with the Velvet Underground, he wrote a handful of songs that he'd played with a number of short-lived bands, including the memorably named Rhythm Assholes. By 1976 the sight of a shirtless, manic Alexander pounding the piano keys had become a familiar one. When he didn't have his own band, he'd sit in with Reddy Teddy or the Boize. "I was Mr. Everywhere—I'd sing with one band at the Rat, then go to the Club in Cambridge and join another," he recalls. "Finally, Fox Pass's manager said, 'Willie, you sleaze, why don't you form your own band?'"

He took the plunge simply by choosing a band he liked, convincing them to sack their front man, and taking over. The result was Willie Alexander & the Boom Boom Band, a mighty outfit that had punk immediacy and some good old guitar heroics, courtesy of Billy Loosigian. And Alexander's songwriting was more daring than the norm. Since his first single, "Hit Her wid de Axe," came out during the bicentennial summer, he told people it was about Lizzie Borden. But it was really a bit of sexual innuendo he'd picked up from a coworker at his kitchen day job. "That was a tough one to explain to feminists," he admits.

Alexander's new group was the first Boston punk band to get signed to a major label, releasing albums for MCA in 1978 and 1979. His shows in that era were considerably looser than they'd been with the Lost. "I threw a lot of my clothes off in those days. I'd write things on my chest, or put a jacket together and throw it into the audience. It seemed you could be your own art, your own painting. I ended up with a lot of cigarette burns on my arms and chest; sometimes you'd come home with a bite mark on your hand from someone dancing with you. That was punk rock."

But the albums weren't big hits, nor were high-profile releases by the Boston bands DMZ, the Real Kids, the Nervous Eaters, the Atlantics, and the Fools. To understand why, you'd have to remember the

Willie Alexander still rocking in 2007. (Photo: Jon Strymish)

antipathy that many felt toward punk rock. "It was us versus them, just like in the sixties," notes WBCN's programmer Oedipus. "We were the anarchists, the adulterers. We wore that scarlet letter A." It didn't help that many of the punk bands had enough bravado to say rude things about established rock stars. As Aerosmith's Tom Hamilton put it, "I heard those bands talk about getting rid of the dinosaurs and I thought, 'Wow, are we one of the dinosaurs? Are we going to be gone?'"

Sometimes punk rock's scuffles with the straight world were pretty amusing. Just one example: Human Sexual Response—a theatrical, multisinger band whose work was daring on a few levels—was booked to play Channel 5's wee-hours entertainment show, *Five All Night Live*. According to Oedipus, who was present that night, the band had every intention of being well-behaved, but they weren't prepared for the amount of jostling and bossing around that they got from the producers. True, the band members didn't have a lot of experience with live TV. But they did have a song called "Butt Fuck," which they proceeded to play with the cameras running. By the time the producers realized what was going over the air, the band had had its revenge.

The Rat was a dump, but it was our dump. And if you did any rocking in Boston from 1976 through the mid-nineties, it was your dump as well. You couldn't have asked for a place that had less to do with the big productions of arena rock or the tinsel and glamour of disco (or for that matter, the wanna-be glamour of Narcissus, the slightly tacky disco across the street). Wedged in the heart of Kenmore Square right next to the Strawberries record store—which was known far and wide as an easy place to shoplift—the Rat was nothing more than a basement that looked and felt like a fallout shelter. Nobody seemed to wear anything but jeans and leather. To get in, you had to be sized up by the club's doorman, the late Mitch Cerullo, who sported a gray beard, spoke by holding an artificial voice box to his chin, wore gray suits on the hottest days of the year, and looked like he'd make short work of anyone who dared start trouble. There's no proof that he had underworld connections, but you wouldn't want to push your luck. On the other hand, if you were a pretty girl or a regular, odds were good that Mitch would wave you in for free.

Sanitary maintenance was never too much of a priority at this place. In fact, you knew you were at the Rat the moment you got down the stairs and your shoes started sticking to the carpet. The men's room toilets finally gave out sometime during 1987 and were never seen again; by the nineties it was down to one working urinal. The women's bathrooms at least had fixtures that worked; they also had

Human Sexual Response done up for Halloween. (Photo: Paul Robicheau)

graffiti that revealed which underground rock heroes were good in bed and which were washouts. There was nothing exclusive about the dressing room, which was a few feet from the bar and had a door that didn't lock, making it likely you'd catch a musical hero in a compromising position. In terms of decoration, there was barely a pastel color in the place. The walls had ominous slashes of dark postnuclear green over black; one painted sign ("The Rat—Boston Rock'n'Roll") was as fancy as it got. During the mid-nineties some temporary managers tried ringing the stage with large stuffed rats with flashing red eyes; regulars immediately started wondering if the place was getting too upscale.

The sign in Kenmore Square said "Rathskeller" in someone's attempt at an old German lettering, but nobody ever called the place by its proper name. On the ground floor, James Ryan, a music fan and college radio DJ, opened the Hoodoo BBQ, which for a time offered some of the most authentic Southern cooking to be found in Boston; every hip Allston kitchen had a few bottles of Ryan's zingy barbeque sauce in the refrigerator. A street rumor had it that the recipe's secret ingredient was heroin—which makes a nice story, but it was in fact coffee, along with any leftover beer the cooks felt like throwing in. The pretty girl taking your order could well have been the manager of the band playing downstairs. (The tall and striking Lilli Dennison, later to manage the Del Fuegos and the Dogmatics and to open a club of her own, was one of the early Rat waitresses.) The jukebox had a couple

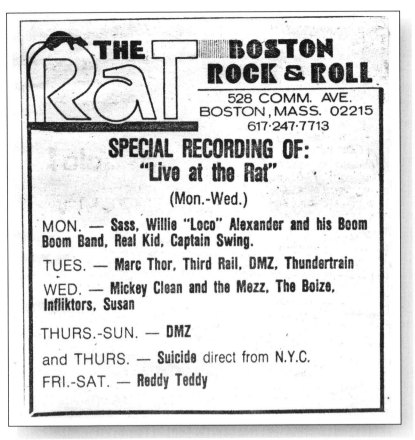

An ad for the shows that produced the *Live at the Rat* album.
(Courtesy Willie Alexander)

hundred songs, but the Nervous Eaters' "Just Head" and the Replacements' "If Only You Were Lonely" were the only ones people ever
seemed to play (unless they were hung over, in which case it was the
Blasters' "I'm Shakin'"). And the guy bumming cigarettes outside the
door might well have been in the band you just paid seven bucks to see.

And the band onstage? Maybe the singer looks like a grade school
brat in a crew cut and short pants, the music is impossibly fast, and the
song is a funny, tasteless bit of doggerel about saving Hitler's brain—
that's Richie Parsons fronting Unnatural Axe. Or the music's still impossibly fast but more snarly, the singer is a Bowie-esque fashion plate,
and the song's a snotty rant about how he's "Better Off Dead"—that's
Peter Dayton fronting La Peste. Or the music is three-chord grit, the

singer's a gutter preacher in blond curls and shades, and the song's a soulful pep talk, "Don't Give It Up Now"—that's Jeff Conolly and his Lyres. Or the singer has a blond pop-star look, the tune's as catchy as a mid-sixties nugget, and the song is "All Kindsa Girls," about how fast he's going to get over his last girlfriend—that's John Felice fronting the Real Kids. Or it's the Neighborhoods with life-affirming kid anthems, or the Thrills with leather-jacket swagger, or the Neats on a blues-rock bender, or even Scruffy the Cat doing jacked-up country music.

It could be a future superstar, or a no-account band that you'd never hear from again; but that barely mattered. The Police played there for four consecutive nights on their first American tour in 1978, but they didn't draw better than the above-named local heroes. (In fact, they barely drew at all, since they had released only two seven-inch singles at that point.) During the summer of 1984 R.E.M. played the Rat on their way to becoming one of the biggest bands in the world. That same summer, the Rat saw the short-lived New York punk-polka band Das Furlines—whose leader, the late Wendy Wild, swung from the club's railings while wailing the lyrics of "Love Power," a song she'd borrowed from Mel Brooks's film *The Producers*. (Picture an upside-down blonde six feet above your head singing, "I gave my flower to the garbage man! He tossed my baby in a garbage can!") One would be hard-pressed to decide whether she or R.E.M. played the more memorable show.

Like the Tea Party in its day, the Rat was never the only game in town. Some scenesters felt more at home in Cantone's, a converted Italian restaurant on Broad Street in the Financial District, which felt less like a fallout shelter and more like somebody's untended living room (complete with hot subs that were sold at all hours during shows). For about a year, in 1979–80, Boston University had its own Allston basement, the Underground, which seemed too dark and cluttered to be anything but a punk club. (It did, however, become a Laundromat.) On the upscale, the glossy punk disco Spit (next to the old Tea Party space on Lansdowne Street) had more money to throw around, and the cavernous Channel on the waterfront by South Station had twice the capacity; both got bigger names in more often. But like CBGB in New York, the Rat was the lowdown, zero-glamour spot most associated with the city. You weren't really in Boston until you hooked up, passed out, or at least got your ears opened there.

Back in 1976 one and only one thing mattered about the Rat: it

A vintage Willie Alexander gig flyer. (Courtesy Willie Alexander)

would give a paying gig to bands who wrote their own material. Such gigs were harder to come by after the loose atmosphere of the late sixties tightened up. The era of disco and arena rock had begun, and live bands were now expected to do sound-alike cover versions of whatever was on the charts. Original bands came with no drawing power and no necessary professionalism—but at least they were cheaper to book. That was good enough for the new owner, Jim Harold, who took over the

Rat in the mid-seventies. And when he took a chance on bands who didn't have the inclination (or even the ability) to learn hit tunes, he opened the floodgates. Punk rock probably wouldn't have happened in Boston if this club—dingy as it was, but in a prime location—hadn't had all those slots that suddenly needed filling.

"It was perfect for music geeks like us," says Johnny Angel, leader of Thrills and Blackjacks. "Before punk, there were only a couple of choices if you wanted to be in a band. You had to audition for blues bands, California soft-rock bands, or disco bands. And I wanted to play guitar, but I didn't want to play any of that. How the hell are you supposed to get a Steely Dan song right when you're only in your twenties?"

Mezz, Thrills, La Peste, Classic Ruins: Let's Go to the Rat

So now audiences had two choices: they could hit a place like Narcissus, where a band in disco suits and music school chops was executing snappy dance steps, doing tight, professional versions of songs by Stevie Wonder and Earth, Wind & Fire. Or they could head to the Rat, where the Mezz's lead singer, Mickey Clean—a rail-thin figure with wild, staring eyes—was ripping off his shirt, jumping on tables, falling on the floor, and crashing into beer bottles. One of the first "Rat bands," Mickey Clean & the Mezz were the polished cover circuit's worst nightmare—the question was whether you wanted professionalism or you wanted fun. For at least a couple hundred kids on a weekend night, that wasn't a question that prompted much thought.

"Sometimes the music wasn't even all that good," notes the former Mezz guitarist Asa Brebner. "It was more the energy, the do-it-yourself mentality. Around 1976 the same kernel of an idea was planted in every city—'Let's open up some nights for bands who want to bring their friends and work for the door.' People at that age want a social life, and the Rat became that for a lot of people. Jim Harold really had horrible taste in music—all he cared about was that the place was full." In short, punk happened because everything else had gotten so dull. "We didn't think to call it punk; to us it was just these cool songs that we wrote in the basement when we were on mushrooms. There was never really a movement; just so many like-minded people that it got dubbed one. We just felt that music had gotten corporate again; I swear that around then I saw the Allman Brothers three times and they played the exact same show. That did it for me."

A Mickey Clean gig flyer with a cartoon by Asa Brebner.
(Courtesy Asa Brebner)

Punk rock at that time still had the feel of something new and slightly illicit, so the very presence of a band like the Mezz was enough to set off the domino effect. Jeff Conolly, who would later front for DMZ and Lyres, wandered into the Rat just because it was near his Boston University dorm; he saw the Mezz onstage and was never the same. "Maybe there's a better word than epiphany, but that's what it was," he recalls. "Probably a Monday night, when you could get in for

Mickey Clean onstage with the Mezz. (Photo: Carol Fonde)

free. And all of a sudden—wow. There it was, five feet in front of me—punk rock! The real stuff is happening here, the same thing that's going on at CBGB in New York. This looks and sounds as good as any Stooges record I own."

Still better for some was the chance to take a new name and reinvent themselves. Johnny Angel, born John Carmen, was a stockbroker-in-training and a former student at Kenmore Square's Center for Alter-

An onstage summit between Eric Martin of the Neats and Johnny Angel,
then of the Blackjacks. (Photo: Paul Robicheau)

native Education, "where they sent the dropouts and reprobates who
couldn't cut it in a public school." Under his new name he became
one of the scene's prominent characters, a consummate wiseass with a
tough-guy streak. "Yeah, but I weighed 140 pounds soaking wet—what
kind of a tough guy is that? But I grew up a little on the defensive, and
maybe I invented the persona so people wouldn't know I was really a
nice Jewish boy from Wellesley. That's too embarrassing." Angel's band
the Thrills (later called City Thrills after a copyright challenge) had a
formidable front woman in Barb Kitson; they hid some classic sixties
pop threads behind their volume and noise. "We'd see other bands and
think, Hey, these guys are still doing mid-tempo rock," Angel recalls.
"So we'd come out and play as fast as we possibly could. That was a
rush, it was magnificent. It's the difference between fighting and fuck-
ing, and we were in a fighting mood. You could do the other thing
after the set."

By the end of 1976, the scene at the Rat and other clubs was already
coming up from underground. The Ramones, New York punk heroes,
had released their debut album by then, so there was a nationwide con-

text. And Boston produced its first real document when a weekend of late-1976 shows was recorded for the *Live at the Rat* double album, with a lineup of bands both now-legendary (Willie Alexander, DMZ, the Real Kids) and long-forgotten (Susan and the Boize—whose tracks are quite good, but them's the breaks). "The scene didn't trickle into existence, it exploded," says the Real Kids' John Felice. "One month there were twenty bands, the next there were two hundred vying for the same gigs." And coming in from out of town wouldn't necessarily do you that much good—especially if you were English, which made you a little suspect. Johnny Angel recalls that when the Damned made their U.S. debut at the Rat—underground hype, U.K. hit single, and all— they drew thirty people, including Thundertrain's singer, Mach Bell, who lobbed ice cubes at them.

Lilli Dennison's arrival at the Rat showed how strong a pull the place could have: then prone to wearing black clothes and glitter make-up, Dennison walked into the Rat when it wasn't even open—but they didn't want her to know that. "I was growing up in Michigan and thought I was about to move to New York," she recalls. "Since I was a punk enthusiast, I'd heard of the Rat; it was one of those places I had to visit. So I walk in one afternoon with a girlfriend; we were a little wet behind the ears. We walk downstairs and see the Thrills playing. They were only doing a sound check and the place wasn't open yet, but we thought we were at the actual show. So we walk to the upstairs bar. They see these two young girls sit down and they give us a pitcher of beer. It was like a little masquerade, everyone trying to make it look like the club was really open! After a couple of hours my friend whispers to me, 'You should ask them for a job.'" She did, was hired, and never moved to New York.

A lot of passions can get unleashed when you have a roomful of youths in a cavernous space getting drunk and listening to wild music. Sometimes that's a beautiful sight; but there were inevitable clashes as well—particularly before the Massachusetts drinking age was raised to twenty in April 1979, which resulted in the crowds becoming older and more collegiate. Before that, the Rat was not a place for the timid. The record producer Rick Harte, who'd later make records with a handful of Rat-seasoned bands, initially came in strictly as a fan. With his rail-thin and decidedly nontough look, he learned it was best to keep to himself. Anyone with a punkish or slightly effeminate look was easy prey for the less-tolerant suburban types, or even for the club's own bouncers.

"Even though it was a place where you'd think a wide variety of behavior was permitted, the bouncers there were scary. If they didn't like the way you were looking, they would literally drag you out by your hair—I saw that happen more than once. I was never scared for myself because I'd learned how to fit in. But I saw people get severely beaten if they acted out in any way. It happened at other clubs, too. One night at Cantone's there were Hell's Angels types from a motorcycle gang. I saw fights with pool cues, things you might see in a movie," Harte recalls. More opportunities to get beaten up were outside, in Kenmore Square, where a rivalry had sprung up between the Rat punks and the disco crowd across the street. Gigs in the suburbs weren't too smooth, either. "It seemed that wherever I went with the Neighborhoods, people wanted to beat them up. Maybe it was because they wore mascara, but security was a problem wherever we went. I think the bands just accepted it as part of the blue-collar, 'live hard and fast, drink all you can drink' ethos. But that's how it was before the drinking age went up," Harte says.

On at least one occasion, the Rat's aggressive atmosphere had an unexpected payoff. Kathei Logue, a band manager also known around town as a college radio DJ and sometime Rat booking agent, was watching Unnatural Axe one night and got a little too close to the stage. The front man, Richie Parsons, was in the habit of kicking his legs around, and during a fast song his foot went directly into Logue's head. It knocked her unconscious, broke her nose, and dislodged a tumor that would have taken major surgery to repair. The accident may well have saved her life.

And the bands kept on coming: the Atlantics had a good-timey appeal; the Classic Ruins benefited from a tight trio sound and the dry wit of their singer, Frank Rowe, a droll Randy Newman type. At one point Rowe wrote an ode to a favorite beer—"Labatt's"—and wheedled some sponsorship money from the brewery in question. A shaggy-dog story about a hard-drinking lumberjack, it somehow managed to sneak the line "He changes his shirt once a year to take the empties into town" past the brewery brass.

The Real Kids: Better Be Good

The Rat also booked plenty of bands who had nothing to do with punk, but peer pressure had a way of separating the wheat from the chaff. So imagine that you're playing the Rat, but you're a new band that hasn't gotten it together just yet. A few songs into your set, you notice that four guys are stationed at both ends of the stage, giving you the evil eye. You're not sure if they're a rival band or a street gang, but they're not happy and they're not moving. Before long you're getting flustered and your set is even more of a mess than it was. Congratulations: you've just met the Real Kids under the worst possible circumstances.

"Man, we were obnoxious," the band's leader, John Felice, now admits without a whole lot of regret. "That was our attitude, though; we really intimidated other bands. They'd finish a song, go looking around for a beer, and see all four of us just glaring at them. Then they'd get nervous and start making mistakes. But we didn't think of ourselves as anything special, just a rock-and-roll band. And we thought rock and roll was something you were supposed to care about." Even today, Felice sports a defiant stare that brings *Rebel without a Cause* to mind. But unlike James Dean in that film—or the young Marlon Brando, who famously explained what he was rebelling against by replying, "Whaddaya got?"—the Real Kids knew exactly what they were rebelling against: disco and arena rock. "Music was so frigging bad then," notes Felice, apparently still rankled by it. "Some really boring, awful shit out there. That's what it took to light a fire under the Real Kids."

In fact, the Real Kids—which Felice formed after a stint in the Modern Lovers and the short-lived Children's Rock and Roll Band—were a real contradiction; tough and street-smart, with a propensity for fighting and drugging, they made some of the most upbeat, wide-eyed music to come out of the Rat. "I had the conviction that rock and roll didn't have to be dark and negative to be interesting," Felice explains. "It's supposed to be fun and positive; anything else is anti–rock and roll. Sometimes it's hard to keep a positive attitude when your life is a mess; but that's staying true to the music, and I think it's something we lived up to, that honesty thing. I never wrote a topical song in my life; I just stuck with cars and girls." Originally called just the Kids, the band had to change its name when another group of Kids got the copyright. It

An early shot of John Felice (center) with the Real Kids.
(Photo: Carol Fonde)

was a famous friend, the New York Dolls singer David Johansen, who
told Felice, "You guys are the real Kids," and it stuck.

The Real Kids started before punk really hit, so few things in early
1976 were less fashionable than a band who wore beat-up leather jackets and cruised used-record stores in search of old Buddy Holly albums. The sense of being permanently out of step gave the Real Kids a
chip on their shoulder that proved useful; one of their albums was even
titled *Outta Place*. The first album cover shows the four band members—Felice, guitarist Billy Borgioli, drummer Howie Ferguson, and
bassist Alan "Alpo" Paulino—sporting a surly look that dared you to
think they could ever be pop stars. "I'd been around people who would
do whatever it took to get famous, and I never trusted people like
that," says Felice. "So we did what we did, we played hard and loud.
People who liked us called us great; people who didn't called us shit.
We weren't a band you could take in small measures; and not many
people were willing to take responsibility for liking a band like us."

More than a few fans pointed out the early similarities between
Felice and Tom Petty: both had baby faces and shaggy blond hair; both
wrote catchy, romantic songs that harked back to the glories of mid-
sixties pop. The first Real Kids album was in fact released within a few

months of Petty's debut, and it sounded no less hit-worthy. "All Kindsa Girls" was on there; so was their attempt at a dance craze, "Do the Boob" (inspired by their scenester friend Bob "the Boob" Colby, who had a peculiar way of shaking his head when he was getting into the music). Like his former bandmate Jonathan Richman, Felice had a way of working local references into his songs that only made them more universal. You don't need to have ever walked Boston Common to hear the post-breakup ballad "Common at Noon" ("Sun shines on the Common at noon / All those girls look like you") and know the feeling.

But someone like Petty probably had a manager who made sure he stayed clean and kept his sights on commercial success. For better or worse, the Real Kids weren't going to be well-behaved if they didn't feel like it. "We were the antithesis of a pop star band. I was twenty-one and anything but innocent, even if the music sounded that way. Sometimes we were lucky to get through a set without passing out. Drugs at the time didn't have the same stigma they have now; people's parents were doing them. I just jumped on with both feet and said, 'Yahoo!' Sounds trite to say, but sex, drugs, and rock and roll were really all I cared about, in no particular order: I just took whatever was available."

The Real Kids' thirty-year history had its glorious moments and its messy ones. There were bitter breakups, short-lived reunions, and inspired shows when even a half-decent one seemed unlikely. Felice wound up making his best album, *Nothing Pretty*, in the eighties, when he temporarily left the cars and girls behind and turned to grittier tales like the dark-humored junkie confessional, "Ain't We Having Fun." The band was hit by tragedy in 2006, when the original bass player, Paulino—who'd kicked his bad habits and was working as a drug counselor—died suddenly at home. Yet the Real Kids carry on, and this scruffy, bad-tempered band that lives for rock and roll is—usually—sounding as good as it did three decades ago.

The Nervous Eaters: Just Head

Many of the Rat-era bands seemed a combination of pop stars, music nuts, and juvenile delinquents—the types who'd pick your pocket and seduce your sister, all while comparing the fine points of their favorite mid-sixties album tracks. Few bands embodied this split personality more than the Nervous Eaters, who sounded like they looked: baby-faced guys with threatening scowls and black leather, clearly guys whom you didn't want to mess with. Even so, they got their name from the bass player's mom, who'd noticed their impatience at the dinner table. The group's two 1977 singles, which would remain their signature tunes, summed up the nice-and-nasty mix: "Loretta" was a lively, Stones-y rocker about innocent love ("When I talk to Loretta, she makes me feel like number one!"). But no talking was involved on the follow-up, "Just Head" (". . . cause I'm in a rush!"). Few have covered the romantic gamut better than that.

"I plead insanity on that one," Steve Cataldo, their front man, says today. "I can't tell you how we came up with those two songs, but I can tell you I'd give anything to jump in the time machine and go back. Funny thing is, the women in the audience liked it a lot when we did songs like 'Just Head.' I think people like what they're afraid of. They can read their own ideas into you. It made them want to pull you into the back room and see what you're all about. Audiences never changed much—you always had to hit them over the head. And if they liked you, you'd build a following pretty quickly."

Bands like this had to wait till 1977 to start happening. But Cataldo was a product of the hippie era who'd expanded his mind, hung out at the Tea Party, and made the psychedelic *Saint Steven* album in 1969— but somehow he got from the Tolkien-esque "Aye-Aye-Poe-Day" to "Shit for Brains" and "You Smell Like Fish" in a mere seven years. The newfound gutter humor was partly due to that music-nut side: the Eaters' bassist, Jeff Wilkinson, in particular was into the Fugs, the cult-hero band of freaky Beat poets from New York. "Jeff was a guy who affected a lot of people. He had this autograph from [head Fug] Tuli Kupferberg—a little ass with what looked like a penis, and it said 'Fuck the Moon.' Jeff thought that was the living end," says Cataldo.

Beyond that, Cataldo didn't have to look far for song inspiration. "We were all pretty wild—I mean, Alan [Paulino, who played in both the Eaters and Real Kids] would have scared the living crap out of you; he looked like he'd rip your head off and run down the street. I had my gentlemanly moments, but I was as crazy as those guys. I remember us stealing hubcaps for absolutely no reason and running down the streets of Beverly in the middle of the night. And then it was, 'What are we going to do with these?' 'I dunno—put them on our car and drive around with them.' We'd have drink holders in our car and drive around with a beer. You had no fear back then."

Indeed, the Nervous Eaters had one of their proudest moments when they freaked out a British musician who'd already worked with bad boys like the Who, the Kinks, and the Rolling Stones. The pianist Nicky Hopkins was called in when the Eaters made their major-label album in 1980, and there were usually joyrides after the sessions. "I think we scared him to death—for one thing, we kept asking him about the Who, and we knew more about the records he played on than he did. We'd drive him home at night, and he'd make us drop him a couple blocks from his place, because he didn't want us to see where he lived."

DMZ, Lyres: Don't Give It Up Now

Somewhere between pure soul and pure chaos, between cheap thrills and three perfect chords, you'll find Lyres. If ever a band seemed likely to self-destruct, this was the one; yet at this writing they've been together, in one form or another, for twenty-seven years. And they've outlasted hundreds of Boston bands for the same reason the Rolling Stones' Keith Richards has outlived many of his contemporaries—whatever that reason may be. Most Lyres fans can recall the night they've dragged some music-snob friend, or maybe just a timid girlfriend, to one of their less coherent shows and gotten only a puzzled look: you really think this could be one of Boston's greatest bands?

Damn right they are. You just have to see them on a good night, when those elemental chords are pounded out like the future of civilization depends on it, and when "Don't Give It Up Now" delivers all the life affirmation that rock and roll ever promised. "Once there was a time, I thought I had a lot to say," their leader, Jeff Conolly, sings, bringing up life's inevitable disappointments before returning, ever more forcefully, to repetitions of the title—an existential crisis resolved in three minutes flat. On such nights they'll be channeling all the maniacs who ever played, from Little Richard to the horny adolescents who bashed out "Louie Louie" in their garages. Conolly will be whipping his unkempt hair around his face as he throttles the keyboard, knocking the tambourine against his jeans hard enough to draw blood, singing like a demon between swigs of beer, then turning around and gesturing with his hands, to prompt the drummer into kicking the energy up just one last notch. Yet fans of this band tend to love the whole shebang—the nights of pure inspiration, drunken flailing, and everything in between.

Exactly what makes Conolly run is another question. Some time in his youth he got the nickname Monoman, a reference to his record collection as well as his single-mindedness, both of which have only grown over the years. The band's fortunes have been up and down—they were highest in the mid-eighties, when "Don't Give It Up Now," "She Pays the Rent," and "Help You Ann" got nationwide college radio play—but Conolly seems oblivious to that, often playing the best shows when nobody but the diehards are around. His bandmates have stayed loyal (drummer Paul Murphy, bassist Rick Coraccio, and guitarist Danny McCormack have all logged decades as Lyres), even though he's sometimes bawled them out onstage.

In all truth, the majority of shows are tight and precise, but the debacles can be pretty spectacular. During a show in 2005, Conolly decided to take a nap before his set—but he did so right onstage, under the opening band's keyboard. He stayed there dead asleep while the Charms played their set; their keyboardist, Kat Kina, had to avoid hitting him with her spike heels. He then woke up and played a Lyres set as if nothing had happened. There were more routine occurrences, such as the night a few months later when a pissed-off Murphy—an on-and-off Lyre for twenty-five years and a born-again Christian for eight—knocked Conolly to the ground in an onstage scuffle, then lectured the audience about Jesus immediately afterward. It's an unwritten law for this band: the more Murphy clenches his teeth and looks like he wants to kill somebody, the harder he'll play and the better the set will be.

There was also one night when Conolly was lucky to walk away alive. That happened in the fall of 1988, the night Lyres hit Seattle. This was by far the wildest era of the band: Conolly was regularly breaking vodka bottles onstage after drinking the contents, calling the audience assholes, losing and replacing band members at an alarming rate. And on this particular night, he had the mother of all onstage brawls with the drummer he'd picked up for the tour.

Seattle always loomed large in Conolly's personal mythology. One of his all-time favorite bands, the sixties punkers the Sonics, hailed from there; and one of the band's favorite tunes is "Soapy," a three-chord stomp borrowed from another early Seattle band. So he was about to fill a longtime goal by performing that song in Seattle, but it didn't work out quite as planned, as the drummer (not Murphy) wasn't used to his perfectionism. "Second song in the set, and the drummer picks that night to forget how to play 'Soapy,'" he recalls, his eyes lighting up with the intensity they probably showed that night. "And here we are in Seattle—home of the Sonics! Home of my heroes! So I turn around and start playing air drums at him—you know, just to get him back on track. That's when he snaps, steps out from the drum kit, picks up this big set of drums, and hurls it right at my face. Hits me right in the eye; there's blood splattering all over the audience. But meanwhile, we're only two songs into the set. Am I gonna start crying for a doctor as soon as we get to Seattle? No way. So I pop my eyeball back in and we finish playing the set."

He points to a horizontal scar below his left eye as evidence that this incident really happened. "But I'll tell you the really pathetic part," he says as a capper. "After I get back from the hospital the drummer says, 'Uh, does this mean I can't be in the band anymore?'"

Despite all the carnage, Lyres (no *the*, Conolly insists) now has only Aerosmith to rival it as Boston's longest-running, never-broken-up band. (True, Conolly played a farewell gig in 1990 and moved to California for two years, but as he later insisted, "I never broke the band up. I just fired everybody and moved.") After dozens of personnel changes, the 2007 lineup is the same as the 1984 model. "This group equals dysfunctionality to the nth degree," he admits. "Repetition. Doing the same thing over and over again. Knowing instinctively what the four-piece combo is supposed to sound like. As sappy as it sounds, the one thing holding us together is our love for the music."

You wouldn't expect this kind of rock-and-roll disturbance to be rooted in a Connecticut prep school, but those are indeed Conolly's roots. Drawn into record collecting at an early age, he was a student at Pomfret School in Connecticut when he made the discovery that the mono version of the Beatles' *Sgt. Pepper's Lonely Hearts Club Band* had interesting variations from the stereo one—thus the birth of his nickname. He briefly attended Boston University afterward, just long enough to have his life changed by Mickey Clean & the Mezz at the Rat. A few months later he found himself fronting his first band, through a combination of happenstance and nerve. He'd befriended Adam Schwartz, a singer who was in DMZ, the band JJ Rassler had put together. Conolly was invited to tag along on a rehearsal. As fate would

Jeff "Monoman" Conolly in a characteristic pose. Note the Hoodoo BBQ T-shirt. (Photo: Paul Robicheau)

have it, Schwartz got kicked out of the band that very night. And Conolly knew an opportunity when he saw one.

"Okay, so I kind of felt bad about it," he confides as another beer arrives, his eyes showing that intensity again. "But there I was at this DMZ rehearsal, and the others were unhappy with Adam. Some words were exchanged, his feelings got hurt, and he walked out of the rehearsal. I probably should have said something sympathetic, but instead I said, 'Hey, you guys know any Stooges songs?' That was very inappropriate, but I didn't care. I saw this opportunity and created my own audition by being a loudmouth. And somehow it came to pass that I wound up taking the microphone."

It also came to pass that DMZ—who hadn't made much of an impression with Schwartz up front—were off and rolling, and for the next few years they'd embody the bad-boy rocker image. They got their first gig at the Rat the same way Conolly passed his audition with the band: through pure chutzpah. Since they looked like glitter renegades—heavy makeup, leather, and ever-present sneers—passing themselves off as English rock stars proved easy. "We were wickedly into *Clockwork Orange,* wearing tons of eye makeup," the guitarist Rassler recalls. "We got dressed up and blew right past the door guy at the Rat, looking like we belonged there. So word gets around the club: 'We better be nice to these guys because they're probably somebody really big.' So Jim Harold comes around with a bottle, and we're getting free Jack Daniel's. We booked a show for the next Monday night, and the place was packed because word got around that we were really Led Zeppelin."

Perhaps appropriately, Conolly's first song for the band was one about taking a girlfriend's virginity: "The First Time Is the Best Time." And here the circumstances weren't quite as sleazy as you'd expect: he wrote it on a skiing trip with his parents. "Right after I joined the band, my dad wanted me to come on a skiing trip to Vail, Colorado. And I did some very punky things, some very non–family reunion type things on that trip. But I came back armed with original songs."

Tempers within the band were already beginning to fray when they went to New York to make their one self-titled major-label album, a trip that coincided with the infamous blizzard of 1978, a week in February when the entire Northeast was snowbound. The band was holed up in a quiet part of Long Island, and being unable to leave the recording studio seldom does an already tense recording session any good.

They also made a most unlikely choice of record producers—namely, the sixties pop stars Flo & Eddie (alias Mark Volman and Howard Kaylan, lead singers of the "Happy Together" Turtles). Sessions were in fact abruptly shut down after Murphy broke his wrist during a take. For all that, the album's better than anyone in the band thinks it is. They were aiming for a vintage late-sixties sound and got it, heavy on the fuzztone and Vox organ. But it didn't turn the same commercial trick that their Sire label mates Talking Heads and the Ramones had managed. On a recent European reissue of the album, Conolly succinctly sums up that experience: "Nobody died, at least."

Lyres were officially unleashed less than a year later, once again at the Rat. The debut single of "How Do You Know" and "Don't Give It Up Now" came out in 1979, followed in the fall of 1981 by a four-song EP (an "extended play" record whose length is between that of a single and an album). The latter was released within months of future superstars R.E.M.'s debut single; Lyres' single placed higher in the *Village Voice*'s critics' poll than the one by those boys from Georgia. To this day, the band always gets brought up whenever anyone talks about a revival of "garage rock" or a sixties-derived punk-beat combo sound. Little Steven Van Zandt—a garage expert who programs and hosts the Underground Garage channel on Sirius satellite radio when not playing guitar with Bruce Springsteen or acting in *The Sopranos*—has named them as one of his favorite bands. He also booked Lyres to play a daylong festival he produced in New York in the summer of 2004. Shortly before playing "Don't Give It Up Now" and "Help You Ann" to an international broadcast audience, Conolly was spotted in the parking lot trying to scalp his extra tickets.

Conolly takes a lot of the band's repertoire from obscure sixties singles that he collects. He has a personal policy that the band will not play someone else's song unless he owns an original copy of the vinyl single. And when he finally drives himself to write a song, he maintains a lyrical wit that the sixties kids didn't always manage. One of the first Lyres songs, "How Do You Know," was his comeback to everyone who told him he'd never be famous. ("That was our crybaby anthem," he now says.) A follow-up, "She Pays the Rent," says more about why musicians stay in relationships than their girlfriends might want to hear, though Conolly's girlfriend at the time, the late Kathy Duff—a glamorous and good-hearted muse who looked like a more exotic Joni

Mitchell, and did indeed have a profitable bank job at the time—wore the song proudly.

Their most famous song, "Help You Ann," shows an equally cheeky sense of how to run a relationship. The singer is in love with a prostitute, and he promises to set her straight. ("Think of all the money I could save!") Yet Conolly swears his real intent was more benevolent. "It was never about a girl named Ann," he insists, despite the title. "It's friends and bandmates. Listen to what the chorus is saying—AN' I wanna, AN' I wanna help you!" So that's a candid statement about how Conolly wants to make a contribution to music, but it's coded. "And I had to write it that way, because I thought the Ramones had already cornered the market on the word 'wanna.'" Of course.

Asked about his status as a local icon, Conolly will invariably reel off a list of the clubs he can't get gigs at. Indeed, at the time of our interview, he admits to having five dollars to his name. Yet the next day finds him taking a trans-Atlantic flight, with the very same five bucks in his pocket, to headline a garage-rock festival in London, where the reunited Remains are also set to play. The rock-and-roll life doesn't always run smoothly, but it would get awfully boring without people like Monoman around.

The Neighborhoods: Fire Is Coming

And so the chain reaction was on: barely a year after Jeff Conolly saw Mickey Clean at the Rat and had his life changed, an Upton teenager named David Minehan hit the same club and saw Conolly with DMZ. "Man, it was an assault. Loud, scary, going for the throat. And that's what did it for me. I grew up thinking that you had to cultivate your position somehow, play your instrument well, and that refinements were needed before you could make your case as a rock star. But with DMZ there were no refinements whatsoever."

A suburban teen who grew up on David Bowie, Minehan had high cheekbones and a thin, androgynous look and was prone to walking into high school classes with spiky, bright-orange hair, a silver lamé jacket, and loads of mascara. "I just didn't want to look like the townie guys, didn't want to act like 'em," he says. As such, he faced two major choices: form a rock band or get beaten up. It didn't hurt that one of his high school friends had done some roadie work with some big local rock bands, and he also happened to play drums. "Mike Quaglia was

The Neighborhoods in 1984. Left to right: David Minehan, Mike Quaglia, Lee Harrington. (Photo: Paul Robicheau)

working for Willie Alexander, and he was a gregarious guy. Just sixteen and he had gotten into the habit of helping himself to drinks behind the bar at the Rat. So he brought all this knowledge of the urban underground scene to my humble high school."

To some extent, younger Rat bands had slightly older Rat bands as role models: Minehan was already looking up to DMZ, Alexander, La Peste, and the Nervous Eaters. But something else happened in the fall of 1977: the United Kingdom's greatest punk band, the Clash, played at the Harvard Square Theater; it was a show that changed the life of everyone who was there (well, almost everyone: Johnny Angel swears that the opening act, Bo Diddley, was better). Still, the night inspired

Minehan and many others to get serious about forming bands. "We got our marching orders that night. If you'd looked into the audience, half the people who wound up in bands afterward were there." And so the Neighborhoods came together with Minehan on guitar, Quaglia on drums, and John Hartcorn on bass (replaced in the early eighties by Lee Harrington).

But since the Neighborhoods were genuine teens with a fairly up-beat outlook, they had more pop-star appeal than the bands they emulated. And they wound up getting noticed in a hurry: Rick Harte put his money and energy behind producing a single and releasing it on his Ace of Hearts label. From their repertoire he picked "Prettiest Girl," a mid-tempo number with a killer chorus hook. At the band's insistence it was released as the B-side—"We had to get one of our little punk-rock songs on the A-side"—but it became the side the radio played. And they played it often: "Prettiest Girl" sounded punk but not overly so, with clean production and that chorus. Having made the Cars famous a year earlier, WBCN went heavy with "Prettiest Girl," which sold 15,000 copies in town. The band also won WBCN's first Rock-'n'Roll Rumble at the Rat, beating La Peste in the finals.

They also opened for their U.K. heroes, the Clash and the Jam. At a Jam show in West Hartford, Minehan got the courage to present all three members of the band with the Neighborhoods' single. Two of the Jam thanked him kindly, but the drummer, in a rude show of bravado, immediately smashed his copy on the wall. Far nicer was the father of Jam's leader, Paul Weller, who doubled as the Jam's manager. Informed the Neighborhoods had the same lineup as the Jam, he nodded and said, "Drums, bass, guitar—I'll give it a listen." This became a catch-phrase among the band members for years.

With one 45 to their name, the Neighborhoods weren't that rich or famous just yet—but to a trio of excitable teens, it sure felt that way. They had a hit, and they could command a grand per show. And they played a good 250 shows a year, so the money was coming in about as fast as they could spend it. Nowadays Minehan gets a dazed look when he even tries to recall that period. "We took all the work we were offered. We imbibed anything that was put in front of us. We got everything that we ever could desire; I mean everything. But what people don't understand is the psychosis that comes with all of those things. Eventually you reach critical mass; you're not even sure who you are anymore. And we never got to make an album during that time, because we just couldn't say no to shows. Eventually we were just pimped out."

Still, punk rock (or even friendly, punkish rock like the Neighborhoods') remained an affront to some, just because the music was different, the imagery was strong, and the musicians looked weird. Minehan recalls opening a show for the Dead Kennedys—a San Francisco band with a strong liberal bent and a barbed, Swiftian wit. They're well remembered now, but in 1979 you didn't just turn up in Boston with a name like that. "The cops were out in force, hundreds of them all over the Rat. They were waiting for the riot, and all they got was a glorious night of rock." But despite his local star status, and not being a tough-looking guy by any means, Minehan managed to get himself beaten up more than once.

The most sobering incident happened outside the Rat after a show; it shows how high the tensions could run between the Rat crowd and the rougher, traditional townies who hung around across Kenmore Square at the disco club Narcissus. "They were professional street kids, the kind who grew up knowing how to fight. Somebody said something smart to my girlfriend; she said something smart back. They slapped her, I stepped in. And the next thing I knew I was lying in front of the Rat bleeding profusely from my head. And I see [the doorman] Mitch [Cerullo] standing over with me saying, 'Hang on David, the ambulance is on the way.'" Minehan recovered after receiving stitches to his head, but the feel around Kenmore got a little tenser—especially since the bloodstains were visible outside the Rat for months afterward.

The original Neighborhoods grew up fast during their two years in the spotlight; when the original trio split (when Hartcorn departed in 1981), they were already feeling like veterans. But the band itself was really just beginning. After a short breather, Minehan threw out the old songs and tried a few different approaches. For a short time he surprised everyone by doing a more challenging, artier sound inspired by Mission of Burma. "That met with such resistance that it didn't last long, but I didn't want to be the cute punk kid anymore." By the mid-eighties the Neighborhoods had taken on a heavier sound and cultivated a tougher image, trading the makeup for black leather; according to Minehan, "We had an unofficial competition with the Bags to see who could be the most cock-rock." Now that they were playing at the Allston club Bunratty's as often as at the Rat, the Neighborhoods' shows had more of an "out with the boys" vibe: "We're going to see the 'Hoods, man!"

It's no surprise that the band formed an alliance with Aerosmith, whose guitarist, Brad Whitford, produced their last studio release. Aerosmith would also turn up in Minehan's future: in the early nineties he got pulled in briefly to do some Japanese dates with Aerosmith when Whitford was dealing with family matters. Both Minehan and Aerosmith were then deeply into their cleaning-up periods, having spent long stretches in overindulgence. But Minehan maintained his preshow ritual of taking a big swig of Listerine before going onstage. This caught Aerosmith's Steven Tyler by surprise when the two wound up sharing a mike. "He catches this alcohol-like substance on my breath and says to me, 'Whoa, man, what you drinking?' I shouted back, 'Listerine, and I didn't even swallow!'"

When the Neighborhoods wrapped it up in 1992, they easily sold out the Rat and played a three-hour show that included virtually every song they could remember. The encore comprised three songs that had inspired them a decade earlier: La Peste's "Spymaster," the Nervous Eaters' "Just Head," and Mission of Burma's "That's How I Escaped My Certain Fate." It was pure Rat-era punk, and at that point it was hard to imagine that anyone ever hadn't liked it.

By 1979 the punk scene was so well established that some bands were already making fun of it. Never known for their subtlety, the Fools produced the greatest parody to come from the era. Talking Heads' "Psycho Killer," an intense psychological study, in their hands became "Psycho Chicken," about a fowl running berserk at a Colonel Sanders outlet. Never known for their sense of humor, Talking Heads nonetheless played it through their PA after some of their concerts, and their leader, David Byrne, called it "a humorous version of a brilliant song." The Fools would score again with 1984's country lament send-up, "Life Sucks . . . Then You Die," by some distance the best song ever to include the line "I cut off my dick with a power tool."

Robin Lane, Bristols, Lizzie Borden: All Kindsa Girls

Freddy Cannon may have sung in 1963 about Abigail Beecher—the history teacher who wanted to be a rock and roller, strutting around school with her electric guitar—but in truth the world wasn't ready for her yet. Didi Stewart found that much out as late as 1976, when she and her band, the Amplifiers, were playing a show at the South Shore's Horseneck Beach. One audience member was so offended to see a front woman that he quite literally took matters in hand: he picked Stewart up off the stage, carried her out the door, and deposited her on the beach. "It didn't even bother me as much as the fact that the band just kept on playing," she now recalls.

The shameful truth is that Boston rock was pretty much a boys' club until the punk era. Boston's first (and for a long while its last) all-female band to make any waves was the Pandoras, who managed a three-year career in the Beatles era. Though not remembered as well as the Remains or the Rockin' Ramrods, they played a lot of the same gigs, including the Surf Ballroom and at least one opening slot at Boston Garden, during a daylong teen spectacular. Later a Northampton band called Lilith made two albums in the mid-seventies, doing a sophisticated jazz-funk blend. Indeed, Lilith's two albums show them to be heavy on technical chops, playing like they had a lot to prove. But that was it, two female bands in twenty years.

Even female singers were in short supply. The sixties band Ill Wind had its front woman, Conny Devanney, whose delivery brought Grace Slick of Jefferson Airplane to mind. In the early seventies Orchestra Luna had its two sirens up front; and Bonnie Raitt was lighting up the blues circuit. But this was still an era when female musicians could get actively discouraged: Didi Stewart recalls being the only woman in her harmony class at the Berklee College of Music in 1972, when a professor told her, "You don't need to be here, you're just going to get married." (She dropped out and joined a band the next day.) Even the first wave of punk did little to level the playing field: City Thrills' front woman, Barb Kitson, was one of the few front women to come out of the late-seventies wave. The leather-jacketed Kitson strutting the stage, proclaiming she was "not another face in the crowd," was an empowering moment. This still put Boston a few steps behind New York's new rock, which had Patti Smith and Debbie Harry at the forefront. New York also had a Providence transplant, Tina Weymouth, whose bass playing for Talking Heads made her one of rock's first great female instrumentalists.

But by now the gender roles were starting to change. During 1977 Linda (Miss Lyn) Cardinal started the *Boston Groupie News,* a magazine

Robin Lane and the Chartbusters (with their manager, Michael Lembo) celebrate their signing to Warner Bros. (Courtesy Asa Brebner)

whose title suggested a very traditional behind-the-scenes role for female rockers. Yet it was also one of the first small publications since the long-defunct *New England Teen Scene* to give local music any serious coverage, and the writing had it both ways—there was serious discussion of local bands' musical merits alongside groupie-ish appreciation of the musicians themselves. Bands that were covered in *BGN* were immediately considered hot, both musically and otherwise; it's no wonder Miss Lyn got some of the best interviews in town.

"We were born and raised during an era in which men were still in charge," she says. "Even though the sixties and seventies brought us women's lib, we were hard pressed to erase all those years of indoctrination. I think a lot of women were just attracted to rockers—and like all well-behaved women, they were doing something to attract a man. Once they got one, they'd give up all their 'doing' and become a wife. I started writing the *BGN* for a couple of reasons, and one of them was to impress a guy," she admits. "But the other was because I wanted to do more than just sleep with guys in bands. It started out as a gossip rag, but I felt bothered by the fact that gossip was more 'women's work.' So I desperately wanted to change the *BGN* to be more about the news on the scene. I felt much better as it grew to something beyond its original gossip-rag status, and that happened because of my personal feminist issues."

Another of the pioneers was Robin Lane, whose band, the Chartbusters, looked to be one of Boston's brightest hopes around 1980–81. When Lane came to Boston in 1977, she already had some musical history behind her: her father was Dean Martin's musical director (and the writer of his signature tune, "Everybody Loves Somebody"); and she'd been friends with Los Angeles' musical in-crowd during the late sixties. As a teenager she befriended Neil Young and sang on one of his classic albums, *Everybody Knows This Is Nowhere*. Yet Boston was looking like a more opportune place to launch a solo career.

"One problem was that only a few female performers were allowed to be on record labels then," she recalls. "They'd say, 'Well, you're really good but we already have Laura Nyro or Joni Mitchell.' Also, Los Angeles wasn't the kind of place that gives you room to grow. I had a reputation from the Neil Young connection, but people like him were also my idols. They were so good and I was maybe too young and not good enough yet. In Boston I could become myself musically and not have to be a commodity just yet."

Boston wound up changing Lane's musical destiny. She came here intending to do the acoustic ballads she'd played in LA. Then she started hanging out with the Real Kids' bassist, Alpo Paulino, who took her to the Rat. "I saw the Nervous Eaters and I thought, This is it! It felt like seeing [Neil Young's first successful band] the Buffalo Springfield back in Los Angeles. I couldn't believe it—a whole new scene that was this vital." Armed with songs and a publishing deal, Lane recruited some of the top local players—including the bassist Scott Baerenwald, who'd been in the Mezz and Reddy Teddy; and Asa Brebner and Leroy Radcliffe, fresh from the retooled Modern Lovers—to play with her. Songs from her folkie days were duly reworked; "When Things Go Wrong" (later a minor national hit) was transformed into a rock song with help from her housemate, Joanne Cipolla, who fronted the band Planet Street.

In fact, the Chartbusters—whose name was Alpo's suggestion, a takeoff on Tom Petty & the Heartbreakers—wasn't really a punk band; it was more a mix of lyrical songwriting with twangy guitars and Rat-bred energy. And when the Chartbusters' debut album came out in 1980, it got some of the most ecstatic reviews in Boston history: Griel

Marcus in *Rolling Stone* went as far as to suggest that, since Johnny Rotten of the Sex Pistols thought rock and roll was dead, he must not have heard the Chartbusters' album yet. "That made us feel good, but we were irreverent about it," Lane recalls. "We had the Bob Dylan attitude; we took it for granted that we were really cool. A lot of people thought we were pretty cocky." They were, but Lane's songs were defined by their emotional generosity. "What I wanted to do in those days was to tell people about Jesus in a different way. Why not do it in the bars, where people are imperfect and they're hurting, where they need it the most?"

The band ran its course over two Warner Bros. albums and a live EP; but in part it was attitudes about women in the music business that busted the Chartbusters. "I had a baby at the end of 1981 and that lost us the record deal. 'Once a woman has a baby in this business, she's done for'—that's an exact quote of something that was told to me. So was 'She'll never work again.' Chrissie Hynde [of the British band the Pretenders] had a baby soon after that, and now it's almost trendy to have babies. But it wasn't back then, and in some ways it put the lid on my career."

Back in Boston, however, things were just heating up. By the early eighties, there was finally a groundswell of all-female bands, who sounded and looked nothing alike. Fronted by the dark Cleopatra-eyed Judy Grunwald (formerly of the Maps), Salem 66 looked like good witches and played haunting, angular music to match. The Dangerous Birds split the difference between Lori Green's pretty pop tunes and Thalia Zedek's darker, edgier ones. Bound & Gagged stomped on traditional gender roles, as did November Group (which had a male rhythm section). Along with a very European electronic sound, November Group had a front woman, Ann Prim, whose androgynous allure harked back to Marlene Dietrich in her tuxedo and top-hat days.

Also among the originals were two very different bands who wound up being packaged together on a lot of live bills: the Bristols and Lizzie Borden & the Axes. The latter (whose leader's name really is Elizabeth Borden) was a modern rock band with a punkish image, whereas the Bristols started out drawing from the upbeat pop of the mid-sixties. Unlike Bound & Gagged, the Bristols chose a suggestive name by accident: They meant to refer to the sixties dance hit "Bristol Stomp," but little did they know that their name referred to a naughty bit of Cockney rhyming slang. (The applicable rhyme, for a female body part,

The Bristols. (Courtesy Kim Ernst)

would be the second half of "Bristol City.") They found this out only when they introduced themselves to a musical hero, the English song-writer Nick Lowe, and he immediately cracked up. The Bristols earned a bit of notoriety when Pat DiNizio of the New Jersey band the Smithereens became smitten with the bass player Kim Ernst and wrote the hit song "Behind the Wall of Sleep" about her, mentioning both her hairstyle ("like [the English model] Jeannie Shrimpton back in 1965") and her bass playing in the lyric.

As Borden recalls, the idea of women being good enough to play instruments proved hard for some to grasp. But having run away from home in her early teens and spent some time "running wild on the streets of Boston," playing in a rock band didn't seem that big a trans-gression for her. "It seemed simple to us: we saw guys out there kicking ass, and we wanted to kick some ass too. But we got hassled, threatened a few times. We got a few things thrown at us. Men didn't know how they were supposed to react to girls in bands. Were they supposed to be fans, groupies, or what? Even if they liked you, they wouldn't talk to you afterwards. Once we drove to New Hampshire to play a show with the Bristols, and the sign out front said 'Girls-Girls-Girls.' We looked at each other and said, 'Okay, do we turn around now?'"

Even the attention that Boston's female bands started drawing was a mixed blessing. The Axes were signed to Capitol, which advised them to act more "girly" and told any lesbian band members to stay in the closet. (Capitol wouldn't have been pleased to learn that the band had gay, straight, and bisexual members.) Even their name, which a Boston band surely had to use sooner or later, came under scrutiny. "And Liz Borden is my real name—what can I say, my parents were crazy. But the label thought the name wasn't fitting for girls. So we wound up calling ourselves Mata Hari—the name of a slutty spy, but I guess they were okay with that."

Along with national stars like the Bangles and the Go-Go's, these early bands broke down some barriers, and there hasn't been a time since when Boston couldn't boast a few vital all-female bands—some of whom, like the early-nineties heavy metal band Malachite, were louder and raunchier than most of the guys. By 1985 the three-quarters-female Throwing Muses were declaring their gender mix a nonissue. "I never cared about it," recalls one Muses member, Kristin Hersh, "But I know that our genders were often stated by journalists, both male and female, who would then sit and wait for a response, as if saying that three of us were women was a question. We never figured out what the answer was supposed to be." Abigail had arrived.

The Cars: Just What I Needed

It was a borrowed guitar lick that introduced Boston's next superstar band to the world. The riff that opened the Cars' "Just What I Needed" was instantly classic (all together now: "Dum-dum-dum-dum-dum-dum-BOMP!") and instantly recognizable, with a taut sound that promised a wild ride ahead. The guitarist Elliot Easton would freely admit that he lifted the riff from the Ohio Express's bubble-gummy sixties oldie "Yummy Yummy Yummy." But that was the Cars in a nutshell: sleek and modern, but with a knowing wink at rock-and-roll history.

The Cars may well be the ultimate new-wave band: For anyone who was around at the time, it's nearly impossible to hear "Drive" or "My Best Friend's Girl" without thinking of the clubs you went to, which classes you cut, or whom you were in love with circa 1980. The Cars looked the part, with a Bowie-esque sense of fashion (a couple of members even got away with the now-unfashionable mullet hairstyle) and sharp outfits. The sound crossed some chic European influences

A Cars poster from 1977, before they became famous. Left to right:
David Robinson, Elliot Easton, Ric Ocasek, Greg Hawkes, Ben Orr.
(Courtesy Asa Brebner)

(Bowie, Kraftwerk, Roxy Music) with a sense of cheap-thrills rock and roll. When the country at large was still scared by the very idea of punk rock, the Cars were part of a small group of late-seventies bands (with Talking Heads, Blondie, and the Police) who convinced mass audiences that new wave was hip and romantic, not to mention fun.

Yet the Cars' roots are far more traditional. And it was an awareness of Boston's acoustic folk scene that brought Ric Ocasek (whose last name was originally spelled Otcasek), the band's leader, to town from his native Michigan. Before making the move in 1972, he'd already begun working with the future Cars bassist and singer Ben Orr as an acoustic duo. "Ben didn't want to leave town right away, so I came to Boston myself. I just decided to go because I knew about the acoustic folk scene, and I wanted to live in Cambridge because Club 47 was there. I remember I was excited to see [the folk-blues artist and Club 47 favorite] Spider John Koerner on Mass. Ave. soon after I came out. It seemed a radical city to me, very 'left,' and I'd just come from Ann Arbor, where everything was always the same. Certainly during the climb up to the Cars I found Boston to be a super-inspiring city, the only place in the country that had so much going on with so many musicians and radio support."

And it had the Modern Lovers, who turned Ocasek's mind from folk music to rock and roll. "I saw them play on Cambridge Common the first year I moved out; and that's what sewed Boston up for me— I was intrigued by them right away. It was just an outdoor afternoon show in the middle of the Common; I don't remember a stage and I don't remember there being any other bands. They probably had a gen- erator they were plugged into. I think they had a cult following by then; there wasn't an overwhelming crowd, but it seemed there were a few people that knew who they were. After that I'd see Jonathan Rich- man a lot; sometimes he'd play by himself on the North Shore and we'd get together and have omelets."

It took a few years of trial and error before the Cars were born, and all five members of the familiar lineup would float in and out of Ocasek's preliminary bands. The 1973 acoustic incarnation (with Ocasek and Orr, who'd by then made the move to Boston) was Milk- wood, which managed one album (whose hippie-Donovan sound would be a mild shock to modern ears). When they disbanded, Ocasek told Jonathan Richman that he was ready to form a rock-and-roll band.

"Then you've got to call it Richard & the Rabbits," Richman replied. So he did, adding a keyboardist, Greg Hawkes, to the nucleus.

Easton, the guitarist, came into the picture for the next and most famous pre-Cars band, Cap'n Swing. This band never released any music; and those who saw them would describe them as an odd mix of gritty rock and long instrumental jams—the Velvet Underground meets Steely Dan. Which is exactly what Cap'n Swing's unreleased, album-length demo from 1976 sounds like. Many of the Cars' trademarks are already there: the cool and detached vocals, the sharp stabs of guitar, even one of the same songs. But at this point the band was more into flaunting its musicianship. There are a lot of fiddly solo breaks that don't need to be there, though the sound is clean and precise. Having no synthesizers yet, they instead used the Fender Rhodes electric piano sound that practically screams mid-seventies. "Bye Bye Love" is the same song the Cars would do, with nearly the same arrangement but with crucial differences—Ocasek rather than Orr sings it, and he tosses away what should be the song's key line ("You think you're so illustri-ous, you call yourself intense!"). Likewise, their attempt to make a charging rock tune out of the Velvet Underground's haunting "Here She Comes Now" is, well, a nice try—but it's significant, because the Cars later referenced the Velvets numerous times while never actually covering them. The mix of elements didn't quite work, and they got told as much after an unsuccessful New York showcase gig.

Turning that into the Cars was partly a matter of keeping what worked (the catchy songs and rock energy) and getting rid of what didn't (the instrumental workouts). It didn't hurt that their drummer, David Robinson, came in as the final piece of the puzzle. Not only did he have a great pedigree as a former Modern Lover and DMZ mem-ber, but he had a background in visual art and could design simple but attention-grabbing images for the band—the early logos and many of the album covers were based on his ideas. He also came up with cheap but eye-catching stage designs that played on the band's name: for one gig at the Paradise he got a full-sized billboard of a '78 Corvette, and he stayed up all night with paint rollers and adhesive. Total cost: eight bucks for the glue.

The Cars played their share of early club gigs, but like the band Boston before them—with whom they had precious little else in com-mon—the Cars made their biggest impression from studio work. In

particular, one of their early demo tapes was a rough version of "Just
What I Needed"—lacking the massive production of the later hit single, but the same song with nearly the same arrangement. Local radio at
the time was loose enough that an influential DJ who believed strongly
in a certain track could run with it. So it was that WBCN's afternoon
air personality Maxanne Sartori put "Just What I Needed" into regular
rotation; it clicked with listeners and became her most requested song,
partly because nobody could go out and buy it yet. That success was
more than enough to convince labels to hit Boston with checkbooks
open, and Elektra Records soon became the band's career-long home.

Yet Ocasek says he didn't peg "Just What I Needed" as a career-
making song when he wrote it. "I was feeling inspired to have a new
band, so I wrote songs for a new band and that was the batch. I didn't
think they were that different than the old songs I was writing; maybe I
was just learning how to do it better. I remember specifically thinking
that my other bands were half song bands and half jam bands, and I
wanted to get rid of the jam thing. Everybody was getting into the idea
of being minimal and playing for the songs' sake. It got more defined as
a band, less loose and more concise; we weren't doing long solos. But I
didn't see any difference between 'Just What I Needed' and another
song like 'Moving in Stereo,'" he says, naming a lesser-known track
from the first album.

To some extent the Cars were initially lumped in with the punk
movement, if only because they didn't really fit anywhere else. "I was
certainly aware of punk because of the Sex Pistols and the Ramones,
and I knew that DMZ and La Peste were happening in Boston. But besides appreciating bands like that, I wouldn't say we were influenced by
them much; I thought that we were more of a lefty pop band. To make
it super simple, it just seemed like music on the radio was boring; it was
all disco and there had to be some alternative to that. That idea was the
whole force. We didn't think we'd be any kind of huge, it just seemed
that music was in one of those stagnant places, and we didn't want to be
stagnant."

With the runaway success of the first album, the Cars would become an international band; and the run of hit singles would stretch
from "Just What I Needed" (released nationally in the summer of 1978)
through 1985's "Tonight She Comes" (the latter featured one of the
raciest double entendres ever to grace the airwaves, though Easton once

pointed out that "it could mean she's coming over to make popcorn") to "You Are the Girl" in September 1987. But the group would always be identified with Boston. In 1981 they purchased the former Intermedia Studios on Newbury Street, in the heart of the Back Bay, remodeled it, and renamed it Syncro Sound. It would survive for more than a decade, though only one Cars album, 1981's *Shake It Up,* was made there. Cars recording sessions tended to happen overnight, so anyone who came to Newbury Street to hit the boutiques—or to buy records at the hipsters' preferred store, Newbury Comics—would stand a fair chance of catching a band member coming out into the daylight.

The mid-eighties would see the Cars becoming a fixture on MTV, though they kept their underground credentials intact by pulling in Andy Warhol to direct his first and last rock video (1985's "Hello Again"). The result again summed up the band as a mix of art and pop influences. And Ocasek feels that it was simply easier for a band to be unique in the eighties, when music wasn't as mass-marketed as it is today. "It was certainly a more open time. You didn't have the influence of the market on everything, the way it is today. Nowadays there's no way to look or sound different—different only means something that you buy at a different store."

One thing the Cars never had was a reputation as a great live band, though bootleg tapes prove they were a lot livelier than history recalls—at least in the early days, when Easton was more inclined to go berserk on guitar. But it's true enough that they toured infrequently and were famous for moving little and saying nothing onstage. And Ocasek made an oft-quoted comment, in *Boston Rock* magazine circa 1985, that he'd rather watch a live sex show than see a band perform. Even today he stands by that general idea: "Well, I was probably playing a lot of bars when I said that. And I have seen a lot of great shows. But for me, I guess a lot of what music is about comes down to writing songs and making records. Even today, if I get a tape from a band that wants to work with me, I couldn't care if they've never played a show in their lives. I'm really more into the records—those are the things that people can hold, or reminisce, or have their lives affected by."

Twenty years after their demise, the Cars remain a touchstone in Boston music. Someone covers one of their songs every few years (most famously, the nineties pop stars Letters to Cleo did "The Dangerous Type" with the Cars' keyboardist, Greg Hawkes, sitting in) or copies Hawkes's synthesizer tones, Ocasek's cool and detached vocals, or Easton's jittery guitar lines. What lingers most, however, is the feel of Ocasek's songs. He wrote about a demimonde that felt very much like the Boston nightclub scene, where all those intense and illustrious types impulsively hooked up. The mood was always romantic, and usually a bit bittersweet.

"It's a weird thing for me, but the night has always been more exciting than the day," Ocasek explains. "When I came to Boston I went to a lot of bars, and I never liked those places very much. It seemed to be a funny meeting ground where people have to drink to become free with their words. I always felt there was a lot of sadness in those places, you see people going through a lot of things, a lot of different relationships, and they're struggling to be happy. I guess I was always trying to figure out how to be happy."

Oedipus, College Radio, and WBCN: We Want the Airwaves

Punk rock wasn't the only thing happening in Boston, but it sure seemed that way.

Even while Aerosmith's new album was easily outselling anything by the Real Kids and the Neighborhoods, punk was muscling its way into pop culture. And by 1981 WBCN had a purple-haired upstart as its program director.

Oedipus, real name Edward Hyson, did something that punk rockers theoretically don't do: he became a big-time player in a major industry. A fast talker with a gift for self-promotion, he was not only one of the most visible figures in town, but one of the most powerful in rock radio during his two decades at WBCN's helm. Criticism comes with this kind of territory, and Oedipus got his share of sellout charges, especially as WBCN edged toward a more homogenized sound in the nineties. But it's easy for cynics to forget that for most of the eighties, WBCN was as good as commercial rock radio ever got. Any number of great, offbeat songs were turned into local hits, and Boston bands were in there to share the glory. Kids who came to Boston to attend college got the national hits they expected, but they heard Human Sexual Response and the Atlantics right alongside them and went to see those Boston bands when they played the clubs. It was no small feat to boost WBCN's ratings while making sure that Boston bands got the exposure they needed.

Oedipus (left) in his early days with WBCN.
(Courtesy Oedipus)

Indeed, the significance of WBCN in those years was high for local bands. It was the next rung on the ladder after a street buzz and college airplay; and a slot for your song on 'BCN would usually mean bigger local shows, larger draws, and the chance for national talent scouts to take notice.

Before his rechristening, Edward Hyson was part of a music-soaked household at 3 Strong Place on Beacon Hill. A six-bedroom brownstone with hieroglyphics drawn on the walls, the place became a frequent crash pad for visiting punk bands—Oedipus recalls stepping over a sleeping Stiv Bators, from the Cleveland (via New York) punk band the Dead Boys, more than once. JJ Rassler was one of the housemates, and DMZ used to rehearse in the basement. "It was the kind of artistic household where people would play music, drink, do drugs all night long," Oedipus recalls. He initially set out to be a photographer—many of the *Live at the Rat* album photos are his—hence the alias. "I liked the juxtaposition, the idea of being blinded by the light."

His first radio show, in 1975—*La Nuit Blanche,* which aired Friday mornings on WTBS, the MIT station—is often credited as the first punk-rock radio show in the country. Though it's hard to verify that Oedipus did it first—and a lot of old-school college DJs would probably argue otherwise—it's significant enough that he did it. And if you were a Boston rebel in the mid-seventies, the very fact that someone was willing to air Patti Smith and the New York Dolls would be enough to win you over—or, just as likely, to make you flip the dial in a hurry. "People forget how much this music was hated," he notes. "It was considered radical, and it was music you just couldn't hear. Even later, when bands like the Police played the Rat for the first time, people forget how unpopular they were."

A writing internship for Charles Laquidara's morning show provided the opportunity for him to approach WBCN in 1977. An ability to think fast under pressure came in handy. "He asked me my name and I said, 'Oedi, and I bet you can't spell it.' He seemed to like that. My first show for them was a midnight to six A.M. slot—I walk in and see Peter Wolf there with [the oldies expert] Little Walter. I'm so nervous, but I look at Wolf and I say, 'Joey Ramone, right?'" Wolf, whose trademark thin and disheveled look wasn't too far from the punk hero Ramone's, got the joke.

As a new staffer at WBCN, Oedipus was around for a turning point in the station's history. In March 1979, its owner, T. Mitchell Hastings, sold the station to Michael Wiener and Gerald Carrus, soon to head the Infinity Broadcasting Corporation. The new owners proceeded to fire more than a dozen employees, most affiliated with the United Electrical Workers Local 262; Oedipus was among the first to get the axe. Such a move might pass without notice today, but in 1979 it quickly became a cause célèbre. The station's major DJs (all of whom had been retained) joined the picket line, the Clash honored the pickets with an onstage dedication, and local bands including Aerosmith and J. Geils staged benefit concerts. And with the help of a girlfriend, Oedipus took matters into his own hands.

"I was a pretty angry young man, especially when I heard the scab DJs on the radio. So I got together with a woman friend and had her call the DJ up—'I like your voice, you're new in town, would you like to go out tonight?' He takes her out, they have some dinner and drinks. The next day he's back on the air, and he gets a phone call. He doesn't know it's me, or that the girl is sitting right next to me. But the voice says to him, 'You were out with this girl Betty last night, right? This is the name of the restaurant you went to, right? Well, if you ever want to see her alive again, you will walk off the air right now.' I think you could hear the needle clicking on the record for a good five minutes after he walked off." Management caved in soon afterward.

Rock radio circa 1980 was a very different animal from what it was in the Woodstock era. Tighter formats were coming into play, counter-cultural spin was toned way down, and familiar songs were starting to be emphasized—in short, the anything-goes FM band was sounding more like hit-oriented AM radio. Groups associated with punk rock—even future icons like the Clash and Ramones—were seen as too risky and largely blackballed. In Boston, WCOZ (which billed itself as "kick-ass rock and roll") was seen as the more traditional station, while WBCN was the maverick. In truth, both stations played a mix of the safe and the risky. Even at its most radical, WBCN was still slipping in the occasional crowd-pleasing Led Zeppelin or Pink Floyd song, whereas WCOZ at least had a Sunday night punk show (*Party Out of Bounds,* hosted by Cindy Bailen). A third local music show, *Bay State Rock,* would debut on WAAF in 1986; its host, Carmelita, would become a much-loved air personality as that station increased its profile in later decades.

In 1980–81, however, the transformation of WBCN was the biggest story in town. Under Oedipus's direction, the station shed some of its freewheeling late-sixties identity; there was less musical variation between individual DJs' shows. "It had become self-indulgent by then; and I had to add structure to the programming. There were still optional tracks on every show, but they also had to play what I told them. I broke them away from free-form radio, because free-form radio would have gone out of business." He put all the new music into rotation, but combined it with the familiar names that drew an audience. "I always said that I'd play the friggin' Grateful Dead if that's what it took to break the Clash."

The DJs themselves took a stronger role as personalities, as the likes of Carter Alan, Mark Parenteau, Ken Shelton, and Charles Laquidara became more famous locally than many of the bands. This too was part of Oedipus's plan: "I thought of radio as an opera of the mind; you're coming in and entering people's heads. I always told the DJs that you don't say, 'Hello, everyone'—you're entering one person's mind. It was showbiz; even the look of the DJs when they went out." Carter Alan made a name with his early championing of U2, with whom he'd remain associated over the ensuing years. A holdover from the station's early days, Laquidara would feature more humor and less overt politics as his show went on. He combined those two worlds in 1980, when his alter ego, Duane Glasscock—a loudmouth teenaged character he created and portrayed—ran for president and pulled in a few thousand votes.

The early eighties were arguably WBCN's glory days, as much for the music as for the personalities. During most of 1984 and 1985, the station ran one of its best-remembered promotions, a series of lunchtime concerts at Avalon with free admission, free beer (one per customer), and free hot dogs. Most of the performers were national acts who were just starting to build a following, notably Jason & the

Scorchers—and the Smithereens, who said a bunch of naughty words onstage before realizing they were on the air. Local bands got to headline too, and one of those shows has to be the most memorable: the Swinging Erudites, a parody band formed by Johnny Angel of the Thrills and the Blackjacks, with the Rat's barbeque chef, James Ryan, as the lead singer. The Erudites' stated goal was to be the worst band in the world. In fact, their irreverence was rather hilarious, especially when the audience wasn't in on the joke. Such was the case at Avalon, when their set included "The Girl from Ipanema" played in three keys at once; a reggae version of the theme from television's *F Troop,* and a good ten minutes of "Tie Me Kangaroo Down, Sport." As Angel recalls, "There were a thousand people in the place, and I swear we cleared them out in thirty minutes."

WBCN also birthed a local tradition with its Rock'n'Roll Rumble, which debuted in 1979, when it was won by the Neighborhoods. (Though 1979 was the first official Rumble, a similar event—called the Spring Rock'n'Roll Festival—had been held the previous year at the Inn Square Men's Bar, with a win by La Peste. That band was first runner-up in 1979; after that bands weren't allowed to compete twice.) Essentially a large-scale battle of the bands, the Rumble has become an annual ritual; a new crop of twenty-four bands competes each year before a revolving slate of judges drawn from bands, the media, and record labels. The prizes of cash, merchandise, and studio time get more elaborate every year, but the real prize is perhaps the chance to make a small bit of local history.

Indeed, the Rumble has been around long enough to spawn its own myths and legends. Did Mission of Burma really come in last in 1979? (The band members swear they did.) And did punk brats Gang Green really destroy a synthesizer onstage while trashing a song by 'Til Tuesday, who'd won previously? (Yes, and I can vouch for it.) It's also true that the metal marauders Slughog started a different kind of Rumble in 1994 by having a punch-out with some audience members right in the middle of their set. Uncle Betty, a finalist in 1991, baited the judges by opening all three of its sets with the un-trendy cover of "Renegade" by the arena band Styx. And that Volcano Suns, the eighties band fronted by Peter Prescott, the former drummer for Mission of Burma, played a 1986 set loud and raucous enough to cause one of the judges, a Capitol Records staffer, to make a beeline out of the Paradise. Though he wasn't

Willie Alexander and the Boom Boom Band at the Rat.
(Courtesy Willie Alexander)

too pleased at the time, that's a story that Prescott now tells with some pride.

High among the legends is the notion of a "Rumble curse," which dictates that nobody who wins the event will ever become famous. In fact, the Neighborhoods did fine, as did 1983's winner, 'Til Tuesday. Seka, winner in 1991, didn't get famous, but the group's drummer, Sully Erna, became a major star with his next band, Godsmack. Cult success was also enjoyed by Gang Green (1986 winner), Heretix (1988), and the Bags (1989). The Sheila Divine (1999), Bleu (2001), and the Gentlemen (2002) remained local headliners for years afterward. Still, the number of legendary Boston bands that crapped out in the Rumble are legion. (Morphine, Letters to Cleo, Lemonheads, Blackjacks, and the Cavedogs all didn't make it past the prelims or semifinals.)

And there's an equal number of winning bands who, deserving or not, went down to obscurity; 1993's winner, Doc Hopper, perhaps deserves special credit for breaking up within a year of winning. An artful pop group, the Dirt Merchants (1994), made a major-label album that wasn't even released. After winning in 1997, the Amazing Royal Crowns became just famous enough to get sued by the West Coast group Royal Crown Revue over the name (they became the Amazing Crowns and razzed the California band by naming their next album "Royal"). Someone & the Somebodies, winner in 1981, didn't get famous, but it did get the honor of being mentioned on a U2 record: the 1981 single "Fire" included three live songs recorded at the Paradise, one of which featured the singer Bono saluting the night's opening act. Twenty-five years later, when U2's members were enshrined as superstars, all those lost B-sides were made available through an iPod promotion, and fans worldwide probably wondered what Bono's ad lib of "Reach out to Someone & the Somebodies!" was all about.

The Scene Proliferates

(1980–1989)

The Early Eighties Scene: Wah-Hey!

There are times when the right scruffy band in the right dingy basement can say it all. And you could find those times at nearly every random weekend in Boston during the early eighties. Let's say you've
stumbled into the Rat, or Jumpin' Jack Flash, or T.T. the Bear's Place, or
Jacks—on a good night they all felt pretty much the same. And let's say
the band onstage was the Turbines, who had a revved-up sound informed by vintage rockabilly. John Hovorka, the front man, had the
look of a factory foreman, and a voice to match. Fixing the crowd
with a no-nonsense look, he'd deliver the message as though he were
issuing an order: "Hey, yeah, there's a party tonight!" And then he's
tense his upper body and let out a howl from somewhere deep inside:
"Waaaahhhh-HEY!"

Boston during the eighties was a whirlwind. It was a decade when
the business just got bigger; when a new influx of labels, studios, and
record stores would turn underground music into a cottage industry
and alternative into a buzzword; when national record labels would
start hitting town in earnest, making national stardom look like a real
possibility for anyone with a hometown buzz. It was an era when bands
proliferated so fast that the Boston sound was no longer possible to pin

down; when doing something illicit in the Rat bathroom became a rite of passage; when newly arrived college students who rode the B train down Commonwealth Avenue would ask why the words "Mission of Burma" were spray-painted on every block. But mostly it was a time that felt like "Wah-Hey!" sounded: a little incoherent, but full of possibilities and wild energy.

Indeed, Boston's reputation was getting so good that one band left its hometown to share a house in Brookline, a few blocks from the Paradise. Nothing unusual there, except that this band, the Red Rockers, already had a hit single with "China." And the town they left was New Orleans, not exactly a musical backwater.

The decade didn't start off that promisingly, however; in 1980 local cynics were already proclaiming the death of the Boston scene. The first wave of punk was already fading, and an initial round of band breakups was under way. La Peste and DMZ were the first to go, followed by Unnatural Axe, the Real Kids, and Willie Alexander's Boom Boom Band. All the major players would stick around, though: Alexander got briefly into spoken word; La Peste's Peter Dayton became a fashion plate with a Cars-like sound (and a local hit, "Love at First Sight"); Unnatural Axe's Richie Parsons formed the short-lived Gremies and wrote the frustrated East Coast surfer's anthem, "No Surfin' in Dorchester Bay."

The national acts were likewise in transition: Aerosmith was deep into its drug period; related squabbles would see the guitarists Joe Perry and Brad Whitford temporarily jump ship. (During his time away, Perry would record and tour with the Joe Perry Project, which borrowed the singers Charlie Farren from Balloon and Mach Bell from Thundertrain.) But the separation would prove short-lived, as Aerosmith made only one album with a couple of stand-in guitarists, Jimmy Crespo and Rick Dufay. When that lineup played the Orpheum, both Perry and Whitford were in the audience. Manager Tim Collins then engineered a meeting at which the original members agreed to reunite—on the condition that everybody cleaned up. "It didn't happen for everyone at the same time; all together it was a period of a year," the bassist Tom Hamilton recalls. "I didn't think at first that I needed to do anything drastic, but I was a daily user for sure. What drying out meant for me was that you could go to a rehearsal, and nobody would be shitfaced or nodding out. We could finally get some work done."

The comeback included a New Year's Eve show at the Orpheum, at which an embarrassed Hamilton was surprised by an onstage stripper for his birthday. Beginning with the 1986 single "Dude Looks Like a Lady," the next decade would bring the biggest success of Aerosmith's career. But even during its down period, the band scored a surprise local hit. During 1984–85 Boston had a short-lived music video channel, V66, co-owned by Arnie Ginsburg and the former WBCN air personality John Garabedian. A locally slanted, lower-budget answer to MTV, the channel made hits of local bands such as the Prime Movers, the Blackjacks, and New Man. Because V66 had only one Aerosmith video on hand, it played "Lightning Strikes"—the one single they'd recorded with the substitute lineup. Though it had flopped nationally, the song became so popular in town that the reunited Aerosmith learned to play it.

Meanwhile, the Cars were branching out; their 1980 album, *Panorama,* was their most experimental (and produced only one Top-40 single, "Touch and Go"). Boston was in limbo as its leader, Tom Scholz, battled with his label, which wanted him to deliver an album before he was good and ready. (Goudreau and Delp had teamed up in the meantime on the former's solo album, which local radio greeted as a surrogate Boston disc.) And the J. Geils Band was coming out of a slump, about to reinvent itself as a more polished MTV-friendly band with "Centerfold" and "Freeze Frame," the two biggest hits of their career—and the last ones, since Peter Wolf would soon fall out with his bandmates, who'd make but one flopped album without him.

The year 1981 saw a beloved club shutting down after barely two years. Tucked away at the crossing of Commonwealth and Brighton avenues, the Underground was the perfect spot for a rock-and-roll basement, just blocks from Boston University and surrounded by the student-packed Allston apartments. In terms of decor, it made the Rat look fancy; the main attraction was a bulletin board with about eight layers of band flyers and gig announcements pinned to it. Yet a lot of action went down in the club's brief existence. According to legend, the place was being run as a tax write-off, so the owners needed to lose money on alcohol. Whether true or not, the place certainly poured generously: this was where one local front woman stepped onstage, looking exotic in tall spike heels and cocktail dress, and promptly fell over backward. The Neats headlined the Underground's closing show in 1981, playing an extended version of their dark blues dirge "Another

Broken Dream" while fans literally brought down the house, or at least large chunks of the ceiling. The space was turned into a BU Laundromat within months.

Another loss hit Boston (and the rest of the world) with John Lennon's killing in December 1980. Local rockers tried to pretend they were too cynical to care—one short-lived band called itself the Dead Lennons—but in truth, everybody did. Oedipus broke the news on WBCN, playing the just-released Lennon song, "I'm Losing You," when word came that he was being rushed to hospital; he cut into the song two minutes later to give the news that Lennon had died. Various Lyres and Real Kids wound up in WBCN's studio with Oedipus, picking out their favorite Beatles records all night. The punk legend Iggy Pop had just wrapped up a show at the Paradise, and the crowd gathered as usual in the club's front bar. It was a rather surreal sight, most of the crowd chatting and drinking as usual—all except for one guy, one of the few who'd heard the news, who was spotted crouched in a corner crying.

But despite those ominous signs, the scene was only beginning to proliferate. When one club went down, two more would spring up in its place; and there were hotspots in virtually every part of town. In terms of atmosphere, all these clubs were variations on the same theme —a dark open room, a bar, a makeshift dressing room, a load of black leather and T-shirts—and sometimes the same bands would manage to play more than one spot in one night. (The Del Fuegos were famous for playing everywhere and anywhere.) Some were only a few doors away from each other. Across Kenmore Square from the Rat stood Storyville, which would helpfully stagger its sets against the Rat so patrons could cross the street and see both headliners. Allston had Bunratty's, initially known for a tougher, noncollege crowd with harder rock tastes—but the punk-oriented Streets was just around the corner on Commonwealth Avenue. The unofficial successor to the Underground, Streets was notable for the local photographer Phil in Phlash's wall-size portrait of the Cramps, a band too big ever to play the place.

The Financial District still had Cantone's until 1984, as well as the short-lived Down Under in Government Center. Just across the street from Boston Garden was the spectacularly dingy Chet's Last Call, a club that lived up to its name one night when a patron keeled over while dancing to Richie Parsons's post–Unnatural Axe group, Stickball. ("This song is for the guy who just bit the dust," joked Parsons, not realizing that he really had.) Chet's also got a moment of fame when a character on the Boston-set TV drama *St. Elsewhere* proposed catching "dinner at Chet's Last Call." (A writer for *Boston Rock* magazine came up with the perfect comeback: "Hope the peanut machine was working that night.") In the Fenway it was Jumpin' Jack Flash, which in 1985 was the site of an especially memorable record-release party for Johnny Angel's band the Blackjacks. In keeping with the band's macho imagery, they roasted a whole pig for the occasion—but misjudged the time it took to cook, so the club was full of hungry rockers gnawing on slices of pink, barely-cooked pork. There's got to be a sexual metaphor in there somewhere.

There was even live music in the sleepy Coolidge Corner area of Brookline, where Beacon Street housed a rhythm-and-blues hangout, the Tam. (For ten years running, the local magazine *Sweet Potato* would describe this place with six well-chosen words: "Brookline's best club. Brookline's only club.") A harder-edged roadhouse feel permeated another area hangout, Ed Burke's, not far from the cluster of hospitals known as the Longwood Medical Area. Even though you had to cross a few dark and ominous streets to get to this place, a steady stream of local bar bands, Gulf Coast bluesmen, and odd comeback tours (the one-hit U.K. wonder Mungo Jerry, some twenty years after "In the Summertime") would play weekly. Alas, the Stuart murder case would help close Burke's at the end of the eighties; after leaving a childbirth class at a local hospital with his pregnant wife, Charles Stuart reported that a black man had approached their car and shot them both. Both his wife and her fetus died. The neighborhood was in an uproar for months as cops randomly stopped young black men in their search for the killer. When Charles Stuart jumped off the Tobin Bridge, the crime was revealed to be a hoax, but the damage had been done.

It wasn't all happening in funky basements, however. Down a side street near South Station, the Channel was the eighties equivalent of those wide-open dance halls on the beaches in the sixties: instead of an urban side street, the picture windows looked out onto Fort Point Channel. If you'd had a couple drinks and the band was great, you could be forgiven for thinking you were looking out at some seaside resort, instead of an unswimmable stretch of dirty Boston Harbor water. Because of its large capacity, the Channel booked a varied batch of shows, so the experience there depended on where one gravitated.

For some the place was synonymous with Sunday hard-core matinees; for others it was the relatively mainstream Boston bands (Extreme, Stompers, Face to Face) that regularly filled the place, not to mention the sixties and seventies comeback acts that seemed to draw better than the hipper ones. I will never forget seeing James Brown play there during a mid-eighties career renaissance; he took his sweet time getting to the stage, so the club stayed open a good hour past the city's 2:00 A.M. curfew.

Cambridge was relatively quiet as the eighties dawned, though that would soon change. The Middle East was still just a restaurant with a bowling alley in the basement; but the family-run T.T. the Bear's Place was starting to experiment with rock shows; both clubs would eventually turn Central Square into a rock hotbed. Also quiet for a time was the building on Main Street, just off Central Square, that had housed the Club in the seventies. In 1984 it would be reincarnated as Nightstage, perhaps the most elegant music club the area saw during that decade. With its plush seating, balcony, and superb sound, Nightstage felt like a classic nightclub and served drinks to match (the club's Long Island iced tea was the strongest potion I ever encountered). Not strictly a rock club, the place booked jazz and folk as well; it also saw the singer-songwriter Lucinda Williams's local debut. There were some proud rock moments here: in the spring of 1989 a smiling Elvis Costello was spotted watching folk-rocker Roger McGuinn's show. He, McGuinn, and Aimee Mann met up backstage after closing and wound up performing a half-hour set for the dozen-odd people still left in the club.

Take a right onto Mass. Ave., and midway to Harvard Square sat Jacks, which saw its share of history for a tiny and tucked-away place. This was Bonnie Raitt's hangout in the late sixties, the site of the Pixies' first show (on a Tuesday evening), and the home base for the late Mark Sandman's band, Treat Her Right—which was booked to play when the club burned down under mysterious circumstances in 1987. Just across the street sat the Orson Welles Cinema, a repertory theater that had a lot of rock-scene overlap, especially during its annual all-night sci-fi and "schlock around the clock" marathons—both of which would invariably feature the campy cult classic *Plan 9 from Outer Space* as the 6:00 A.M. finale.

Even Inman Square was rocking, with the Inn Square Men's Bar (the name a clumsy play on "Inman Square Bar," which had to be quali-

JACKS

952 Mass. Ave., Camb.
491-7800

Fri., April 10

NOVEMBER GROUP

ELECTRIC TOYS
CUE

Sat., April 11
All day benefit for Grass Roots International
**All ages show 2 p.m.
& evening show**

BALL & PIVOT

with special guests

THE BUDDY SYSTEM
CERTAIN CIRCLE
& in evening only
FREE TIME

Sun., April 12

SONGWRITERS' NIGHT

**Benefit for the Boston
AIDS Action Committee**
featuring
Kevin Connelly (The Great Divide),
Laurie Sargent & Angelo (Face to
Face), Johnny Angel (The
Blackjacks), Jaime Rubin (The
Rain), Johnny & Beth A. (Hearts on
Fire), David Champagne (Treat Her
Right), Randy Black (Dr. Black's
Combo), Dennis Brennan (Push,
Push), Garr Lange (The Big Rig),
Digney Fignus, Dave Herlihy (O+),
Ron Scarlet
Open Mike from 8-10
Enjoy a unique music
treat & help a vital cause

Mon., April 13
LOWER WACKER
DRIVE
TIBET
B

TIBET
BIG BARN BURNING

Tues., April 14
INSOMNIA
SLIM CHANCE & THE
RHUMBA RANCH HANDS
MILES DETHMUFFAN

Wed., April 15
BIRD SONGS OF
THE MESOZOIC
with guests
WILLIE LOCO ALEXANDER
and
THE PERSISTENCE OF
MEMORY ORCHESTRA

Thurs., April 16
**College Night • 18+ admitted
with ID**

GARR LANGE &
THE BIG RIG
plus
TREAT HER RIGHT

plus
LISTENER

Fri., April 17
Rounder Recording Artists

NRBQ
Two Shows
9:00 to 11:30 p.m.

Sat., April 18

THE GREAT DIVIDE
with special guests
OCTOBER
RUNAWAY DAN

Sun., April 19
IN THE STYLE OF THE
GRATEFUL DEAD

Open 'til 2:00 a.m.

MAX CREEK

A typically diverse lineup of
shows at Jacks. (Courtesy Asa
Brebner)

fied with the slogan "Ladies invited"). Despite the lack of subway access and less-than-ideal setup (imagine a long shoebox turned sideways), the club saw a lot of overlap with the Rat and the Channel, often bringing rock musicians in for an acoustic "Nebraska night" (the name a nod to Bruce Springsteen's 1982 bare-bones album). Upstart national bands also wound up here, notably the Minneapolis legend the Replacements—whose mid-1984 show lived up to its reputation for drunken onstage shenanigans, but it was also impossibly tight as it played unrehearsed cover tunes that the audience called out. Fans of the Replacements' scruffy image, however, will be glad to know that they were plenty sloppy when they played the Channel in 1985—a few days after being on *Saturday Night Live*—and pulled Barrence Whitfield, a local rocker, up to sing Chubby Checker's "The Twist."

If you wanted to experience punk from a safe distance, there was a place for that, too. At 13 Lansdowne Street, right next to the disco Boston-Boston (formerly the second Tea Party and later to become Avalon), stood Boston's first, last, and only punk disco, Spit; here the scene was a weird combination of glamour and squalor. Instead of disco balls, there were glaring purple and yellow lights, which gave everyone's face a postnuclear glow. There were even live bands in the upstairs room—officially called 13 Up, but referred to as Spit Up by just about everyone. "For a lot of the people who went there, it was: 'I'm a punk on the weekend, then I'm going home,'" notes Liz Borden, who worked the door for two years. You could say something similar about the relatively straight people who danced at the 1270, a multistory gay club at that address on Boylston Street. Sundays were new-wave nights, and there are many who will never be able to hear the Romantics' "What I Like about You" without picturing the view of the skyline from the club's rooftop deck in the summer of 1982.

One prime Boston venue wasn't a club at all: the house at 38 Thayer Street, a ramshackle loft in the South End, became a hotbed in more ways than one. Many of the era's favorite bands—the Dogmatics, the Neats, the Prime Movers, the Del Fuegos, Lizzie Borden, Chain Link Fence—all lived and practiced there, and the parties were known to be some of the wildest in town. The Dogmatics even went so far as to write a song about it and name their debut mini LP *Thayer Street*. The local promoter Billy Ruane recalls waking up there one morning to find his body was being used to mop up beer. "It was a combination

Road warriors Barrence Whitfield, Asa Brebner, and drummer Joe Donnelly of Del Fuegos and Swinging Steaks. (Courtesy Asa Brebner)

dormitory and army barracks, a real bohemian crash pad," recalls the Prime Movers' guitarist, Dick Tate. "One typical night I hear 'Everybody duck!' and the next thing I see is a forty-ounce beer bottle headed straight for somebody's face. The place was only a block away from the Pine Street Inn [a homeless shelter], and that irony wasn't lost on us."

The proliferation of clubs was one incentive for forming bands; another was the possibility of airplay. Commercial radio was no longer the only game in town, as college radio started making more noise— quite literally, in the case of the MIT station, WTBS. This lowly ten-watt station had been the home of Oedipus's original show; in 1977 it gave birth to the Late Risers' Club, the city's first daily underground rock show. It aired weekdays from 10:00 A.M. until noon—an ungodly time slot for punk rock, but one that was open because no MIT students wanted it. So you could now wake up and hear a dispatch from the club world you'd visited the previous night. If you were stuck studying or working a dull job, the show was your lifeline. As Mission of Burma's guitarist Roger Miller put it, "You listened to those two hours every single day. That was why you lived."

WTBS engendered this loyalty by playing all the music that commercial radio was still scared to touch—local 45s, English imports, and all shades of punk. And sometimes the colleges were scared of it too: Oedipus briefly lost his slot for playing the Dead Boys' naughty "Caught with the Meat in Your Mouth"; he got reinstated after convincing the MIT brass that the song was about hamburger.

The station's future was in jeopardy in 1978, when, after a six-year legal battle to increase its signal's strength, the FCC granted the power increase. At that point, though, the station did not have the money to buy a new transmitter. As if on cue, WTBS got a call from a guy who wanted to buy their call letters. It was the media mogul Ted Turner, who wanted call letters that stood for Turner Broadcasting System—he called the Cambridge station himself. Though call letters are generally not for sale, the lawyers for both parties found a loophole, the deal went through, and in May 1979 ten-watt WTBS became 200-watt WMBR— still small potatoes as far as commercial radio was concerned, but enough juice to reach all of Boston. A move to stereo and two subsequent power upgrades took place in the eighties and nineties, the latter of which brought the signal to its current 720-watt power.

Some of its original DJs—Carter Alan, Tami Heide, and Albert O.— went on to commercial radio. Greg Reibman became an editor at *Boston Rock* and the *Boston Herald;* others, such as Tom Lane, Paul "Blowfish" Lovell, and a later addition, Joanie Lindstrom, became local icons. Joining 'MBR at the left end of the dial were Emerson College's WERS, Tufts' WMFO, and Harvard's WHRB, and as college radio DJs graduated to the commercial stations, they'd take some of the college radio aesthetic along with them.

Having earned credit for its role in the Cars' success, WBCN was airing local songs right alongside those of the superstars and airing a local Top Three after its national Top Ten every Friday afternoon. The more conservative competing station, WCOZ, was getting in on the action as well with a weekly new music show, *Party Out of Bounds,* hosted Sunday nights by the hip music fan Cindy Bailen. Local bands now had a path to follow: they'd release a song on tape or a self-produced 45, and if it got enough college radio spins, they could graduate to the big stations. "We all knew the routine," says Billy Conway of Treat Her Right and Morphine. "You made a record, you got in line, you hoped to make the countdown. That population of big radio stations with local music really helped spawn a scene."

Sometimes local success happened quicker than overnight. In the fall of 1980, a teenage Worcester band called the Vejtables cut "Ed King," a parody of "Wild Thing" that lambasted the governor for raising the drinking age. ("Wild thing, you make my heart sing" became "Ed King, I think that you stink!") The producer, Ray Fernandes, gave a call to Mark Parenteau, WBCN's afternoon DJ, who always loved a good novelty; the song was on the air within twenty-four hours of its recording.

The local music industry was expanding in other areas as well. In 1978 Mike Dreese, an MIT dropout, and his roommate, John Brusger, opened a small Newbury Street shop with two grand in savings and Brusger's collection of rare comic books. Business at Newbury Comics took off when the store started selling local, punk, and import singles and albums that were hard to find at mainstream stores. Enlarging its stock and its size over the years, Newbury Comics became a major success story; today it has two dozen stores (including the anchor store a block away from the site of the original) and does more than $70 million of business annually.

Along with hip stores like the used-record spot Nuggets in Kenmore Square and Discount Records in Harvard Square, Newbury made record buying an adventure. That happened at the bigger and less hip stores as well: I will never forget hitting the Strawberries in Kenmore Square at midnight in December 1980 when the first copies of the Clash's triple album *Sandinista!* went on sale. The album never even hit the racks; instead, the pretty, punkish checkout girl handed everyone a copy straight from the box.

Other ventures made less money than Newbury Comics, but they were just as essential to the growth of the scene. By 1980 two monthly music magazines were up and running: *Boston Rock* (which was supported financially by Newbury Comics) and *The Noise,* founded and run to this day by the writer and musician Timothy "T. Max" Maxwell. Not only did both papers cover the local scene—with a tone alternately gossipy and musicological—they also prompted the mainstream dailies, the *Globe* and *Herald,* to beef up their local music coverage. The arts weekly the *Phoenix* has been on the bus since its writer James Isaacs punned a Frank Sinatra song title to create the long-running *Cellars by Starlight* column.

Independent record labels likewise played a major part in the growth of the scene, giving an outlet to bands that weren't quite commercial enough for the majors. Rick Harte's Ace of Hearts label and

Varulven (a more eclectic label run by the musician Joe "the Count" Viglione) both started in the late seventies and sold to underground music fans nationwide; they were soon joined by Newbury Comics' in-house label, Modern Method, and by Curtis Cassella's punk-oriented Taang! And in 1984, a former WMBR DJ and local entrepreneur, Chuck Warner, came up with the overdue idea of collecting some of the most-played local songs on college radio and putting them out as a compilation album. The first release on his Throbbing Lobster label— *Nobody Gets on the Guest-List!*—thus became a small local classic.

Other labels were shorter-lived. Radiobeat ran out of the Kenmore Square recording studio of the same name and released highly regarded debuts by the Proletariat, Deep Wound, and Sorry, besides coreleasing the prescient *Bands That Could Be God* compilation with the even shorter-lived Conflict Records. The latter label, which also released the Flies' first single, was an outgrowth of Gerard Cosloy's more enduring fanzine of the same name. Cosloy, from Wayland, moved to New York City in the mid-eighties to run Homestead Records and later cofounded the Matador label. He has probably signed or reissued more records by Boston bands than anyone else alive, including Dinosaur Jr, Mission of Burma, Lyres, La Peste, GG Allin, Uzi, Big Dipper, Sorry, Salem 66, the Flies, Proletariat, Christmas, Helium, Volcano Suns, Thalia Zedek, Kustomized, SSD, Dredd Foole & the Din, Sebadoh, Come, and the Flying Nuns. Salem's Eat Records, which originally touted itself as making "Imperfect Records for an Imperfect World," put out vinyl from Rhode Island's Rubber Rodeo (one of the first bands to cross country with punk sensibilities), Human Sexual Response, Men & Volts, and the Incredible Casuals; the label's founder, Don Rose, went on to launch the first CD-only label in 1984, the Salem-based Rykodisc. And paying tribute to the sixties band the Barbarians and their hook-handed drummer, Victor "Moulty" Moulton, the Prime Movers released their first single on Moulty Records—where every song has a hook.

More clubs, more labels, more stores, and more airplay (and, ideally, more money) inevitably meant more bands. By 1980 all bets were off in terms of defining the local sound. Too many punk bands? Someone would form a polished mainstream pop group. The mainstream polished pop group gets too popular? A backlash arrives via scruffy garage rock—or folk-rock, country, or heavy metal. Then some unruly kids came up with hardcore after getting sick of all of the above.

One of the most popular early-eighties bands had a more timeless sound: the Atlantics had the tough guitars and jittery rhythms of the era's new-wave rock; but behind that was a wide-eyed, romantic feel that harked back to Beatles-era rock. By most accounts their one major-label album, 1978's *Big City Rock,* didn't catch their live sound (and accordingly didn't make them stars), but they rebounded two years later with the single "Lonelyhearts," a song so danceable that it got equal play in punk clubs and discos.

Some familiar names got louder as the decade went on: the Neats started out with a chiming guitar sound and folk-inspired melodies, then discovered the blues and guitar distortion pedals. Human Sexual Response morphed into the Zulus, toning down the offbeat humor and turning up Rich Gilbert's guitars. And Thalia Zedek, who'd played fairly sweet pop in Dangerous Birds, would go on to the darker and edgier Uzi.

But if one style or approach took precedence in the eighties, it was a nebulous thing that came to be called post-punk, and which was later the foundation for the equally nebulous "alternative rock." Put simply, this was punk-inspired music with added musical sophistication and a bit of art damage, loud and subversive in a more intellectual way. Boston had been doing this since the late seventies, and the Girls (who were, of course, all guys) can probably take credit as the first local band to cross punk energy with jagged art noise. La Peste also employed the odd time signature and cerebral lyric, and Human Sexual Response made good use of Larry Bangor's dark-toned humor and Rich Gilbert's budding guitar ferocity. Even the Atlantics, usually an upbeat rock-and-roll band, played with dissonance in their early gigs.

They all helped to push Boston music in unpredictable directions. But it was three bands in particular—all loved and hated in their time and influential over the years—that embodied the best of what can happen when aggressive music comes out of a brainy college town.

Mission of Burma: Academy Fight Song

When people saw Mission of Burma for the first time, they were most likely overwhelmed. The sound was big and imposing, with lots of feedback, jarring tempo changes, crashing dissonant chords, razor-sharp guitars, and urgent vocals—and the odd catchy tune, though you could barely hear it above the din. It was loud like punk, but more complex and challenging; and somehow it just felt more threatening. The three musicians looked all business, not a smile in sight. You could either love or hate them, but hardly anyone thought Burma was merely okay.

Like most influential bands, Mission of Burma didn't have an easy time of it. Just as the Velvet Underground had been marginalized and Bob Dylan was booed for going electric, Burma cleared its share of rooms. The band became legendary only after the fact, but when it broke up in 1983, it left behind some rabid fans, many equally rabid detractors, and more than a few shredded eardrums. Famous bands later played tribute: R.E.M. recorded "Academy Fight Song" on a fan-club single and performed it onstage during the height of its stardom. The band's early-eighties output—an EP, a studio album, a live record, and a couple of singles—has for the most part remained in print since its release. Heard today, the music sounds like exhilarating rock and roll, if more cerebral than the norm. But at the time, it was more severe than most ears could handle.

"We were loved by our fan," Clint Conley, the band's bassist, deadpanned recently at their rehearsal space. "There was a certain buzz about us, and a few visionaries that were willing to give us shows." "I remember playing to people and feeling anger emanating from them," adds the drummer Peter Prescott. "That was still happening as recently as . . ." ". . . Last week," chimes in the guitarist Roger Miller.

Though straight-ahead punk acts were getting most of the attention at the end of the seventies, Burma had a precedent in an artier stream of bands that were more under the radar—ones that drew from the energy of punk but were a little weirder in their approach. Some of those played in alternative spaces outside of bars, spaces where mixed media could occur. One of those shows, at the Modern Theater in the city's Theater District, drew Roger Miller out in 1978. A recent transplant from Ann Arbor, Michigan, he was planning to pursue a career as a piano tuner. "It was the Girls, La Peste, and movies. And you couldn't tell what was a band and what was a movie. My mind was blown and I said, The hell with tuning pianos."

The same theater was the site of Burma's debut on April Fool's Day 1979. Lou Miami, a local scenester and tastemaker (and front man of the campy Kozmetix, probably the first band with a male singer to cover "To Sir with Love"), put together a bill that included Burma, his own band, and Bob Lawton's Boots (whose namesake leader went on to

Mission of Burma in 1981. Left to right: Clint Conley, Martin Swope, Peter Prescott, Roger Miller. (Photo: Paul Robicheau)

become a successful booking agent). "The place was choked with asbestos and rat droppings. It had no business being open. We fit right in," Burma's Conley recalls. "At the time there was such excitement around anything new—'A night of all new bands? I'm there!' Nowadays you'd rather stab yourself with an ice pick." Out of those eclectic shows came bands that were a bit too ambitious for the louder-faster confines of punk. "The artier stuff always has some sense of struggle—like you know nobody's going to hear you, so you had better do something," notes Prescott. Adds Conley, "There was a sense that people making rock could be thinkers, appreciators of art—not 'Let's get fucked up and play.' Not that we didn't do some of that."

In fact, Burma was a more straight-ahead rock band than was first intended. Miller came in with a number of quirky, angular songs left over from his previous band, Moving Parts, but Conley and Prescott pushed the group in a heavier direction. That was clear near the start, when Miller came up with an early version of the Burma song "Nu Disco." "I came in with this complicated song that was a bunch of bullshit, but I didn't know that at the time. And they said, 'We like those two chords in the middle, can we keep that?' So that was perfect. It's like they were saying, 'That song's really great, you just have to throw out ninety-seven percent of it.'"

Miller remained Burma's most prolific writer, but Conley tended—at first, anyway—to come up with the songs that put the bluster into a more tuneful package. So his first song, "Peking Spring," found early support on MIT's WMBR, which aired it virtually every day in the latter half of 1979. At that time, radio tapes had a life of their own; they were made just for airplay and not released on vinyl—so if you really loved the song, you had to either request it on-air or go see the band. "Clint pulled 'Peking Spring' out of nowhere, and we started shifting away from the overthinking, conceptualized stuff," says Miller.

Soon afterward, the producer Rick Harte, just off his local triumph with the Neighborhoods' "Prettiest Girl," approached Burma about putting out a single. "People were telling me it would be my first mistake," Harte recalls. "I got told so many times that they were Mission Impossible, they were horrible, they would never amount to anything. And I thought, Well, they must be pretty good to get that reaction. When I saw them live, I thought they had at least two good songs. And in those days that was all I needed."

Harte chose Conley's "Academy Fight Song" for the A-side—a song as noisy as anything in Burma's repertoire, but with an infectious, shout-along chorus—and Miller's salute to the Dada art movement, "Max Ernst," for the flip side. In the studio "Academy" became something of a production epic. "There are several guitar tracks, tracks of feedback, and there's an acoustic guitar in there; it's almost like a symphony," Harte says. "The band felt I'd gone overboard, but they were happier with it when it became successful."

Now that they had a real vinyl single, commercial airplay was possible. WBCN got behind the recording, and it also proved direct enough for Boston's other commercial rock station, the less punk-friendly WCOZ. If Boston wasn't fully ready to buy into Burma's aesthetic, it could at least relate to one killer tune on the radio. Around this time the band also added a fourth member, who didn't play a conventional instrument: Martin Swope worked a tape machine and wove taped loops into the live mix from his place behind the soundboard, as well as contributing the same sounds to the records in the studio. He would capture moments of the trio's performances, loop and doctor the sound, and feed it back into the live mix.

"Academy" was joined a year later by Burma's most anthemic song, "That's When I Reach for My Revolver"—a four-minute bullet that built a liberating statement out of murderous frustration. The song took on a life of its own, and the nineties techno star Moby recorded his own version more than fifteen years later. He had to assuage MTV, however, by changing the chorus to the less threatening "That's when I realize it's over." Notes Prescott, "It's funny—when the MTV flap started up, that was the first time I ever noticed it was about shooting someone with a gun."

Burma was now selling records and gaining a fan base; and the college airplay gave the group a strong underground cachet. One fan even took matters to extremes: during the summer of 1980, someone spray-painted "Mission of Burma" and "MOB" in dozens of locations all over Boston—over freeways, at main intersections, at colleges, you name it. It took more than ten years before the graffiti disappeared, and the perpetrator was never caught. The band members swear they had nothing to do with it. "Some people that liked us went on a bender," Prescott explains. Adds Miller, "I was fearing for my life, because I lived in the North End [Boston's Italian neighborhood] at the time. Some of the graffiti showed up right where I lived, so I had to take all the stickers off my guitar case. I didn't know what the hard-core Italian crowd would make of my being associated with it."

Despite their reputation, some of the band's gigs were quite successful. They recall sharing a Paradise bill with the Stompers—about the most traditional of popular Boston bands—whose fans surprisingly warmed to Burma. On the other hand, the nightmare gigs could be fairly spectacular. "The worst was in Cleveland," Miller recalls. "'Revolver' had just come out, so they'd heard of us. We start playing and . . . nothing. People were just pinned to the wall. Nobody made a single sound. After a while we started taunting the audience. Hurrah's in New York was another one. The place was packed, a good five hundred people there. By the fifth song, I swear there were twelve people left." It's no surprise that the band started fighting back. "Around then in Philadelphia, we did a set that started with 'Dead Pool,' 'Einstein's Day'—all our slowest songs right in a row. Just our way of saying, 'This is who we are, there's no hope!'"

Another show in Los Angeles went so badly that Jello Biafra, the singer for that night's headliner, the Dead Kennedys, took the band aside and apologized. "Everybody there was a skinhead or had a Mohawk," recalls Prescott. "We were getting 'You suck!' and large amounts of expectorant. Jello comforted us and said, 'They're not exactly open-minded.' So that shows that we pissed off punks as much as we did suburban kids. And you know, all we were doing was playing rock music. We weren't physically attacking people. Somehow the sound we made did this to them.'"

The onstage volume took its toll on Miller, who developed tinnitus, a severe ringing in the ears. "I started hearing a sustained tone, like the sound in the monitor when a heart stops beating. It had a bad psychological effect." This led directly to his breaking up the band, a move that seemed especially ill timed. They'd recently put out their first (and, until their reunion nearly two decades later, only) studio album, *VS*—a timeless record that worked the tunes, the noise, and the soundscapes into something both beautiful and brutal. Audiences were finally coming around, and a national breakthrough seemed possible before Miller dropped the bomb. "I remember not being heartbroken," Conley says. "Much as people say about *VS* now, I thought the reaction was a little bit tepid. It didn't have the jump-out hits of the singles." Adds Miller, "I remember walking into Discount Records in Harvard Square, and [store manager] Decibel Dennis explained that our single 'Trem Two' wasn't selling—it was a pretty peculiar single. So even at that stage we were a disappointment."

Undertaking a farewell tour (which was later documented on *The Horrible Truth about Burma* live release) and true to their history, Burma played at least one triumphant show and had one near disaster. They got a hero's sendoff at Boston's Bradford Ballroom (now the Roxy); Miller wore the protective headphones that he'd use at every show from then on. A few nights later, they played their final show in New York, opening for the bad-tempered John Lydon's post–Sex Pistols band, Public Image Ltd. Notes Rick Harte, "The two bands were on a collision course, and I think PiL was threatened by Mission of Burma. They come onstage and the house sound got killed; the amps stopped working and Burma had to play through just the onstage monitors. I think PiL wanted Burma to sound tiny."

Sure enough, the acclaim started rolling in once the band split up. The CD era brought their music back into print, this time with more recognition. "When the reissues came out, I remember seeing the reissue column in *Rolling Stone,* and four albums were in there: Van Morrison, Miles Davis, Jimi Hendrix, and Mission of Burma. And I'm think-

A post-reunion Mission of Burma (Conley, Prescott, Miller); facing them is a fan and Burma authority, Eric Van. (Photo: Jon Strymish)

ing, What the hell? Shouldn't we be over in some also-ran column?" While Conley went into TV production and Swope joined the chamber-rock ensemble Birdsongs of the Mesozoic, the other two members were very visible in the next decades. Prescott made six albums with his next band, Volcano Suns, before moving on to front Kustomized and Peer Group. And Miller juggled art and rock in a handful of bands and solo projects (including Birdsongs of the Mesozoic, No Man, Alloy Orchestra, and Binary System), often playing electric piano. "I heard a lot of 'Why aren't you playing guitar? Why aren't you playing rock music in the traditional sense?' The only time it bothered me was once when I was standing with my wife, and somebody was talking to her about 'the legendary Roger Miller.' Like I was standing right next to him, but he couldn't talk to me because I was legendary."

When their reunion occurred, it caught fans by surprise. During the summer of 2001, the English band Wire—an equally experimental group of kindred spirits well loved by Burma's members—was playing the Roxy, the venue of Burma's local farewell. Prescott was opening the show with his psychedelically inclined Peer Group, which Conley had lately joined. During a particularly trippy jam, Miller wandered onstage with a trumpet, and all three core members were onstage for the first time in eighteen years—a brief hallucination of Burma. The true reunion was announced soon afterward, with a small handful of shows planned in New York and Boston for January 2002. Martin Swope chose not to participate, and Bob Weston, who had played both with Prescott in Volcano Suns and with Miller, was deputized to fill his looping-mixing role behind the board. The first performance was a secret open rehearsal at Lilli's/Club 608, the short-lived club Lilli Dennison ran near Porter Square. (The show couldn't be advertised, so the band was listed in the papers as Myanmar, a geographical joke that fooled no-body.) Never claiming that the reunion was permanent, Burma instead booked a few shows at a time and steered clear of long-term plans. As a result, the band has been together at this writing for five years and two albums, more than doubling their original output. "It looks like re-unions have become a trend," notes Conley. "And that's funny, because we've never been part of a trend before."

Throwing Muses: Delicate Cutters

Rock and roll may have been invented by teenagers, but by the mid-eighties, actual teenage bands were in short supply, both nationally and in Boston. With the drinking age set at twenty-one, most bands making any kind of local impression—at least outside the youth-oriented hard-core scene—had at least a year or two of college (or of avoiding college) under their belt. There were young upstarts playing weeknight audition shows, but a teenage band doing anything exciting was rare. A teenage band as rare as Throwing Muses was just about unheard of.

It wasn't merely their ages—they were all minors at the time of their first single and demo tape—that made Throwing Muses stand out. Their sound was just as jarring as Mission of Burma's had been a few years earlier, though the Muses overwhelmed more with messy emotion than with pure volume. The songs raced along with tricky rhythms that initially made no sense but were all carefully considered with guitar parts that pushed and nudged against each other. Stepsisters Kristin Hersh and Tanya Donelly had pretty voices, but they didn't sing prettily. Their harmonies went askew with theatrical shrieks and gasps, the moments of straightforward beauty coming only in glimpses. Likewise, the lyrics hid some strong material—sex and betrayal, obsession and identity issues—behind an often baffling stream of images.

Finally, there was the band itself. Hersh, the front woman, exuded a strange beauty onstage with a perpetually haunted look, drawing into

A fresh-faced Throwing Muses in 1985. Left to right: David Narcizo, Kristin Hersh, Tanya Donelly, Leslie Langston. (Photo: Paul Robicheau)

herself between screaming fits. Donelly, an angelic blonde who sang the sweeter parts, looked unsuitably cheerful. A tall, dreadlocked bass player (Leslie Langston) and a hard-hitting, head-down drummer (David Narcizo) added to the study in opposites: this was a misfit's club making good. Like Burma, they tended to inspire an immediate love-or-hate reaction. Johnny Angel of the Blackjacks—whose testosterone-heavy rock seemed to hail from a different universe—was among those won over. "As soon as I saw Throwing Muses at the Rat I thought, That's it, it's all over for me. I don't know how to do this, it's everything I can't adjust to. The drummer doesn't play a beat; he just accents everything the singer does. The chords are weird. The melodies don't make any sense, and yet they're really good. If this is what's coming next, then I'm finished."

Hersh wrote most of the songs, and when reporters asked where she got this material, she'd say that she simply didn't know. And she wasn't being coy; as she'd explain later, she never got her songs in the usual way, by sitting down with a notepad or guitar. Rather, the songs would appear to her as auditory hallucinations. She'd awaken in the middle of the night to music blasting in her ears; these would be the songs she taught to the band. Eventually she went through therapy and was diagnosed as bipolar, but all she knew at the time was that the music came to her already formed. Thus, she was seldom inclined to analyze her songs or even take credit for writing them, and this added to the slightly otherworldly feel of this band. As she's pointed out many times since then, it would have been more of a problem if those unknown forces were sending lousy songs.

"There was this lightning bolt that happened in my head at some point, and it revolved around music," she explains. "Suddenly, I could 'see' music and it was huge and it told me what to do and it could make me sick, yet it was supremely beautiful. I thought it was gods, I suppose. It was probably craziness, but I don't like being called crazy." It's also worth noting that she grew up on both punk rock and spooky Appalachian lullabies, and elements of both would find their way into her songs. She and Donelly began playing together in their early teens, launching the band at high school parties. If the songs weren't going over, they'd attempt to pass off their odd, elliptical songs as Led Zeppelin covers. "At first it was just making sounds we'd heard before and liked listening to. We wrote our own material, but it wasn't really songs yet. We probably sounded like anybody else, just young and with female vocals."

The mysterious appearance of the songs may have been unsettling, but it also gave Hersh the impetus to get the band noticed. At that time, she says, "I became obsessed with writing real songs, and yet felt less and less in control of the songwriting process. And lacking pride or shame, I began to book us into clubs in Providence, where, I'm sure, people were initially confused—God knows I was. But the students from Brown and RISD [Rhode Island School of Design] embraced us and we packed clubs; we were spoiled by smart people. Or maybe they were just arty." Less often noticed was their equally quirky sense of humor. Their first vinyl single officially had each side on a different record label: Blowing Fuses and Spewing Mouses.

With their formative stages already behind them, Throwing Muses moved to a Somerville apartment once everyone had graduated from high school. "We felt we'd outgrown Providence and the reception in the Boston clubs was even better than what we were used to, so we moved there. The other bands in Boston all spoke their own language too, so we didn't feel like weirdos—and yet there was that nice, garage-y undercurrent to everyone's sound. We had been considered a hardcore band before we moved to Boston because we used distortion and played fast, but that wasn't really accurate, given that quirky country-punk thing we were into. The Boston scene allowed us to sound like that and not be breaking any rules."

The buzz spread fast once the band was in town. It didn't hurt that Gary Smith, the co-owner of Fort Apache Studio who had produced their limited edition *Doghouse* cassette album, was waxing enthusiastic about them to anyone who'd listen. When they got signed, it was to 4AD, an English label known for artful, somewhat abstract rock. The local hit from the first album was "Green," Donelly's only song on the record. This led to the idea that Donelly was the band's more pop-inclined songwriter—though in truth, each of the women wound up writing her share of commercial and not remotely commercial songs. "She, being more extroverted, wrote attractive, prettier songs," Hersh says. "My songs were as barbed and shy as I was. But we were, and still are, very close. Our guitar parts intertwined in ways that made it impossible to call one *rhythm* and the other *lead*."

In 1986 the group saw their first official album—recorded while Hersh was well into her first pregnancy—and their first overseas tour; a revelation in itself. Though hometown crowds had taken the band highly seriously and paid close attention at shows, fans in England were jumping up and down and yelling, "Yeah, Boston! Rock and roll!" As Hersh recalls, "We were used to looking at the audience from the stage and seeing what we called 'the sea of glasses.' Nobody danced. Some people actually took notes. We had never played outside of Boston, Providence, and New York. Then we went to the U.K. and there were drunk, sweaty, screaming boys jumping all over the place. I have no idea where the girls were—maybe in the back so they wouldn't get knocked over."

Yet the English tour was also the end of Throwing Muses' honeymoon as a Boston band; after they returned, the shows were bigger but fewer. (For a time their opening band was the newest client of their manager, Ken Goes, a group whose adventurous nature made them an obvious match: the Pixies.) Hersh has mixed memories of that era: "It was sad to come back after a world tour and find that we no longer fit in; we weren't 'local' anymore. Our shows had to be booked in advance and we couldn't play more than once every few months. We couldn't just slide into the weekend bill with five other bands we loved at the Rat, like we used to. The scene just disappeared for us then, and the rest of the world was a flimsy consolation prize."

Unlike Burma and the Pixies, Throwing Muses didn't flame out early. They remained prolific for a decade, becoming a trio after Donelly's departure in 1990. (Donelly first formed the Breeders with Kim

Deal of the Pixies, then took the spotlight full-time in Belly.) Hersh became more prolific than ever; her songs were divided among spectral
acoustic solo albums, the occasional Muses reunion, and 50 Foot Wave,
a second rock band with an even louder and more basic approach. If she
still hasn't figured out what brings those songs to her, she has at least
made peace with the disturbances. "I started hearing these songs, or seeing them, or whatever it is I do, twenty-five years ago, and I'd say it took
me twenty of those years to come to terms with it," she says. "I still don't
understand it and I don't know if I'm gonna write the song that kills me
today, but I do feel honored to have hung out with this wild, brutal
thing. Writing and playing songs is the most intense high I've ever felt."

The Pixies: Bone Machine

When the Pixies reunited in 2004, they got to be something that they
never were before: rock stars. On their first go-round they were cult
figures, local heroes, and alt-rock trailblazers. They played huge stadiums
as U2's opening act; but they were only headlining theaters, including
Boston's Orpheum, by the time they broke up, never making it to the
arenas. And yet here they were, the hit of the Coachella festival in May
2004. Playing to a massive outdoor audience in Indio, California, they
looked even less the part than before: some hair had been lost and
waistlines expanded since the eighties, and even their bassist, Kim Deal,
had shed the dark glamour she wore in her twenties and now sported
a more wholesome, midwestern look. Yet the crowd of fifty thousand
gave a hero's welcome to a band it knew mainly from records and by
reputation; the next night's headliner, Radiohead, even honored them
with a dedication. In the eighties, songs like "Vamos" and "Wave of
Mutilation" had been the stuff of the alt-rock fringes; now there they
were in the middle of the mainstream, being rock stars.

It's hard to mention the Pixies now without hauling out the familiar
accolades: they were the band that embodied alternative rock, the band
that Bowie and U2 admired, the band that Nirvana stole from. ("I was
basically trying to rip off the Pixies" was Kurt Cobain's comment to
Rolling Stone about "Smells Like Teen Spirit"—Cobain was less inclined
to mention that he'd also nicked the chords from Boston's "More Than
a Feeling.") It's worth remembering though, that the Pixies made perfect sense in the context of late-eighties Boston—and that the first gig
was at least as modest as anybody's.

The Pixies' Joey Santiago shows the finer points of guitar technique.
(Photo: Paul Robicheau)

That happened at Jacks in Cambridge, a watering hole midway between Central and Harvard Squares. The occasion is nothing, just a Tuesday new-band night when a few young outfits are getting their first gig. Second on the bill, taking the stage at 10 P.M., is a band that just formed a few months before. And man, are they noisy! The baby-faced singer may look innocent, but he's screaming his head off, singing weird stuff about incest and mutilation. The guitar player is making god-awful feedback; the female bass player with jet-black hair softens things by singing in a come-hither tone. The small crowd gives them a favorable reception, but nobody thinks this is the future of rock. If you've heard of this band at all, it's because of the posters they stuck around town a few days earlier, with the attention-grabbing slogan "Death to the Pixies."

The Pixies' sound fit perfectly in a time when any kind of edginess was very much appreciated. Noisy guitars, jarring tempo changes, provocative lyrics, and overall weirdness were all familiar to local ears by now. Mission of Burma had become a time-honored role model, and bands such as Volcano Suns, Sorry, and the Zulus had expanded the possibilities of extreme sonics and daring songwriting, all while still sounding like fun rock and roll. Frank Black (then known as Black Francis, his real name is Charles Thompson), the Pixies' front man, was in particular a fan of the Five, whose singer, Reid Paley, would convulse onstage screaming his guts out while the guitars wailed away. (Paley is still a friend and sometime collaborator of Black's.) All Boston needed was a band that could take the jarring sound and harness it to something resembling a hit single. By the time they came up with "Monkey Gone to Heaven" and "Here Comes Your Man," the Pixies were it.

"It seemed to be an arty atmosphere," recalls Black. "You could be more extreme in whatever you were trying to do. It was all about being super aggressive, or super jangly, or super bombastic, or super comedic. All of it was more extreme. It didn't seem that a lot of bands were trying to sound like whatever was on the radio." The Pixies had a lot of fans from the start, but Boston already had a context for what they were doing. Kurt Davis, who sang in Bullet LaVolta, was a fan in the early days. "At that time the Boston scene was as diverse as it's ever been. I checked the Pixies out and I'd like to tell you that it was a revelation, that the world shook. But the fact is that they were yet another really good band with something special going on."

Yet the Pixies' story is full of the kind of storybook details that make a band legendary. Even their formation was different, as they were arguably the first band hatched by mail. "I was in Puerto Rico, and Joey Santiago was at UMass. And a letter was written and plans were made— 'Dear Joey: I'm thinking of going back to school, let's form a band.' 'Dear Charles: Sounds good, let's get together in January.' And that was probably the last time I wrote a friggin' letter in my life." They stuck with their plans to form a band, but the college career fell by the wayside. "I had my plan worked out: I'm gonna drop out of school, go to Boston, and become a rock musician. Joey had to lie to his parents, because there was more pressure for him to finish school."

Having done some loose jamming before leaving Amherst, Black and Santiago were soon hitting the Boston clubs and keeping an eye on the competition. The Rat became a favorite hangout, Black recalls.

We made an almost scholarly effort to pursue it. We'd go to the Rathskeller and time the band's set, then say, "Okay, this is how much material we need to come up with." It was really a confidence-building exercise—seeing bands and saying, "Yeah, we can

do that!" You'd see a band you liked, the Zulus or the Classic
Ruins, and you'd think, Maybe we can get up to their level. Or if
the band wasn't your cup of tea, you'd think, Yeah, we can do better. It was a combination of critiquing the bands and feeling inspired by the better ones. What I really loved was that it wasn't
just about the bands and their music—it was about their personalities, their sweat. You'd go to the club and they'd be three feet
away from you onstage. "Oh, it's a short guy, a fat guy, a quirky
guy, a confident guy, a guy with no confidence." But you got a
sense of who they were, and that was exciting for me.

One of the Pixies' legends hinges on the way Kim Deal joined the
band. Black and Santiago put an ad in the *Boston Phoenix,* looking for a
bass player who liked both Hüsker Dü and Peter, Paul & Mary. Given
those two reference points—a very hip independent band and a long-
unfashionable folk trio—it's no surprise that Deal was the only one
who showed up. Aside from that, Black remembers, she had one obvious point in her favor: "She was a girl, and I really wanted to have a
girl in my band—not sure why that was, maybe because of Tina Weymouth in Talking Heads. Also, when I was younger, I used to do a lot of
singing and harmonizing with one of my aunts, who was younger than
I was—about the same age as Kim. When Kim walked in, my main reaction was feeling happy that someone wanted to talk to me and sing
my songs."

Their early posters attested to the Pixies' twisted sense of humor,
which came out in more than one song. Strange sex and flying body
parts were the stuff of Black's early songs (outer space would enter the
picture later on), and the band raised some eyebrows by covering "In
Heaven (The Lady in the Radiator Song)," from David Lynch's bizarre
Eraserhead. Where did this sensibility come from? "From me, I guess.
Midnight movies like *Eraserhead* that were popular at the time were a
pretty big influence on me—the combination of horror and humor.
The sex thing wasn't meant to be shocking, just psychologically honest,
à la the Violent Femmes' first record, or back to Jonathan Richman.
Then again, I think those kinds of feelings go back to older bands like
the Who—that 'I'm so confused and messed up in my mind that I
don't know what to do.' It's that kind of desperation, as opposed to trying to be titillating." And to some extent, his songwriting simply came

down to necessity. "To me a song just equaled two minutes. Your gig needed to be at least a half hour long, and we didn't have that many yet. So it was never really, 'Let's write this type of song'; it was more like, 'Let's write a song because we need three more.'"

The short-lived Green Street Station in Jamaica Plain was a favorite stomping ground. This was a fairly remote local club; the subway went there, but the change from the Green to the Orange Line made it a fifty-minute commute from Allston. "It ended up being the place where we could make our couple of hundred bucks and have a good time playing," says Black. "What happened onstage was really all this pent-up energy and nervousness we had because we were so green. We'd get on-stage and, WAAAHH! It would all explode. And, yeah, it was exciting."

Deal wasn't even present for the show that landed the Pixies their record contract. A family emergency had called her out of town, so the Pixies played as a stripped-down trio. (Ironically enough, they played the Newport Folk Festival in 2005 and billed it as their first-ever acoustic show, but circumstances had forced them to do something similar this night at the Rat.) The English label 4AD, which had signed Throwing Muses, was in town, and the Pixies had to come up with something. Black recalls, "David [Lovering, the drummer] played a kick drum and a snare, and it got stripped down to just the songs. Everyone knew Kim was missed, but people knew the band was handicapped and they went along with it."

Unlike the majority of Boston alternative bands, the Pixies took naturally to the studio. Steve Albini, who produced their debut, 1988's *Surfer Rosa,* was experimenting with dry, razor-like guitar sounds that built an atmosphere around the songs. Jon Lupfer, who engineered the record, heard it as a precursor to the "low-fi" sound that became trendy in the nineties. "It's about getting away from the corporate sound, say-ing that records don't have to sound good, as defined by Fleetwood Mac, to be great records." The English producer Gil Norton's work on the follow-up, *Doolittle,* found a meeting of those sounds with arena-rock grandeur. Both discs had jarring cover art—images built around a topless dancer on one cover and a monkey with a halo on the second. The West Coast songwriter Scott Miller, who led the great under-ground bands Game Theory and the Loud Family, found the packaging to be especially influential. "Maybe it's just me, but I found the album art essential to the whole experience," he says. "With the picture frames and decoration improvised from hair and detritus, it almost literally suggested reframing of the personal landscape."

Most people would pick one of those two as their favorite Pixies album, though Black has said he was more keen on the third, *Bossanova*. Both that album and the band's swan song, *Trompe le Monde,* are stronger discs than their reputation suggests, but in retrospect they sound like rehearsals for Black's solo career; there is less of Deal but a more crafts- manlike approach to the songwriting and fewer manic outbursts. In other words, the Pixies had grown up. In later years they'd get more re- spect from insiders: U2 had them open the mega-hit Zoo TV tour in 1992, and David Bowie covered their song "Debaser"—not especially well, it turned out—in concert with his early nineties band, Tin Ma- chine.

In later days the lack of camaraderie in the band was apparent on- stage, and there was never much attempt to hide it. There was a show at the Boston-area outdoor arena Great Woods in which the Pixies opened for the British band Love & Rockets, and Black and Deal stood at opposite ends of the stage, singing in harmony while staying safely out of each other's field of vision. Also notorious was a show at the Paradise during which the songs were played in alphabetical order. By most accounts, the longtime friction between Black and Deal comes down to the most mundane of reasons: he's a stickler for punctuality and she was chronically late. The Pixies ended much like they started: not being in a mood to confront everyone directly, Black faxed his manager's office in January 1993 to announce he was quitting. So a band that started by mail broke up by fax.

The Pixies spent the next dozen-odd years swearing they'd never reunite. Black proceeded to have a musically diverse and unusually pro- lific solo career, coming out with as many as two albums in a year. And Deal had a brief fling at post-Pixies stardom with the Breeders, a band she formed with Tanya Donelly of Throwing Muses and in which she was later joined by her twin sister, Kelley. But the Pixies seemed to get talked about the more they stayed away, Cobain's oft-quoted statement (and more support from Bowie, who covered their "Cactus") serving to keep their name alive. At this writing they're three years into one of rock's odder reunions: finally talking about making a new studio album while still not hanging out together much. Yet whenever the Pixies play—assuming they get together to do it again—their standing as a

few semi-ordinary musicians who got to together to do something ex-
traordinary is borne out: they are rock stars.

'Til Tuesday: Voices Carry

But while all this loud, cerebral, and rough-edged music was taking
over the clubs, a very different band was outstripping them all for national success. And how different 'Til Tuesday was became clear to the
drummer Michael Hausman when he showed up at a friend's barbeque
in the summer of 1985. "I was hanging out with the Bristols and Treat
Her Right, real down-to-earth, blue-jean kind of bands. We'd just flown
in from doing [the TV show] Solid Gold a day before, and I was there in
my stage clothes—shoulder pads, my pants halfway down to my ankles,
paisley slippers with chartreuse socks. And I'm looking around thinking,
Hmm, wow—maybe I should have changed for this!"

But that was 'Til Tuesday in a nutshell: the glamorous quartet crashing the garage-rock barbeque. "We were kids playing dress-up, trying
things out, being excited about being in a band," Aimee Mann, the
singer and bassist, recalls. With the tall, striking, and platinum blonde
Mann up front—and a redheaded guitarist, Robert Holmes, who was
nearly as pretty as she was—'Til Tuesday was among the first Boston
bands to hit during the MTV era with the over-the-top dramatic video
they did for "Voices Carry." This led local cynics to dismiss them as low
in substance—but Mann had the last laugh, going on to a long-running
career as a critically acclaimed songwriter.

Forming 'Til Tuesday (whose name came from an obscure, early
David Bowie song) was something of a contrary move on Mann's part.
She'd already put in two years at Berklee and fronted a more punk-
friendly band, the Young Snakes. Then it occurred to her that playing
pretty, emotional songs might be a more radical thing to do. "After the
Young Snakes I realized that there were still rules [within the underground rock world]; they were just unwritten rules. You couldn't write
a love song, you couldn't write about a relationship, you had to be detached. That was as limiting as anything else." The flashy, new-wave dress
was initially a part of the package, though Mann says she never noticed
that she had sex appeal. "I'm sure I wasn't aware of that. We just knew
we were sick of bands who just wandered onstage. And I'd see fashion
magazines and think, This is great—these new designers doing crazy
ideas. So we did a low-rent version."

Aimee Mann fronts 'Til Tuesday at WBCN's Rumble in 1983.
(Photo: Paul Robicheau)

Initially, 'Til Tuesday was a very English-sounding band; their first local hit, "Love in a Vacuum," had an elegant, electronic feel similar to that of the new-wave hits coming out of Britain at the time. Writing "Voices Carry" was really the beginning of Mann's finding her own voice. Though still danceable, the song was actually more about the melody than the rhythm. The lyric zeroed in on one painful moment in a relationship—something Mann would become quite good at doing. At this point her songs weren't yet autobiographical; "Voices Carry" was in fact written about a male friend. "He was telling me about a girl he went out with who was affectionate when they were alone, but wouldn't talk when they were out. I originally sang it from a man's point of view, until our record label said, 'What is that, a lesbian song? We can't have that!'"

The band caught on fast, with local airplay and a win in WBCN's 1983 Rumble; they were signed to Epic soon after and had an English producer, Mike Thorne, at the controls when they recorded their debut. (Thorne had previously worked with Wire, the experimental band whom Mission of Burma idolized.) Though the title song, "Voices Carry," was looking like an obvious hit, the label initially tried to give it to one of its other artists—Cyndi Lauper, a big hit maker at the time. "They told us we could make a lot of money if she did it and we said, 'Nah, we want to do it ourselves,'" Hausman says. "We didn't think it was going to be a hit; we just didn't want to give it to her."

This was probably a smart move, since "Voices Carry" became a national hit, both on the strength of Mann's voice and her star turn in the video (she plays a punk type who is told to be quiet by her straitlaced boyfriend, only to have a shouting outburst in the last chorus when he takes her to the opera). "The one sour note was the guy they cast to be my boyfriend—I would never go out with a guy like that. But other that that, we were really proud of it," she says.

That song and video marked the commercial peak of 'Til Tuesday's career. More notably, it began a long tradition of Mann's rebelling against the music industry. Their second video was a send-up of the first one, beginning with Mann's bandmates insisting they get equal time on camera. And the second album, Welcome Home, was an improvement on the first in all ways but one: it was less obviously commercial, toning down the dance rhythms and pushing the melodies up front. "Look, we were naive," Mann says. "We thought that being a musician was all about getting better—you write better songs, you change, and you grow. But that's exactly what they don't want you to do. I remember visits from people at the label. One of them said, 'I want you to write a song like this,' and started tapping out a rhythm on his knees." One can only imagine the withering look he probably got in return.

By the time of their third and best album, Everything's Different Now, Mann was turning to sixties pop for inspiration, writing a song with

Elvis Costello, dressing less glam, and using the word *fuck* in the single—none of which sat well with the record label. More notably, she was starting to write more personal songs; the album largely chronicles the end of her romance with her fellow songwriter Jules Shear. The result was better reviews, more devoted fans, fewer sales, and more battles with the label—which wanted her to cowrite with commercial songwriters and rush another album out right away. "We thought that was preposterous," she says. "It was like, 'We don't like what you're doing, so why don't you do more of it?'"

Yet 'Til Tuesday's local audience remained devoted, and the band carried on for four more years with shifting personnel. Jon Brion, a multi-instrumentalist and later a big name on the Los Angeles pop and soundtrack circuit, was a mainstay of the later lineup, as was the guitarist Buddy Judge. They took to playing a loud, chaotic version of "Voices Carry"; this was the final song of the last official 'Til Tuesday show at Ovations in Saugus, on April 10, 1992. When a new album did appear the following year, it was Mann's solo debut, *Whatever*—the start of a solo career, with Hausman remaining on board as her manager. But her turning point really came with 'Til Tuesday, when she had a taste of pop stardom and reached for creative satisfaction instead.

Now based in Los Angeles, Mann looks back with mixed feelings at her video-star days. "It got weird, and it got weird fast. I can remember walking into clubs and hearing people say, 'God, who does she think she is?' But the fact is that I'm a really shy person and always was. I didn't really know how to interact, and I probably suffered from a lot of clinical depression. And because I was so quiet, I probably pissed off a lot of people at radio stations who expected me to put on a dog and pony show. So I didn't really know how to be a rock star; that was never the right job for me. So it probably helped me that 'Til Tuesday got so successful, because I was so unprepared for it."

New Edition, New Kids on the Block: The Right Stuff

But for some, Boston in the eighties would forever be associated with the biggest and most surprising success story of them all. It began innocently enough with the Jonzun Crew, who in 1981 were one of Boston's few successful R&B acts. The disco era had largely passed Boston artists by, with two major exceptions: the long-relocated Donna Summer became a disco superstar, and Tavares, a quintet of brothers

from New Bedford, had a handful of soul hits through the seventies.
They were labeled a disco group only after "More Than a Woman"—
a song written by the Bee Gees and appearing on the multiplatinum
Saturday Night Fever soundtrack—became their biggest hit of all.

With a futuristic high-tech sound, the Jonzun Crew scored a string
of slightly goofy club hits—including "Pack Jam (Look Out for the
OVC)," which combined the vogue for offbeat dance singles with the
emerging video-game craze. Two of the Florida-born brothers who
helmed the group, Michael and Larry Johnson, ultimately went separate
ways. Working under the name Michael Jonzun, the former teamed
with Peter Wolf after he left the J. Geils Band. The resulting album,
Wolf's solo debut, *Lights Out,* was a successful mix of rock and techno-
soul sounds that was a few years ahead if its time.

But it was his brother Larry who was really about to make waves.
Going by the name Maurice Starr, he styled himself as an all-around
star maker who harked back to the Svengali figures of earlier decades.
He produced a regular series of talent shows at the Strand Theater in
Dorchester. With the impeccably dressed Starr always commanding the
spotlight, these contests were presented as glossy events at which dreams
of stardom came true. And stardom did indeed come to New Edition, a
teenage Roxbury quintet who sang an old Jackson 5 hit at one of those
shows. Starr signed them up as his management clients. Still patterning
New Edition after the Jackson 5, he and Jonzun wrote and produced
their first number-one R&B hit, "Candy Girl." Soon thereafter the
group rebelled and broke away from Starr, dropping the Jackson 5 pose
after their voices changed. But Starr's credentials as a hit maker were
now secure.

Starr continued to hold his talent shows and to work his showbiz
magic on an expanding roster of bands. Not all of those groups made it
big; another teenage group, the Perfect Gentlemen (which included his
son Maurice Jr.), had only one small hit single, and Rick Wes—a white
rock singer whom Starr saw as a new Elvis Presley—was a quick fizzle.
But Starr was nothing if not ambitious, and he continued to take inspiration from earlier decades of show business—another of his acts,
Margo Thunder, was something of a Tina Turner figure. So his next big
idea after New Edition made a perverse kind of sense: in the early seventies the Jackson 5's success had briefly been usurped by a white

group, the Osmond Brothers. Since Starr had already done his own Jackson 5, why not his own Osmonds as well?

That was roughly the idea behind a group that debuted locally on May 13, 1986. The occasion was a Starr-produced afternoon show at the Sportsmen's Tennis Club in Dorchester—a family event with a relaxed, early-summer vibe. The main attraction was the singer Bobby Brown, who'd just left New Edition and was headed to an uncertain future as a solo artist. (At that point, nobody could see the tabloid fixture that he and his future wife, Whitney Houston, would become.) But Starr was on hand to introduce his latest discovery: an all-male, all-white, all-cute teenage vocal group that he'd dubbed the New Kids on the Block. "I wanted a white group that could play to a black audience and kill 'em," he told me at the time. "Once they get through the ghettoes, they'll be able to play anywhere." Indeed, they already seemed ready for the world: "If any of you girls are interested in me, I'm a Capricorn," announced New Kid Joey McIntyre, who was all of thirteen years old at the time.

A few years later, the New Kids were back in the area on a national tour, this time headlining at the Worcester Centrum. It didn't happen overnight (the first album bombed), but by this time the New Kids were synonymous with teen mania; if you strolled the lobby of the Centrum, you'd find teenage girls arguing heatedly over whether Donnie, Joey, or Jordan was the most awesome. The Dorchester teens had taken the world by storm; everyone under sixteen knew the songs "Hangin' Tough" and "You Got It (the Right Stuff)." Their live show on this day was part serious and part cornball: they proved their mettle by playing all the instruments for a song or two. (On this occasion it was the Jackson 5 song "I'll Be There"—Starr's old loves apparently died hard.) There were lasers and explosions and some comedy based on Donnie Wahlberg's rocker-dude persona. Then they promoted their latest hit album—a Christmas record, of all things—by singing in sequined suits, flanked by inflated snowmen.

This kind of fun was the last thing that the denizens of the Rat wanted to hear about, but their little sisters clearly understood. The New Kids' reign lasted roughly three years, from 1988 through 1990—about right for teen idols—and they went on to mixed fortunes afterward. (Wahlberg has had the most success, as an actor.) But people who were teenagers at the time have to smile when hearing about the "boy band" sensations of today: they've already seen five Dorchester kids do it all.

The Del Fuegos: Don't Run Wild

Between Mission of Burma's exploratory noise and 'Til Tuesday's elegant pop, it would already seem that Boston in the eighties was covering a lot of ground. Still, there was always more. The new phenomenon of MTV was also influencing Boston bands, if it was only to dress down, look scruffy, and thumb their noses at it. But some decided it was no crime to look stylish, play stylish music, and capture their appeal on three minutes of videotape. 'Til Tuesday was the most successful, but other area bands hit MTV as well. Providence's Rubber Rodeo did so with an odd mix of high-tech pop and country music, and New Man got airtme with the naggingly catchy "Bad Boys." The former club promoter Digney Fignus, who had an elegant Bowie-esque look, got MTV play in 1984 for "The Girl with the Curious Hand," one of the few worthwhile Cars sound-alikes. Face to Face had a lead singer, Laurie Sargent, who was both vocally and visually impressive. The band's MTV hit was "10-9-8," but Sargent stood out in another video as well: in "Sun City"—an antiapartheid benefit song produced by Little Steven Van Zandt—she can be seen singing and strutting alongside Bruce Springsteen and Lou Reed.

'Til Tuesday's success led the way for a handful of ambitious bands whose sound was more sophisticated than the punk norm. High among them was O Positive, whose singer, Dave Herlihy, could go head-to-head with any of the golden throats on MTV. The band's moody, textured sound had a European tinge; their lyrics were often literate and not often upbeat. But it's no small feat to be angst-ridden and seductive at once; O Positive managed that with "With You," a major local hit in 1985. That song hooked fans into the longer, exploratory material they'd do onstage.

More traditional rock and roll was also alive and well. The Stompers' leader, Sal Baglio, was a true believer whose songs would have been AM-radio staples in a more innocent era; as it was, the band maintained a strong local following for nearly two decades. Another anomaly was born when the guitarist Peter Greenberg, formerly of DMZ and Lyres, wanted to play manic late-fifties rock and roll; he chose a fellow record store employee as the front man, "just because I knew he could sing."

He was right, though the front man had to change his name because there already was a music star named Barry White. So Barrence Whitfield and the Savages featured one of the most wailing, soulful voices in town. Led Zeppelin's Robert Plant was among his fans. Whitfield also managed to dig up plenty of wild, little-known songs from the fifties; and "Mama Get the Hammer (There's a Fly on Baby's Head)" would be one of his most requested tunes—especially when he played weddings.

Boston proved friendly to roots rock, a catch-all term for music that harked back to country, R&B, and fifties rock and roll. The best of these bands put a fresh spin on the old sounds. Treat Her Right benefited from an inventive harmonica player, two low-strung guitars, and the vocal interplay of David Champagne and Mark Sandman (the latter eventually in Morphine with the drummer Billy Conway). Scruffy the Cat was the greatest Boston rock band ever to include a full-time banjo player; the cleverly named Condo Pygmies worshipped at the altar of Jerry Lee Lewis. Also much loved in some quarters was Lazy Susan, an acoustic band whose two front women sung with a haunting Appalachian twang. And in the nineties came the New Orleans–inspired Slide and the raunchy blues duo Mr. Airplane Man.

Another rootsy band also made national waves. If you were one of the millions who watched MTV's telecast of 1985's Live Aid concert, you saw a whole lot of the Del Fuegos—not onstage, unfortunately. The Boston quartet was just a little too young and little known to make Sir Bob Geldof's guest list. But the Del Fuegos had the mixed fortune of having done a Miller beer commercial that was aired throughout the telecast. There was the band straight out of Boston clubs—maybe looking a little too hip in their leathers and shades—noting that "rock and roll is folk music, it's music for folks." They'd get kidded about that line for the rest of their days. And for better or worse, they'd be forever associated with that commercial—pretty ironic for a band whose front man, Dan Zanes, is now a big name in children's music and a confirmed teetotaler.

But in their eighties heyday, the Del Fuegos did a lot more than sell beer. During a time when Boston was still intoxicated with punk and hard rock, they reminded local crowds that you could go back to the roots—Elvis, the Everly Brothers, Eddie Cochran—and get good and intoxicated just the same. Not that Boston had ever forgotten completely about country or pre-Beatles rock; even Lyres and Real Kids did Elvis Presley and Eddie Cochran songs, respectively. But the Del Fuegos seemed the most likely for a national breakthrough when *Rolling Stone* named them the best new band of 1984 and Tom Petty picked them as his opening act a short time later. These days there's a big audience for roots rock and alternative country, but the Del Fuegos were playing that music long before anyone knew what to call it.

Back home in New Hampshire, they probably just called it sloppy rock and roll. In fact, it took only one bad gig to convince the Del Fuegos to pack up for Boston. "We were booked at the Hawaiian Isle II, a Polynesian restaurant in Concord, New Hampshire," Zanes recalls. "We were doing our usual set, lots of Drifters' songs, some Elvis and Sam & Dave. We were supposed to be doing four sets a night but we cleared the room after one set, and got fired after two. We had nothing against playing well; we just weren't always able to do it. And we couldn't tune our instruments, so it became more of a punk-rock experience."

It was precisely this experience that made them right for Boston in 1983. "We knew there were some rockabilly bands around, which meant something to us—more meaningful than all the kids at home who were singing in English accents," Zanes says. The Boston clubs gave them a chance to polish their musical chops while getting into the occasional drinking contest with their musical heroes. One such spree happened at Cantone's, the converted Italian restaurant in the Financial District. "We got to open for the Real Kids, who were heroic figures to us. The best way to get them to pay attention to us was to get into a drinking contest. That one went on for most of the evening, and it was finally settled with the two bass players drinking some pink liquid. I believe it ended up as a Quaker tie, which means that everyone made it out of there in one piece."

Despite—or maybe even because of—such evenings, the band became far tighter than they'd been in New Hampshire. By the time they signed their record deal, they were tight indeed: their 1984 album, *The Longest Day*, is tough and twangy, boozy and big-hearted. But the following year brought *Boston, Mass.*, with a local anthem ("The Sound of Our Town") and a minor national hit single, "Don't Run Wild." They were recording for the LA-based Slash label, home of a few great West Coast bands (Los Lobos, X, and the Blasters), which also had a foot in punk and one in the roots tradition. By then the band was accustomed to living on the road. A story circulated in Boston that the Del Fuegos were spotted at an all-night truck stop by Bruce Springsteen, who gave them an approving look and said, "Hey, you guys look like a rock-and-roll band." (As it turned out, the story was embellished just a bit: the rock star who spotted them was only the less-hip Huey Lewis.)

Even for a band that *Rolling Stone* liked, life on the road wasn't exactly glamorous: Zanes recalls one New York gig, in a winter snowstorm, where they made just enough money for either one hotel room or one case of beer. (They slept in the van, clutching very cold bottles.) Which is why the beer commercial didn't seem like a bad idea. "We knew our rock history pretty well," Zanes points out, "so we knew that the Rolling Stones had advertised Rice Krispies. Otis Redding had done commercials. We didn't realize how it would put us at odds with everybody else, though. It debuted at the time of Live Aid, so there's everybody raising money for this cause; and there we were hawking beer. Critics wrote us off, but it was worse to hear bands saying, 'We'd never do a beer commercial.' And we knew that what they meant was, '. . . like the Del Fuegos!' "

But they really were the salt-of-the-earth band portrayed in the commercial. When a writer for the *Boston Phoenix* razzed them for wearing sunglasses in the ad, Zanes responded, writing that they were too ugly to appear otherwise. When the Del Fuegos and Los Lobos shared a bill at Boston's Paradise, both bands put so many friends on the guest list that the sold-out show wound up losing money.

Other problems were brewing, too. The two-year party was catching up with them, and it led to much infighting. (Two original members, including Zanes's brother Warren, were gone by their swan song, *Smoking in the Fields*—a disc that's better than Zanes thinks it is.) The Rock 'n Roll Caravan with Petty and the Georgia Satellites didn't help much. "We were living the American dream, and I was so uptight that I couldn't appreciate a minute of it. I was fighting with my brother and feeling intimidated by the whole Petty camp. I had everything I wanted, but I wasn't ready to appreciate it. And the band felt we were ready to go to the next level. . . . Only problem was, it was a level below."

But the Del Fuegos got out with their nice-guy credentials intact; their very last gig—a reunion at the Middle East in 2002—was a benefit for a food bank back in New Hampshire. Dan Zanes, now in the children's music business, says that when he cranks up the tremolo on his guitar and leads the kids through a rocking version of "Polly Wolly

Doodle," it doesn't feel a million miles from an old Del Fuegos gig. "It's really very similar," he told me before one of those shows. "When we played the Rat and Cantone's, it felt very communal. To us it wasn't a show if people didn't dance; it didn't even count. It's the same thing now; the whole experience is about people getting up and being part of it. But now we can have a full-throttle dance party before lunchtime." In other words, when you've spent years playing for drunk twenty-five-year-olds, playing for sober five-year-olds isn't that big a stretch.

Hardcore: The Kids Will Have Their Say

By 1982 punk rock was almost mainstream; the Cars had made new wave respectable, Mission of Burma's name was written all over the city, and there were Mohawks on every street. There wouldn't seem to be any way left that rock could be shocking or rebellious. Then hardcore came along.

If fifties rockabillies had sung about gang war, hardcore sounded like one: it was punk rock played as fast and loud as humanly possible, with no regard for subtlety and even less for melody. And gang war was exactly what the shows looked like. To the untrained eye it simply looked as though the audience members were beating the crap out of each other. The mosh-pit phenomenon had struck, and the fans were doing pretty much what the music demanded: slamming into each other, jumping on each other's heads, flying knees and elbows in all directions—slamdancing. To any over-the-hill, senior citizen rock fans—say, to anyone pushing twenty-five—it looked easy to get yourself hurt out there.

"Yeah, but you would have been initiated," points out Curtis Casella, whose Taang! record label became the main outlet for Boston hardcore.

> It was like being in a gang; you had to get knocked around to get accepted. I wouldn't call it an innocent kind of bonding; it was not a safe environment. If a more innocent person walked into a hardcore show that had never seen it before, they would run out the door the other way. If you'd been brought up on the Clash and thought that was edgy, you'd come in and see kids with bald heads and Xs on their hands, flying through the air; and you'd think it would look like a massacre. All you'd want to do is lean up against a wall and hide. The bouncers certainly freaked out;

they thought it was just kids beating up on each other. But if you talked to them, these kids were all friends. They'd huddle beforehand and say, "We're going to show this out-of-town band that Boston audiences are the craziest in the nation."

In any case, hardcore was a prime example of Boston taking another city's ball and running with it. Hardcore originated in Los Angeles, where the band Black Flag caused enough disturbance to get banned from clubs on a regular basis; soon afterward the all-black Bad Brains and the politically and socially conscious Minor Threat sprang out of Washington, D.C. But Boston arguably took hardcore more to heart than other cities. By 1982 there were enough Boston hardcore bands to merit a compilation album, the seminal *This Is Boston, Not LA;* and a handful of bands—DYS, Gang Green, Jerry's Kids, the Freeze, the Proletariat, the F.U.'s (later to morph into the more metallic Straw Dogs), SS Decontrol (originally Society System Decontrol, its name was later shortened to SSD)—were at the forefront. The local *xXx* fanzine chronicled and supported the scene.

At first the shows were strictly do-it-yourself. The Gallery East, just across from South Station, was already operating as a gallery and performance space with a taste for the avant-garde; for the first year it was virtually the only spot that dared to book hardcore. But the shows moved around a few corners to the cavernous Channel, and by 1983 all-ages hardcore matinees at the Channel had become a weekend ritual; a Boston band usually opened for a national act. When Jerry's Kids opened for Minor Threat and the show drew fifteen hundred, other clubs were more willing to take a chance.

Everything about hardcore—the straight-edge lifestyle (no drugs or alcohol), the brutal speed and volume, the violent image and disregard for catchy tunes—seemed a reaction to the old and stodgy forms of rock from . . . maybe six months before. But hardcore was also a reaction to the fact that those under twenty couldn't drink legally, which meant that teenagers were no longer allowed in clubs to see those older bands (unless they played a rare all-ages show). The Xs on hands were originally a mark for underagers who weren't allowed to drink at clubs, but it became a symbol of the movement. "Hardcore made its own rules, that's why it was unique," says Casella. "Cocaine, women, making a million dollars—that wasn't part of the whole prescription. Hardcore was more like a cult: you lived it, you absorbed it, you didn't listen to anything else."

In fact, the first band to incite slamdancing in Boston wasn't even a hardcore band, but the relatively good-natured garage punk group the Outlets. Their best-known tune, "Knock Me Down" (which appeared on a seven-inch single split with Malden's Boys Life), was simply about the effect that a pretty girl had on the singer; but fans started taking the song title literally. "It looked pretty cool when you were safe onstage," the guitarist Rick Barton, then with the Outlets, points out.

For a certain age group and hormone level, the idea of risking life and limb for rock and roll didn't seem too bad. And even some musicians who wound up forming non-hardcore bands made a few trips to the pit. Kenny Chambers, a singer and guitarist who would soon form the punk trio Moving Targets (and who was later with Bullet LaVolta), managed to have Dicky Barrett (who later fronted for the Mighty Mighty Bosstones) stage-dive onto him at two different shows. "It seemed there were always the same ten to fifteen people stage-diving at every show," Chambers recalls. "I did it myself once or twice. There was an element of showing off, looking big for your friends. [Black Flag's singer] Henry Rollins used to say it was homoerotic, but I never thought there was anything sexual about getting knocked down watching a band."

Not everybody remembers the Channel shows as being quite that raucous. Evan Dando, the future leader of the Lemonheads, was a regular at those matinees, and he recalls a more communal vibe. "There was no aggression at all; it was about having fun. Back in the day there was some kind of etiquette. Everyone was bouncing off each other, but they'd pick each other up when they fell. People would form a circle during the slow parts, and then freak out in the fast ones. But I never saw spikes in the pit or anything like that. Everyone seemed pretty cheerful. A lot of that got lost when hardcore got into the mainstream, but at first it wasn't about anyone getting hurt."

But Dando never tangled with David "Springa" Spring, the fifteen-year-old lead singer of Boston's first important hardcore band, SS Decontrol—a band he formed soon after seeing the group's future guitarist crash through a plate-glass window. "It happened at the Main Act in Lynn. I was trying to sneak in underage; and I see someone smashing through the glass; someone had pushed him right through. That was the first time I ever laid eyes on Al Barille, our guitarist. People were pretty afraid of him, but we got along fine. I was good at taking stuff apart, and he was good at blowing stuff up. One of the first things we did together was to blow up the toilets the night the Underground closed. We clipped wires, unscrewed doorknobs, and generally manhandled the place."

Though Springa was a short kid with a fairly slight build, when he got into the pit he didn't mess around. "I would always put carpet tacks inside my spiked bracelets, so anyone who'd bump into me would jump back in a hurry. It was always my thing to make them stay away from me, rather than to inflict pain. People were in there with steel-toed boots; sometimes they had kneepads under their pants. You had to wear defensive mechanisms to get out alive. I'm sure everyone wanted to kill me, but I could always get onstage before the bouncers got me." His unhinged energy as a singer, with arms striking and legs kicking, wasn't much different from his displays in the pit. "We're young kids, we're smart, we hate everybody outside of our school and we're tired of getting pushed around. By the time you get to the Sunday all-ages show, you're ready to vent and get it all out of your system. You'd come back to school on Monday feeling all tired out, then by Friday you're ready to do it again."

SS Decontrol started as a straight-edge band, but not everybody followed their lead. Gang Green laid their own philosophy on the line with "Alcohol," a major local hit that threw a new spin on a familiar Miller beer jingle ("You got the beer—We got the time! You got the coke—Gimme a line!"). Arguably the most popular of the lot, Gang Green was in 1986 the first hardcore band to win WBCN's Rumble; a journalist for the *Boston Herald* even gave them a hundred-to-one chance of winning. Their set in the final round included their other local hit, a cover of 'Til Tuesday's "Voices Carry"—which was, despite their disrespectful intentions, a pretty good version. While playing that song in the Rumble, they brought a synthesizer onstage and trashed it—the synth representing all that was slick, MTV-oriented, and uncool in their world. And, sure enough, they won.

Other leading hardcore bands had preoccupations ranging from Marxism to hockey. The Proletariat was the most political band of the lot and one of the most sophisticated musically. Their debut album, *Soma Holiday,* borrowed its title from Aldous Huxley's *Brave New World* and includes some well-turned attacks on the Reagan era. Though the readers of *Boston Rock* magazine named it the best local album of 1983, it's since become a forgotten classic of the era. Putting fury above finesse was Slapshot, whose love for hockey imagery was well suited to the gutteral delivery of their singer, Jack "Choke" Kelly. Their cover of Jefferson Airplane's "White Rabbit" was about as far from Grace Slick's original vocal as one could imagine. Slapshot's 1985 formation made them a relative latecomer to hardcore; but they outlasted most of their contemporaries, recording with the famed Chicago producer Steve Albini in 1994. In 1999 twenty-two Boston bands honored them with a tribute album, *Boston Drops the Gloves.*

Many of the more traditional Boston bands at least liked the idea of hardcore, even if they didn't all brave the shows. Mission of Burma—one of the few pre-hardcore bands that the kids liked and respected—recorded a short, loud, fast, hardcore-ish song, "OK / No Way." And the Dogmatics—garage-rock wise guys—poked fun at the phenomenon with "Hardcore Rules," a song that might have been taken as a serious anthem ("No such thing as rock and roll! Only SS Decontrol!") if it hadn't been sung to the tune of "Skip to My Lou."

The first wave of hardcore officially ended during a Paradise show in late 1984, when Springa took the stage with Jerry's Kids and pronounced, "We started hardcore in Boston, and we're ending it here and now!" Some original bands split up and some changed their style; others simply discovered that cocaine, women, and making a million dollars weren't bad ideas after all. Originals like SSD, Gang Green, the F.U.'s, and DYS all went for a change of style as they became technically better players. (Only Slapshot dared to put this trend in its place with their song "Crossover Sucks.") Once they slowed their tempo down and began to employ guitar solos, the sound became a little more familiar. The last line in that Dogmatics song said it all: "Hardcore's dead, let it settle. Now I'm into heavy metal!"

Dinosaur Jr: Freak Scene

Hardcore also hit western Massachusetts, but in a different form. Long a stronghold for (Grateful) Deadheads, the Five College area wasn't likely to come up with hard-moshing, straight-edge bands. In fact, some of the western kids were a little bummed when the tougher Boston bands came to town. "The Boston crowds were always these big scary guys;

they came in and up went the Marshall stacks. When SS Decontrol would play at the Grange in Greenfield, I'd be thinking, Hoo boy. Party's over," recalls Lou Barlow, a Westfield townie. "Their scene seemed to have no tolerance for anything but straight-edged hardcore. And the guys were so huge that you couldn't slamdance, because you would really get hurt." The area's homegrown bands weren't exactly that threatening. There was the proudly goofy Pajama Slave Dancers, and Da Stupids, a particular favorite of Barlow's. "That band had a couple older hippies playing with the young kids—It was the weird townies who formed bands like that."

After playing in the hardcore band Deep Wound, Barlow's next group, Dinosaur Jr (initially just Dinosaur, before a California band sued over the name), was itself a weird townie band, but a great one. Barlow on bass and Emmett "Murph" Murphy on drums were the rhythm section, even though Barlow admits they didn't know the first thing about being one. And on vocals and guitar was J Mascis, a hardcore refugee (and, like Barlow, formerly of Deep Wound) who'd become a fixture at the area's college radio stations, despite the fact that he'd never enrolled in a college.

Before they had a real sound, Dinosaur Jr at least had a mission: play loud. Really loud. This is no exaggeration: one of their first shows at the Rat was the most ear-splitting I've ever heard; the sound carried down the hall, up the stairs, and out the door. "That wasn't just typical, it was a prerequisite," Barlow says. "If we had a manifesto, that would have been number one: above all else, confuse people. And the volume presents the whole confusion factor. One thing we got out of hardcore was that it wasn't about setting the world on its ear. You were in it for the musical integrity; it was about being part of something."

And besides, playing loud was fun. "We'd all had our formative experiences with extremely loud bands. For J it probably came from growing up with Kiss and AC/DC records. For myself it probably came from having seen [the legendary Minneapolis band] Hüsker Dü play the VFW in Easthampton. There was nobody there, maybe thirty people, and the volume was just unbelievable. You couldn't even recognize the songs you knew. And that feels really great when you're fifteen and sixteen years old."

The members of Dinosaur Jr were well steeped in Boston bands by the time they formed in 1983, thanks partly to the Ace of Hearts sin-

gles that came into Northampton's musical hangout, Main Street
Records. "The Neats were a favorite of mine—they were the soundtrack of my senior year in high school. Also, I'd somehow seen Mission
of Burma play 'Academy Fight Song' on Channel 38 and thought,
That's amazing." Still, he admits that Dinosaur Jr didn't have much of a
specific sound, or much of an audience, in their early days. "At first, we
were all over the map, and we learned just by playing shows—we
weren't much for practicing. We did college shows but didn't play to
many people; the older people were just disgusted. We had our friends
who would follow us around; I met my wife because she was doing
radio at Smith [College]. There were maybe three or four girls at Smith
who liked us."

Dinosaur Jr found their sound once they broke away from the
loud-and-fast boundaries of hardcore—particularly as Mascis learned
to play long and wild guitar solos that were actually interesting. "He
began his search for the perfect guitar sound. It all involved high-
wattage amplifiers. He was buying whatever he could afford, and that
was usually abrasive-sounding transistor amps. When he got those vintage Marshalls, I think he'd found his sound. That made it easy for me
to play bass, because I never really thought I could be heard."

By their second album, *You're Living All Over Me,* Dinosaur Jr had
found its footing. And they'd signed with the California label SST,
home to noisy misfit bands from around the country—New York's
Sonic Youth, Los Angeles' Black Flag, San Pedro's Minutemen, Arizona's
Meat Puppets, and Barlow's old heroes, Hüsker Dü. "From a critical
point of view, that second album was where we arrived at a sound.
Until then our Boston shows hadn't done too well; we'd go to Chet's
Last Call and play to nobody. But then there was a show at Bunratty's,
after the album, where it was totally crammed with people. But we
could barely tell, because we never looked up. Instead, you'd be onstage
thinking, Are we rocking anybody? or, Are we playing this song right?
At first you'd just take it for granted that there was nobody paying attention, but we saw some momentum happening."

The band also came to embody a certain slacker appeal. Since they
never talked onstage or looked at the audience, you couldn't be sure if
they wanted to be there or not. If you wanted an antidote to rock stars
preening in the spotlight, there it was. "It's partly that we were extremely young and self-conscious," says Barlow. "Fun was not one of our ob-

jectives. We just acted like everything was a huge drag. I'm not sure what the source of that vibe was, but J is such a low-key person and he was the leader of the band. The leader of a social clique always determines the tone, and his tone was so laid back—to the point where it felt a little risky to be really excited about anything."

A fallout between Mascis and Barlow would end Dinosaur Jr's original lineup in 1989; both went on to write nasty songs, notably Sebadoh's "The Freed Pig," that were presumed to be about each other. Both would go on to greater success, at least for a time—Mascis with Dinosaur Jr (now effectively a solo act) and Barlow with Sebadoh and Folk Implosion. Yet 2005 would find Dinosaur Jr joining the string of bands who had reunited and played to larger audiences than ever.

GG Allin: [Censored] My [Censored]

Most rock and rollers think of themselves as outlaws, but a few of Boston's quite literally were. In the late fifties a band called Myles & the Wild Ones played a number of local hops; the singer, Myles Connor, made a convincing juvenile delinquent with his shades and no-nonsense look; the band had a nifty, nasty single called "Hey Little School Girl." But Connor became better known in later years as Boston's most notorious—and successful—art thief. By his own count (on a 1998 ABC News profile), he masterminded "thirty-plus" art robberies; he is widely assumed (but never proven) to have been involved (though in prison at the time) in the spectacular, still unsolved heist at the Isabella Stewart Gardner Museum in 1990 (during which three Rembrandts, a Vermeer, and numerous other works were taken). Connor served twenty-three years in prison and was nearly fatally wounded in the sixties in a shoot-out with police. He was freed in 2000 and three years later he even appeared briefly at a benefit show at Arlington's Regent Theater. Arnie Ginsburg introduced him as "a man who left music to join the world of art collecting."

When you're talking rock-and-roll outlaws, however, all roads lead to GG Allin. And it may be the ultimate irony that a town with Boston's puritan heritage was home to the most extreme rock monster who ever lived. We live in a culture in which anyone with a slightly daring act is branded as edgy, outrageous, dangerous. But GG Allin truly was all of those things, and it was not a pretty sight.

Allin's performances are the stuff of legend. He'd charge onstage, looking like a demented pro wrestler with his hulking figure, handle-bar moustache, and manic stare, while the band slammed into some ill-rehearsed punk riff. The song would be something suitably foul; "Bite It You Scum" and "I Wanna Fuck Myself" were among his most-requested numbers. Maybe he'd be wearing a diaper or a jockstrap, which would come off during the first tune. Whether he chose to masturbate, roll around in broken glass, urinate, or cut himself and spray blood, there would definitely be body fluids involved. If someone got too close to the stage, Allin would attack the guy with his fists, or coldcock him with the mike. A brave soul might hand the singer some pills and he'd take them without asking what they were. By the third song, the Ex-Lax that he'd downed before the show would start working, and the shit would quite literally hit the fans.

The show would last until the cops showed up, which usually wasn't long. And with any luck, someone in the band would have the presence of mind to smuggle Allin out of the club in an equipment case before he was arrested. The indie film *Hated* includes a recording of the drug-fueled, filth-smeared spectacle that was Allin's final show—all seven minutes of it. The same film shows Allin beating the hell out of a woman who chides him for not making good on a promise to die onstage. Allin is then kicked and punched by her companion before the police break the whole thing up.

Don't bother asking whether the music was any good. Some of it was, most of it wasn't, but that's hardly the point. Allin's life—which ended on June 28, 1993, after he scored some after-show heroin in New York and passed out at a party—was a performance in itself. It did take a certain sensibility even to attend his shows; and in fact he didn't play Boston that often. His last local show, at Green Street Station in Jamaica Plain, ended nearly as soon as it began, after an unidentified someone—fan, bandmate, or crew member—urinated on the couch. But despite the very real dangers of his shows, he did manage to get booked and to draw crowds. "Clubs sold drinks when he played, I can tell you that," notes Joe Coughlin, a Boston writer who befriended him.

Allin did manage to play with some of punk rock's greats—the Ra-mones' bassist, Dee Dee Ramone, and Sonic Youth's guitarist, Thurston Moore, among them—and there are serious fans who'll argue whether "Outlaw Scumfuc" or "Gypsy Motherfucker" was the superior work. But those who dared attend the shows were a different breed. "Some

truly lost souls were into him," says Coughlin. "I met one guy who
drove eight hours just to get hit in the head. The people who didn't
have anything else to do had GG."

Born in Lancaster, New Hampshire, to an apparently abusive
father who saddled him with the name Jesus Christ Allin (later legally
changed to Kevin Michael Allin), GG wasn't originally any more ill be-
haved than any of the other misfits who played punk rock in the late
seventies. Indeed, he got thrown out of his first band, the Thrills (with
his brother Merle on bass), for missing too many rehearsals because he
wanted to be home with his wife. This earned him the nickname of
PWK, for Pussy Whipped Kevin. "He was a great drummer, but he
wouldn't move to Boston to be in the band," the Thrills' Johnny Angel
recalls. "He was a good egg all around—just a big, nice, goofy guy from
New Hampshire."

His first album, released in 1980, was merely misogynistic and in
fact rather catchy. Then something apparently snapped. By 1983 he'd
disbanded his band the Jabbers and formed the Scumfucs. Out went
songs like "1980's Rock & Roll," and in came "Hard Candy Cock" and
"I Don't Give a Shit." Initial copies of his second album, *Eat My Fuc*
(later truncated for reissue to *E.M.F.*), came with a hand tracing of
Allin's private parts. According to Coughlin, the onstage mayhem started when one of his bandmates needed to urinate and didn't feel like
leaving the stage. Soon afterward, a fan on tour gave Allin some pills
that turned out to be horse laxative; the results likewise were visible to
all. He also engaged in oral sex with strippers onstage at least once; he
had another stripper urinate in his mouth and filmed it for posterity;
and once in San Diego he ripped out the ceiling pipes and flooded the
place.

The long-running local music magazine the *Noise* will always have
a warm spot for Allin, whose band was the first ever to pay for an ad.
Recalls its editor and publisher, T. Max, "He bought an eighth-page ad
in issue number seven—late spring, 1982—for his 'Gimme Some
Head' single, then a half-page ad in issue number twelve that said, 'Buy
our EP and fuck yourself with it.' He appeared to be a very polite
young man. In July of 1986 we did a cover story on him, and he was
still polite when I met him at the Rat to do a photo shoot. Behind the
Rat there was a festering Dumpster, and I asked if he would get in
there for the shoot. Before the sentence was even out of my mouth he

dove headfirst into the trash without even examining what might be in there. He thrashed around like he was in the ocean, then hopped out as if nothing had happened."

Ensuing years would find him in two familiar environments: TV talk shows and jail. He did time for his onstage exploits and for an alleged assault on a woman he was involved with. (She pressed charges after he burned her with a lighter; he claimed he was trying to revive her after an overdose.) During one of his incarcerations he recorded an album that included the song "Shove That Warrant Up Your Ass." On the Geraldo Rivera and Jerry Springer shows, he came off as an odd combination of sideshow barker and cult leader as he talked up his mission to bring danger back to rock and roll.

Exactly what made GG run will never be an easy question to answer, though his upbringing was likely a factor, as was his determination to live up to his image. Yet those who knew him say that he remained surprisingly affable offstage. "You create a persona that you start to inhabit, then you start to believe it's the person you really are," says Johnny Angel. "To me he could have just been a nice guy raising a family. As for the onstage thing—he could have been way high, or just saying, 'Hey, why not?' I've done unbelievably stupid things onstage myself; you just forget yourself."

According to Coughlin, "If you treated him like a person, you'd get it back twice. Even when he was a derelict smelly toothless bum, he'd still talk to you if you talked to him." He even claimed to like his audience, for all the physical harm he inflicted. "They knew what they were getting into," Coughlin points out. "And those who didn't got the hell out of there quick. A lot of his fans were lost souls, kids that no other band would lay claim to."

Allin's accidental death wound up preventing his stated mission to die onstage and take as many audience members as possible with him. He set dates for this at least twice, but he wound up being behind bars when the dates rolled around. "I don't think he would have been afraid to do it, but he kept saying, 'I've got to put it off for a while, I still have too much to prove,'" says Coughlin. "He would have been humiliated to go out the way he did." Still, he notes, Allin in later days also talked about toning things down. "I think he was getting tired of beating the shit out of himself. I could see him getting into country music—both because he loved it, and because it would piss people off."

The Underground Goes above Ground

(1990–1999)

Cavedogs, Dumptruck, Big Dipper, O Positive

In the summer of 1994 the West Coast punk-rock band Green Day hit Boston for a show at the Hatch Shell. Green Day had just caused a celebrated riot at the Woodstock '94 festival, and the band was well on its way to superstardom. The guy carrying the bassist Mike Dirnt's bags at the hotel was a former punk rocker himself and recognized a kindred spirit. He introduced himself as Pat Leonard and said he used to play bass in a Boston band, Moving Targets. At this the Green Day star's eyes lit up: "Moving Targets! I started playing drums because of you guys!" Leonard got to hang with Green Day backstage for the rest of the night, and he made a frantic call to Kenny Chambers, the leader of Moving Targets, the next day. "I'm sure there was a lot of talk about trying to put the band back together," Chambers recalls.

It was a typical story for the early nineties, when Boston bands were becoming legendary for garnering more influence than money. Those who had looked like surefire superstars in the past few years— Aimee Mann, Throwing Muses, Treat Her Right, O Positive—were still stuck at cult-hero level. And it seemed the streets were littered with careers that should have been huge.

There is, for example, no way to explain the failure of the Cavedogs, a fresh-faced trio who were one of the purest power-pop bands (in the irresistibly tuneful sense of the early Beatles and Who) that Boston ever produced. By the time the California label Enigma signed them and released their debut album, *Joyrides for Shut-ins,* in 1990, half the songs had already become familiar to Boston audiences as radio tapes, so the album was practically a greatest hits collection. There was only one problem: around the time of its release, Enigma threw piles of money into an attempted comeback album by the seventies' teen idol David Cassidy. Though that album spawned a Top-30 radio hit, it tanked saleswise, and it took a lot of Enigma's resources with it. (The end of the label's partnership with Capitol Records also contributed to the situation.) The Cavedogs wound up playing shows with "For Sale" signs hung around their necks, and at one show they had themselves introduced as "Hindenburg recording artists, David Cassidy & the Cavedogs." (Cassidy was, of course, nowhere in sight.)

The Cavedogs did get to make a second, equally overlooked album for a bigger label (Soul Martini on Capitol, which had absorbed Enigma), but they continued to thumb their noses at the industry. During one all-important showcase gig in Hollywood, schedules went awry and a curfew cut their set short. Pleading with the venue's management for time for an encore, they swore they'd play a quick one. And that's exactly what they played: the Who's mini rock-opera, "A Quick One." All ten minutes of it.

Another band that surely should have made it was Dumptruck, whose leader, Seth Tiven, wrote some of the saddest lyrics in town. But he always set them to buoyant pop melodies that either lightened the depression or just made it more enticing. Having built a small national following in the mid-eighties, the band was set for a big breakthrough, but instead the group wound up as poster boys for bad record deals. After their third album—*For the Country,* a small classic of downcast, rustic beauty—they'd finished their commitment to the independent label Big Time and were ready to sign with a larger company. Big Time's head didn't see it that way, however, and he sued the dirt-poor band for five million dollars, claiming he still had them under contract. The band would spend the next two years playing legal benefits for itself. In the

A quiet moment with 0 Positive. (Photo: Paul Robicheau)

end, Big Time defaulted on the suit—the owner simply didn't show
up—but by then Dumptruck had lost the pending deal, their savings,
and their career momentum. They did pull an appropriately bitter and
jagged album, *Days of Fear,* out of the mess. And even after a move to
Texas, Tiven proceeded to keep Dumptruck alive with various lineups
for another fifteen years (and counting)—in part, no doubt, to prove
that he could.

And the near misses just kept on coming: after a couple of successful independent releases, Big Dipper and O Positive, both at the forefront of local bands with good tunes and smarts, made national albums
for Epic that went nowhere. (Big Dipper's album perhaps tried too
hard to be commercial; O Positive's maybe didn't try hard enough.) In
fact, both bands did their best work on independent labels. Big Dipper's
previous album, *Craps* (on the smaller Homestead label), spawned a
local hit in "Ron Klaus Wrecked His House"—a true story about a
raucous eviction party thrown by the singer Bill Goffrier's former
bandmate. That album's finale, "A Song to Be Beautiful," featured a
roomful of guests shouting out the memorable chorus, "For a song to
be beautiful, the artist must be free!" It was deep thought with a beat.
As for O Positive, they rebounded and did their best album—*Home*

Sweet Head, inspired by depression over the Epic fallout—and released it on their own label.

The Bags and Bullet LaVolta, heavier rock bands, likewise failed to set the world alight. Both were well loved at home. The Bags were essentially a punk band with a few extra notches of volume, tongue-in-cheek bluster, and a flair for offbeat song angles. (Few bands could match their "Waiting for Moloney," a twenty-minute mini-opera about commuting through Allston for rehearsal, complete with B-line sound effects.) Bullet LaVolta sported two pile-driving guitarists (Clay Tarver and Kenny Chambers, the latter moonlighting from Moving Targets) and a singer, Kurt "Yukki Gipe" Davis, whose onstage intensity brought the national punk hero Iggy Pop to mind. Both bands would have fit well into the mid-nineties musical climate, but in 1989–90 the world at large wasn't sure if they were punk or metal. (In Boston we at least knew that the answer to that multiple-choice question was "Yes.") Equally surprising was the relative failure of Tribe, an elegant, European-sounding band, whose single "Abort" was three minutes of beautiful neurosis and about as unsettling as a catchy tune could get.

One of Boston's best nineties bands would also fall prey to record-label skullduggery. The Shods had a great sense of rock history—with hints of the Clash, David Bowie, and farther back to rockabilly—and a stack of killer tunes from their front men, Kevin Stevenson and Dave Aaromoff. Clearly poised for success, the Shods were the first band signed when the local studio Fort Apache—by then a hotspot for forward-thinking bands—launched a custom label with MCA Records. They spent two years recording and fine-tuning their album—finishing it just in time for MCA to pull out of the deal; legalities at that point dictated that they couldn't release the album at all. (They did, however, get the rights back five years later.) Undaunted, they quickly recorded an entirely different album and released it on their own label; it got the topical title *Bamboozled, Jilted, Hoodwinked & Hornswoggled.* The band would continue into the new millennium.

Others made a long-standing impression without a real commercial breakthrough. Thalia Zedek, who'd started the Dangerous Birds in the early eighties and subsequently recorded an EP with Uzi, had evolved into an experimental rocker with a raspy, whiskey-soaked voice that would have fit well in a cabaret. In 1990 she and the guitarist Chris Brokaw formed Come, which combined some warm guitar sound with

The Shods' front man, Kevin Stevenson, makes a point.
(Photo: Roy Rubinstein)

many seductive hints of danger. (They both continue to record and
tour as solo artists.) Galaxie 500 had a more dreamy sound with a psychedelic flow; this endeared them to U.K. audiences in particular. Indeed, Galaxie 500 proved how important a band can be without commercial airplay, a major label, or mainstream attention: since their
breakup, they've been honored with both a four-CD boxed set and a
posthumous album of sessions they recorded for the BBC. The guitarist
Dean Wareham moved to New York, where he formed Luna. The
rhythm section of Damon Krukowski and Naomi Yang first explored
psychedelia in the band Magic Hour; then they became the ethereal
folk-rock duo Damon & Naomi. They remain cult heroes on at least
two continents.

One band that did make it, however briefly, was a group that had
played the Channel frequently under the name of the Dream, before
selling that name to a TV series and taking the punning name of Extreme. Always an arena-ready band, Extreme's trademark sound was a
mix of heavy guitars, wailing vocals, and a funky backbeat—yet their
one big hit had none of the above. Instead, "More Than Words" was a

Naomi Yang of Galaxie 500 and Damon & Naomi. (Photo: Jon Strymish)

gentle ballad with Beatles-type harmonies; its difference from anything else on the radio made it a left-field hit in 1991. Recapturing their heavy image afterward proved more of a problem, and their singer, Gary Cherone, was on the hot seat when the superstar band Van Halen briefly took him on as lead singer in 1997, replacing the loudmouthed Sammy Hagar. To say that Cherone had to work hard to win over hostile audiences would be a severe understatement.

Morphine: Cure for Pain

The biggest anomaly to come out of Boston in the nineties—and iron-ically enough, one of the most successful bands—had to be Morphine, which Mark Sandman, a singer and bassist, and Billy Conway, a drum-mer, put together as their band Treat Her Right was winding down. Though the previous group had a stripped-down lineup, Morphine worked with even less: Sandman played a two-stringed slide bass; Dana Colley played baritone sax; and Conway (who alternated drum duties with Jerome Deupree) at least got to play a full kit. For the most part, nobody played anything else. "We call it low rock," Sandman would duly explain to anyone who asked what kind of music it was; he'd then insist that he didn't need all four bass strings, since one string already had all the notes on it.

In fact, Morphine's sound, a kind of sexy film-noir funk, benefited from the limitations of the lineup. "It freed us up because with two bass strings, your triad's not complete; there's already negative space in there," Conway explains. "As a trio we could turn on a dime, and the flexibili-ty lent itself to Mark's writing. He would always say things onstage like, 'Welcome, music lovers and curiosity seekers.' We were happy to see fifty-five-year-old jazz guys in the audience next to a state-of-the-art, black-clad indie rocker. To us the greatest success was when people didn't notice what was different about us; they just liked the music."

In 1991 the band signed with the small, local Accurate/Distortion Records, which released its debut, *Good*. Soon thereafter they moved to the Salem-based Rykodisc, whose roster then included the David Bowie, Elvis Costello, and Frank Zappa catalogs. The label would go on to issue releases from Throwing Muses and Kristin Hersh, as well as reissue Mission of Burma's Ace of Hearts titles and comprehensively bring Galaxie 500's recordings back into print.

One breakthrough for Morphine came when their music was fea-tured in the hit independent film *Spanking the Monkey,* which made good use of both the band's sexiness and its darker undercurrent. A similar sly personality was projected in Sandman's lyrics. "Someday there'll be a cure for pain; that's the day I throw my drugs away," he wrote in the trademark tune that shares its title with the band's break-through second record, *Cure for Pain,* thus invoking the spirit of the blues while giving a wink to those in the demimonde. "A great song is

Morphine plays outside the Middle East at the Central Square World's Fair in 1997. Left to right: Billy Conway, Mark Sandman, Dana Colley. (Photo: Paul Robicheau)

hard to write," says Conway. "When you have one, it's not too hard to present it in a pop format, no matter what the instrumentation."

Still, it took Sandman's charisma to transform a trio of creative players into a band that hit the lower reaches of the big time. Sandman's short black curls and heavy-lidded look gave him matinee-idol appeal; and he had bohemian cool to spare. "You don't have that by mistake," Conway points out. "You had to want to be there in the spotlight, and he did. But he reminds me of someone like Peter Wolf, in that you could see him out catching a band on any given night." Indeed, the members practically lived in the clubs, whether it was Colley doing solo saxophone sets at Charlie's Tap, or Sandman playing in an endless list of side projects (one of which, *Like Swimming,* paired him for one 45 with the nineties rock star Beck). If nobody was playing, Sandman could be found kicking back or holding court at his favorite seat at the Middle East—the upstairs bar, second stool from the right.

The rise of the Middle East was one key to the amount of action this decade saw. The initial credit goes to Billy Ruane, a beloved local character who never did anything quietly. Indeed, the sight of Ruane in full glory—shirt hanging open, feet flying in all directions, drinks toppling in his wake—was often more interesting than whatever band he was watching. In early 1988 he booked himself a birthday party at T.T. the Bear's Place in Central Square, only to wind up with more bands than the club could fit. So he arranged a second stage at the family-run Middle East restaurant next door. Danny Mydlack, a performance artist who was known to shave his own chest while playing the accordion, was the first act to appear, followed by the Blake Babies; and a fine time was had by all. By the mid-nineties, the Middle East would convert its downstairs bowling alley into another, larger live venue. With T.T.'s and the artsy dance club Man Ray all within half a block of each other, Central Square would turn into something of a rock-and-roll theme park.

Mighty Mighty Bosstones, Upper Crust, Sebadoh, et al.: Gimme Indie Rock

How do you know that your band's suddenly become a big deal? When you're still living in a dinky apartment in Somerville, and a white stretch limo shows up to take you to the airport. Bill Janovitz, Buffalo Tom's singer and guitarist, woke up to find that monstrosity outside his Davis Square house one morning in 1992, soon after their song "Taillights Fade" became a left-field hit. The limo was so out of sync with Buffalo Tom's roots as a rough-edged, club- and college-bred band that the bass player refused to get in. "Chris Colbourn was mortified. He grabbed his suitcase and said, 'I'm taking the subway,'" Janovitz recalls. "I got in, because I'm all about convenience. My feeling was, Hey, we're not paying for this, so let's enjoy it."

Scenes like this happened to countless bands in 1993, the year of the indie-rock gold rush. Suddenly it seemed that the major labels were everywhere, throwing money around. So you're in a proudly underground, punk-inspired band that you thought was too raw for radio, too weird for pop stardom? No problem. They'd still find a place for you on MTV, on a film soundtrack, maybe even in a teen magazine. You too could get a major label record deal with a six-figure advance. Maybe you could even quit your day job.

The moment had been a long time coming. During the eighties there was still a clear division between the commercial bands and the independent ones; if you were doing something a little raw, weird, or punk-inspired, there was only so far you could go. Many of the eighties

bands that history remembers as great and influential—Sonic Youth
from New York, the Replacements and Hüsker Dü from Minneapolis,
X and Black Flag from Los Angeles, and, of course, the Pixies and Mission of Burma from Boston—never made it to the top. Most signed
with major labels and wound up playing theaters, but none found superstardom, sold platinum, or made it far on commercial radio, which
was still busy wearing out Led Zeppelin albums from the seventies. The
mid-eighties success of the Georgia band R.E.M. at least proved that
one great band could crash the commercial gates; but R.E.M., as much
as it wanted to, never managed to drag dozens of other misfit bands into
the spotlight.

The band that finally changed the world wasn't even trying. The
Seattle trio Nirvana had already been around for two years before most
of the world noticed. At one of Nirvana's first Boston-area shows, in
1990, the band played the tiny Jamaica Plain rock bar Green Street Station, sharing a bill with the noisy Boston band the Cheater Slicks.
(Asked about that show years later, Dave Shannon, the Cheater Slicks'
guitarist, said, "We figured, big deal—a bunch of hippies from Seattle.")
Yet Nirvana's second album, *Nevermind,* nearly changed the climate
overnight when it was released in September 1991. Nirvana's leader,
Kurt Cobain—a disheveled cynic with a heroin problem and bad taste
in clothes—was nobody's idea of a pop star. But there was something
hugely affecting about his songs and hugely energizing about the band's
guitar sound; *Nevermind*'s producer, Butch Vig, knew how to exploit
both. And the music business reacted to Nirvana's runaway success the
only way it knew how: by looking everywhere for more of the same.

Much as the Beatles had in the sixties, Nirvana provided a rallying
point for bands around the country—but this being a more cynical
time, as many young bands made fun of Nirvana's success as tried to
emulate it. (Nirvana originally recorded for the Seattle label Sub Pop; in
Boston there turned up two small, short-lived labels called Sub Shop
and Pub Sop.) In one case, Nirvana's influence was more hands-on:
Mary Lou Lord, a hip street singer who knew and loved underground
music, met Cobain at the Rat shortly before his album took off. The
two struck up a relationship, though Lord wound up jilted when
Cobain met Courtney Love, whom he would marry, soon afterward.
Lord would field interview questions about the affair—and onstage ver-
bal attacks from Love—for years to come.

What happened in Boston post-Nirvana was the equivalent of that white limo pulling up at Bill Janovitz's house. Sometimes it seemed that youth culture was being recast in Kurt Cobain's image: soulful, alienated, and streetwise teens were turning up on MTV, in mainstream television shows (*90210* and *My So-Called Life*), and newly aware teen mags such as the late, lamented *Sassy,* with its coveted "Cute Band Alert." (To its eternal embarrassment, Buffalo Tom could manage only a "Cute Drummer Alert.") Two area bands, Boston's Green Magnet School and Providence's Six Finger Satellite, were also signed to Sub Pop. According to the guitarist Chris Pearson, the former band was signed because the label owner thought they recalled English punk. "But of course, when our album came out, all the English critics compared us to Nirvana."

Combining with Nirvana's rise—and to some extent causing it—was the fact that a younger crop of music fans, raised on club gigs and college radio, were getting positions of influence. Once-prominent local scenesters were now working behind the scenes at major labels (the Rat's former booking agent Julie Farman was now working A&R at Epic/Sony; the former WERS DJ Debbie Southwood Smith was at MCA; and another local, Steev Riccardo, went from Enigma to A&M). Also moving up in the world was Mark Kates, who had answered phones at WBCN and worked at Rick Harte's Ace of Hearts label. In 1991 he was working promotion at Geffen Records, when Nirvana was about to be its flagship band.

It wasn't just Nirvana soundalikes getting record deals; it was anyone with a cult or club or critical buzz that could conceivably translate into Nirvana-like sales; the old ideas of what was and wasn't commercially viable temporarily went out the window. As a prime example of how the rules were changing, Capitol Records was signing—and a former member of Led Zeppelin was producing—a Texas band that disc jockeys had previously been afraid even to name on the air: the Butthole Surfers.

Boston could always be depended on to provide the major labels with bands that would get some good reviews and cult success, if little else. Yet coincidentally or not, in the era after Nirvana, some of those same artful bands started scoring hit singles. Gigolo Aunts, once shunned as too Beatle-esque for their own good, got onto a Hollywood film soundtrack. (Their song "Where I Find My Heaven" was in

Dumb and Dumber.) Two singer-songwriters, Jennifer Trynin and Tracy Bonham, found themselves the objects of separate major label feeding frenzies. The buzz on Bonham brought Chris Blackwell—the man who'd broken both U2 and Bob Marley to America—into the Rat. (Bonham signed with Blackwell's Island label; the alliance was short-lived but got her a 1996 Grammy nomination for best alternative performance.) A similar buzz brought Warner Bros. sniffing after Trynin; and Warner formed a million-dollar alliance with Squint Records—the label Trynin had started in her living room.

And the hits kept on coming. The abstract pop groups the Dam-builders and Fuzzy both got signed to Atlantic Records. Jonathan Richman was hip again, as the Farrelly brothers built their comedy hit *There's Something about Mary* around his troubadour persona. The experimental guitarist Reeves Gabrels, who'd played in the theatrical rock troupe the Bentmen, got a plum gig playing guitar with David Bowie. Tanya Donelly, once of Throwing Muses, and her dreamy pop band Belly found themselves with national airplay for "Feed the Tree" (whose title came from a New England expression meaning "pushing up daisies"—hardly the usual stuff of pop songs). Throwing Muses themselves got some commercial radio airplay with "Bright Yellow Gun," and Kristin Hersh found herself amused by the "grunge" revolution: "The Parisians finally liked the way I dressed!"

Also scoring a left-field hit were the Mighty Mighty Bosstones, whose gravel-voiced lead singer, Dicky Barrett, would seem to make them unlikely for airplay. But the band had come a long way since Barrett learned his chops at those early Channel hardcore shows. The band had latched onto ska—the Jamaican dance music that had evolved into reggae and already been revived by a handful of eighties bands in Britain. But the Bosstones had a decidedly hometown take on ska, with a strong punk flavor and an onstage camaraderie that harked back to that of the J. Geils Band. This was a group with a strong "out with the guys" appeal. Barrett's writing became more thoughtful around the time he kicked a drinking habit, and "The Impression That I Get"—a song about meeting life's random trials—struck a chord to become their hit; it sparked a ska revival nationwide. True to their name, the Bosstones kept strong ties with Boston after hitting nationally; their multinight "Hometown Throwdowns" became a Christmas tradition.

During one of those swings, they became the first nationally known band to record a live album at the Middle East.

Even the outlandish Upper Crust made it to the national spotlight via Conan O'Brien's late night television show, where they appeared in 1994. It was Nat Freedberg, the former Flies and Titanics leader and a man with a famously snotty sense of humor, who came up with the timely idea for a band doing songs about the joys and pitfalls of bring filthy rich. (Their repertoire includes "Let Them Eat Rock" and "Can't Get Good Help Anymore.") They wore business suits for their first show, which Lilli Dennison booked for them at Green Street, but they wound up taking the conceit further and dressing in eighteenth-century outfits, complete with powdered wigs and velvet knickers. The original lineup included Ted Widmer, a singer and guitarist who left after scoring a job as speechwriter for President Bill Clinton—the closest that any Boston rocker has gotten to the presidency.

Conan O'Brien (a Brookline native) allowed them two songs, "Little Lord Fauntleroy" and "Minuet," both of which contained in-jokes for hometown fans. Nobody outside Boston would have laughed when Widmer sang, "Gonna dance the minuet, gonna dance like Dave Fredette"—the name of their guitarist. And Freedberg had to play a loud guitar lick to cover up one line of the first tune that local fans knew well: "I saw him playing with his hard-on, in the formal garden." O'Brien, who'd been a member of the Harvard Lampoon, recognized a kindred spirit and interviewed the band on his couch, where Freedberg introduced the members by their assumed names: Lord Bendover (Freedberg himself), the Duc d'Istortion (Fredette), Jackie Kickassis (the ex-Bags/Lyres drummer Jim Janota). To which O'Brien cocked his eyes and deadpanned, "You guys work way too hard on the names."

Another of this era's best bands was among the toughest to categorize. Helium began when Mary Timony, a singer and guitarist who'd recently moved from Washington, D.C., teamed up with Dumptruck's rhythm section (the bassist Brian Dunton and drummer Shawn Devlin; the two had lately played with Mary Lou Lord and Jason Hatfield in the short-lived band Chupa). At first Helium evinced the familiar jagged guitars and angry vocals of alternative rock; Timony's lyrics were both feminist and surreal, with frequent references to witches and prostitutes. As the band went on (and Ash Bowie replaced Dunton on bass),

Timony got more interested in fairy-tale imagery, and the band's sound got warmer and more offbeat. Helium's 1997 album, *The Magic City*, is full of rich melodies, fantasy-based lyrics, and carnival-like keyboards; it's one of the more original albums of its time.

The early nineties were also the only time when two popular Boston rock bands were strictly instrumental. The guitarist Rich Gilbert was fresh from the Zulus breakup (and a few years from taking a lead-guitar gig with Frank Black) when he formed Concussion Ensemble, whose lineup—two guitars, one bass, and four drummers—played some of the most overwhelming shows in town. More refined was Combustible Edison, whose leaders, Michael Cudahy and Liz Cox, had played in the pop group Christmas before falling in love with sixties bachelor-pad music. Referencing long-forgotten bandleaders like Martin Denny and Esquivel, their sound was a celebration of breezy melodies and strong martinis.

The national spotlight wound up landing in some unlikely places, giving brief stardom to the self-effacing likes of Lou Barlow. The former Dinosaur Jr bass player, Barlow was a perfect early-nineties type of rock figure: sensitive and bespectacled, the kind of guy you can imagine staying up all night writing lovelorn songs in his living room. And, indeed, the first few albums by his new band Sebadoh were made largely at home, wearing their low fidelity as a badge of honor: forget the studio polish and let the song stand on its own. "I felt I needed to record at home and make songs that sounded really honest. Everything can get extinguished in a studio. I'd rather be alone to figure out exactly what I want to say," Barlow explains. By the time it did acquire studio polish, Sebadoh's songwriting had reached an impressively high level—even if the songwriters (Barlow, Jason Lowenstein, Eric Gaffney, and later Bob Fay) did insist on putting sensitive country-rock tunes, surf instrumentals, and avant-punk demolitions on the same album.

Yet Barlow, who had moved from Northampton to Boston, got his hit song from a more offbeat side project. He'd been hired to score the 1995 independent film *Kids*—a disturbing teenage fable that was hardly cut out to be a hit but became a left-field one anyway. Instead of recording the soundtrack with Sebadoh, he did so with his cowriter, the singer John Davis, in a loose project dubbed Folk Implosion—the name a jokey tribute to a New York band they liked, Jon Spencer's Blues Explosion. The breakout song, "Natural One," didn't have much to do with the film itself—in fact, it's barely in there at all—but it did have the kind of aching melody that had become his trademark. The difference was a modern electronic sheen that came from Barlow and Davis's experiments in Cambridge's Fort Apache Studio. It became a Top-40 hit, the first and only one of Barlow's career.

"The main thing for me was that London Records was bankrolling the soundtrack, so I had a week to work at Fort Apache, where I already felt really comfortable, and it was on their tab," Barlow recalls. "The song came together incredibly quickly; the instrumental track took a couple of hours. Wally Gagel, our engineer, was enough of a tech-head that he knew how to work the samples. We didn't go into the soundtrack feeling like an indie band; we also had this love for what would become known as trip-hop [i.e., drum machines and loping electronic rhythms], and we wanted to explore that."

Barlow doesn't necessarily buy the idea that a whole new audience was coming along after Nirvana's success—and if there was, he had mixed feelings about going after it. "I don't think that punk broke or the climate changed because of a band called Nirvana. We'd seen the audiences build with Dinosaur Jr in 1988—and then again with Sebadoh, we were doing well and our audience was starting to coalesce; it didn't suddenly get bigger after Nirvana happened. What happened with Folk Implosion and 'Natural One' was, we got a faceless radio hit. The song was getting all this radio play and going to the top but nobody knew who we were; there was no new audience that went along with it. And really, we weren't losing any sleep over that."

So there was no soundalike follow-up to "Natural One," and Barlow's now more inclined to write off the single's success as a fluke. "We just ignored all of the attention. I felt we'd already done years of touring, and our partnership and our creativity needed to be respected. So we didn't need to skip any rungs on the ladder in order to milk our single. Looking back on it, that may have been my problem." One who did get a big career boost from "Natural One" was Wally Gagel, who was approached soon afterward to work with another guitar-oriented band that wanted to explore some electronics. They were the Rolling Stones.

Buffalo Tom: Taillights Fade

The feedback that opens Buffalo Tom's first album was probably enough to scare some radio programmers away: squalls of feedback

Buffalo Tom in the limousine era. Left to right: Tom Maginnis, Bill Janovitz, Chris Colbourn. (Photo: Paul Robicheau)

weren't getting a lot of airplay in 1990, unless they came from time-worn Hendrix albums. True, Buffalo Tom was a fairly traditional rock band—one that liked power chords, catchy choruses, and emotive lyrics—but they were as yet too raw and punk-inspired for the main-stream. Besides, they started at UMass–Amherst, where all three members (Janovitz, Colbourn, and a drummer, Tom Maginnis) were attending school, and Amherst didn't boast a whole lot of rock-and-roll history. These were the dark days of 1986, before many people cared that the Pixies had formed at UMass (or before most people cared about the Pixies, period). An Amherst townie, J Mascis, had formed Dinosaur Jr, at that time a band of weird, unpopular guys who played too loud; in the nineties they'd become a band of weird, semipopular guys who still played too loud.

In all, Amherst's scene was largely seen as a poor country cousin to Boston's. But UMass and the surrounding colleges did have a scene that could be tapped into if you were resourceful enough. "I joined the student union concerts committee—that's the group students would join to spend other students' money on bringing bands to town," Bill Janovitz recalls. "We had to beg for gigs. Our best ones were at the Bay

State Hotel, which was kind of an old men's bar. Any shows that were punk or alternative would always draw the same twenty or twenty-five people—mostly dudes, one or two women."

At the time Buffalo Tom's members had their ears on Boston bands like Moving Targets and Volcano Suns—the brainy noise contingent. Throw in the Hendrix and Neil Young they'd grown up with, add some English moodiness, and you'd get what Buffalo Tom was after. "Some of the songs we started out with wound up becoming songs on our records. But we also had a couple of borderline joke songs, big epic things with tongue-in-cheek lyrics—the word *sophomoric* comes to mind. That was before we became the introspective, angst-filled guys we are today," remarks Janovitz.

But the band signed with the Dutch independent Megadisc, which licensed their debut to the impeccably hip LA label SST (run by Greg Ginn, the guitarist from Black Flag, and then also home to Dinosaur Jr), and their subsequent records to the long-standing U.K.–based indie powerhouse Beggars Banquet. With help from J Mascis, who produced the self-titled first disc, the band was able to play Boston and, once they had an internationally released record under their belt, to tour the United States and Europe. And that brought them as close to big-time success as they'd ever imagined getting. "When we got back from the first European tour, I had a phone message from Grant Hart [of Hüsker Dü], who told me he'd heard our album and liked it. So that was it: someone we cared about said we were good, so we must be a real band. The other thing that happened was we were in New York to play, and went to meet J Mascis at the Café Olé on St. Mark's Place. We walked in there and they're playing our album, which had just come out. As we got bigger we kept moving the goalpost back—'Let's see if WBCN will play us during the day'; 'Let's try to be an MTV buzz band.' But that café is really what I remember the most," Janovitz recollects.

It would be too easy to say that Nirvana's success affected Buffalo Tom's fortunes—for one thing, Buffalo Tom's third album, *Let Me Come Over*, had "Taillights Fade," their most obvious hit to date—but then, it didn't hurt. Janovitz explains: "I think they caused America to pay more attention to bands like us; at first, our fans were a lot more Eurocentric. Suddenly we were playing to fifteen thousand people, striking bigger deals. I thought we could maybe make a living. But it wound up getting bigger than we imagined."

That was when limos started showing up at their door, and when Hollywood beckoned. Their fourth album, 1993's *Big Red Letter Day*, was made in Los Angeles with somewhat slick, seasoned producers, which resulted in a few close encounters in the studio, including one with a prominent film director and two rock stars at once. "There was one mixing session where David Lynch [the filmmaker], Slash [Guns N' Roses' guitarist], and Gene Simmons [of KISS] all came around to see our producers. What I remember is that someone started talking about the movie *Town without Pity*, and Gene Simmons stood up and started belting out the title song," says Janovitz. Later they were written into an episode of *My So-Called Life* in which Claire Danes's character goes to a Buffalo Tom show and makes out with her boyfriend to one of their songs.

"I remember watching that last scene, where they see us at a club playing 'Sodajerk,'" Janovitz recalls. "But then, all of a sudden the music fades up, and there's this guitar solo that we'd never done, this wanky kind of solo that I wouldn't have played—obviously something they'd added after we weren't around. So that's what I remember about that episode, along with the feeling of being in the trailers, backstage on *My So-Called Life* with Claire Danes walking around, and us giving each other looks like, 'You better not get carried away here, or else I'm going to kick your ass.' We always felt outside of our bodies at times like that. But really, I saw a lot of great energy in Los Angeles, creative people making films. In Boston it just wasn't cool to be ambitious.

"I could see how bands would succumb to drugs—like when you get flown in to play a show in London and you haven't slept all day. I was wishing I could take speed at that point, but before we went on-stage I said, 'Nah, I'm cool.' We all had girlfriends, so doing the drugs was less of a temptation. Besides, we'd gotten all that out of our system going to school in Amherst."

Eventually things got less heady and many of the mid-nineties bands wound up back in Boston. For Buffalo Tom it was a gradual winding down, and probably just in time. "The experience does leave you with a lot of existential questions," Janovitz notes. "Like, what if I'd put the same amount of work into anything else? Sometimes I think that if I'd worked as hard on anything as I did with Buffalo Tom, I'd be ruling the world."

The Lemonheads and Juliana Hatfield: It's about Time

As Boston bands got their turn in the spotlight, a few inevitably became nationwide crush objects. Even before they became famous, Evan
Dando and Juliana Hatfield were two of the more crush-worthy figures
in town—in a soulful, grunge-era kind of way. He was a roguish type
with an easygoing manner and fashionably unkempt hair. She was a
willowy beauty with charming shyness and a slightly tragic air. And it
didn't hurt that both wrote emotive pop songs that were perfect to fall
in love by.

Both grew up with obscure showbiz connections: Hatfield's mother
is a fashion writer for the *Boston Globe,* and Dando made Jell-O commercials as a child and lived off the residuals for years afterward. (An instrumental he recorded with the Lemonheads was named "The Jello
Fund.") So it's no surprise that they became an underground rock
glamour couple, even though they were never really a couple. And for
anyone who knew them in Boston, it seemed only natural that both
wound up rebelling against the spotlight and carrying on as idiosyn-
cratic songwriters.

During the height of his career, in 1993, Evan Dando got a call from
a reporter at *People* magazine informing him that he'd been chosen as
one of the publication's fifty most beautiful people. This sounded good
to him, especially since he misheard the woman on the phone. "She
told me I was one of the dishiest people in the world," he recalls. "And
I thought, busiest people in the world? That's probably right; I've been
on tour for a long time." Two months later, there he was in *People* —on
a list with the likes of Catherine Deneuve, Tom Cruise, and John F.
Kennedy Jr.—which proclaimed him "a classically handsome, Boston-
bred preppy, blessed with beach-smooth features."

Things like that just seemed to happen to Dando—a man who, he
swears, wanted only to write good songs. A onetime hardcore kid who
cut his musical teeth at those afternoon shows at the Channel, the
Lemonheads' leader found himself a certified pop star, without ever
seeming to take stardom halfway seriously. Nor did he claim to be a
model for clean living: his drug-fueled exploits spawned many a song.
("My Drug Buddy"—actually a tender, country-ish ballad—was one of
the Lemonheads' best.) A few years after the *People* piece, a less flatter-
ing photo of Dando made the tabloid rounds: a grainy black-and-white

Evan Dando during the Lemonheads' set at the Paradise during WBCN's Rumble. (Photo: Paul Robicheau)

that showed him, Todd Phillips (Juliana Hatfield's drummer), and the recently widowed Courtney Love, all in one hotel bed and looking suitably disheveled. Whatever Dando was up to, it's safe to assume that he had a good time.

"It was a laugh, basically—I was in the right place at the right time, and I was decent at some things like singing and songwriting. People these days only see the negative side of [drug use], and I was seeing the positive side. I made the mistake of being honest about that and, yeah, it haunted me forever. I'm sure I did some perverse, silly stuff that took away from people's perception of me as a musician, but I don't regret it. There was a year when I lived in Gramercy Park in New York, basically being idle. I had the money to do nothing, so I needed to get rid of it as soon as I could so I could get back to work."

The Lemonheads began life with a 1986 seven-inch EP, *Laughing All the Way to the Cleaners,* which was financed by the money that the three original members—Jesse Peretz, Ben Deily, and Dando—got from their parents for graduating from high school. And the inspiration came from local radio: Harvard's radio station, WHRB, has a long-standing tradition of exam-period "orgies"—exhaustive, multihour sessions devoted to a particular style or artist. It was the punk orgies, with their focus on lesser-known late-seventies bands, that caught the young trio's ear. "Our band would not have existed if not for the punk orgy," Dando says. "There was one in our senior year that had punk bands from all over the world, maybe two hundred hours' worth, and we all taped it. To me that music went back to the Everly Brothers, the early Beatles in its simplicity. We started covering songs by punk bands like the Users and Slaughter & the Dogs. We thought we'd be the band that would keep the older, English style of punk going."

That style of music—aggressive, but friendlier and catchier than hardcore—became the Lemonheads' early calling card. Their second show, on a Tuesday night at T.T. the Bear's Place—part of a "Nu Muzik" series devoted to unknown baby bands—was also the Pixies' second show; roughly thirty people caught that historic bill. Like many of their punk role models, the Lemonheads had a wise-guy sense of humor. Dando played the occasional gig in his girlfriend's dress; and when they played WBCN's Rumble, they announced that the Rumble was fixed and played a few bars of a very unhip Phil Collins song. (They made it to the semifinals anyhow.) Regular personnel changes also became a tradition: by the time the Lemonheads signed to Atlantic Records in 1990, Dando was the only full-time member.

The album that made the Lemonheads famous wasn't even the one the label had in mind. Having gotten punk rock out of his system, Dando was getting back to the gentler music he'd grown up on, and hanging out with friends in Australia had put him in an easygoing mood. And with the post-Nirvana boom under way, the labels were looking for more loud, disheveled bands. They probably weren't looking for the lilting, acoustic-based songs Dando was writing. Recorded in Los Angeles with Juliana Hatfield playing bass, and a trio of producers (the Robb brothers) who'd been behind a number of hits since the mid-seventies, *It's a Shame about Ray* was full of short, hummable tunes—maybe an obvious hit in another year, but not in 1992. He and Hatfield did their romantic duet on "My Drug Buddy," a song from Dando's time in Australia. "People think it's about Juliana because she sang it so well, but it's a totally honest account of a night with two friends in Australia—actually doing speed; it's not a smack song. I was missing them when I wrote it, so I tried to tell a little story about one night, not to worry about rhymes but to just tell it accurately."

It took a fluke to launch the album. With *Ray* already in the stores, plans were under way for a twenty-fifth-anniversary reissue of the landmark film *The Graduate*. One of the new features would be a re-recording of "Mrs. Robinson" by a modern band, and the Lemonheads got the nod. "We recorded it in three hours, and it was the silly cover song that put us over," Dando notes. "I love the movie and wanted to do my part to help people find out about it. Suddenly we're selling as many as twenty thousand albums per day." It didn't hurt that the video for "Mrs. Robinson" established Dando's sex-symbol status, which he'd later put to comedic use in the film *Reality Bites*. The album was immediately reissued with "Mrs. Robinson" added, as well as a cosmetic change for the newfound audience: the first two words of "My Drug Buddy" were dropped from the title, though the song remained the same.

Dando certainly made the most of his time in the spotlight. He'd tell journalists of his exploits driving around Los Angeles in a "Nissan Crack Finder." A bootleg recording exists of an after-hours Lemonheads show in Hamburg, Germany—apparently playing for strippers and their customers—on which Dando audibly falls down onstage and the bassist Nic Dalton takes over the vocals. Their follow-up album, *Come On Feel the Lemonheads*, was considerably messier than *It's a Shame about Ray*, but wilder and better as well. One track finds Dando sharing a bit of soul searching—"Don't wanna get high / But I don't wanna not get high / . . . But I'm not gonna not get high"—with the late R&B singer Rick James, also no stranger to the subject matter.

Now living a somewhat calmer and cleaner life, Dando says he re-

Juliana Hatfield after going solo. (Photo: Paul Robicheau)

grets nothing. "I was a contrary kind of person. Far as stardom goes, there were occasions where I may have sabotaged it a little bit. I ran into a couple of phases, but in general it wasn't that bad—I had fun with it." After a solo album released under his own name, in 2006 he released an album with a brand new band—called, of all things, the Lemonheads. "I figure, why not add to the legacy? Hey, there's been a lot of worse bands."

Juliana Hatfield was one of the local teenagers who snapped up the first Lemonheads EP upon its release. Soon afterward she formed the Blake Babies, who already had a few distinctions on their side. For one thing, they were the only rock band ever named by the poet Allen Ginsberg. This happened when John Strohm and Freda Love, the group's founders, went to a reading and asked him to suggest a band name. (He saw their youthful faces and recalled his love for William Blake, and the die was cast.) Hatfield, who'd been a student at Berklee, took her own inspiration from hearing Dinosaur Jr and from seeing Aimee Mann behind the counter at Newbury Comics.

Initially gentle and folkish, the band gradually turned up the volume over the course of their three albums (1987's *Nicely, Nicely,* 1989's *Earwig,* and 1990's *Sunburn*), and an eccentric streak came out as well. Just in time for their last tour, the band members shaved each other's heads in a video—quite haunting in a *Heavenly Creatures* way, but Hatfield warns against reading too much into it. "If anything," she says, "it was symbolic of us wanting to shave each other's heads for the hell of it."

A couple of other notable things happened on the last tour. For one thing, they fell in love with Neil Young's proto-grunge album, *Ragged Glory,* and played as many as four songs from it per show. For another, Hatfield wrote a song called "Nirvana," about her love for that then-unknown band, a good year before *Nevermind* was released. Both pointed to the tougher stance Hatfield would take on her solo albums, as did the confidence she'd developed. "I was always intimidated by everything around me; but on the other hand it was a thrill. We had the rock-and-roll dream that we'd take over the world, step out on a stage and blow them away. When I went solo, I was naive and unaware—I was a kid in a candy store, I had a record deal! I'm sure I had rock-star fantasies in the back of my head, but I knew my music wasn't really suited to that."

In fact, *Become What You Are*—her second solo album and her major label debut—represented the best of early-nineties pop culture. Rougher-edged and more direct than her earlier work, the songs were perfect for a time when commercial radio was loosening up playlists in Nirvana's wake. She even had an obvious hit in "My Sister," about a love-hate relationship with a sibling who's alternately "such a bitch" and "the best." Some nonfans snickered when word got out that Hatfield doesn't have a sister (more likely she was writing from her brother's perspective), but the all-ages rock show that's mentioned in the lyrics, a double bill of Violent Femmes and Del Fuegos, really happened at the Kenmore Square club Storyville in the summer of 1983.

It didn't hurt that she'd grown her hair back and was starting to look more glamorous; she had a preference for black T-shirts and shades. Her long-standing friendship with Dando was making the pair look like a less tragic version of Kurt Cobain and Courtney Love. Dando and Hatfield had been housemates in Allston, even members of each other's bands; Dando had played bass in the Blake Babies in the early days, and Hatfield had done the same at different times with the Lemonheads.

Both were coy when the "are they or aren't they?" questions started coming out; Hatfield let slip (in the British paper *New Musical Express* and elsewhere) that she was still a virgin, a remark that followed her around long after it stopped being true. "It was bizarre to us, all this speculation on whether we were a couple. But the fact is that Evan and I never defined our relationship to each other; that's why we never defined it to anybody else. I would say I wasn't his girlfriend and he wasn't my boyfriend. And it's true that I was a virgin until I was twenty-six; I'm proud of that. I was just naive enough to think it wouldn't be a big deal if I said so." As for Dando, he not only wrote a song apparently urging Hatfield to take the big step ("It's About Time"); he even got her to sing in it. While Dando admits he may have had his friend's virginity in mind, he says the song was "just for fun" and an attempt to write in Hatfield's musical style, with chord changes she might have used. (For the record, Hatfield did not lose her virginity to Dando.)

Like Buffalo Tom and other early-nineties acts with teen appeal, Hatfield wound up on *My So-Called Life*. But she had a full-fledged acting role, playing a teenage runaway on a Christmas episode. Her character is revealed to be a ghostly angel at the end of the show, a role consistent with her musical persona, and Hatfield's performance made the episode the tearjerker that it was. She was also doing some modeling and it seemed likely she'd emerge as more of a personality, until she decided it wasn't her thing. "I wasn't suited for fame, not equipped for it, and I really didn't know how to maneuver it. They put you in stupid trendy clothes, put gunk in your hair—I didn't know how to say no. But my songs were on the radio, and that's all anyone wants. I knew I was okay, but I could do better. I was at the beginning and the attention wasn't justified yet."

The bottom fell out after her next album, 1995's *Only Everything*— a deeper and more ambitious record, if a less obviously commercial one. A longtime battle with depression welled up during the tour.

"Soon as it started, I found myself more seriously depressed than I'd ever been in my life. We were supposed to go on to Europe and I knew I couldn't do it; so we played a show at New York University, and I told them I couldn't go on until I dealt with it. The record label called it nervous exhaustion, whatever that means—I'd rather they just said I was depressed. Everybody needs a muse, and for a long while depression was mine. At the same time, I made a record I loved and it wasn't received as enthusiastically as the one before it, so I hate to think that may have contributed. So I knew the ride was over and I'd have to deal with it, even if I didn't enjoy the ride that much."

Mainstream stardom never called back; yet she's been unusually prolific ever since, making at least an album every year or two (either solo or with a reformed Blake Babies or a spin-off called Some Girls) for a still substantial cult following. "I guess I decided I'm not good at being a celebrity and I'm not good with attention. I'm not a socially affable person; basically, I'm on my own. And yet I write these really catchy pop songs sometimes, so I'm trapped in this paradox. The songs do need an audience, but maybe I need them to come to me."

Letters to Cleo: Here & Now

Unlike some of the bands that got famous in the early nineties gold rush, Letters to Cleo really did look like an obvious pick for stardom. They wrote catchy, summery pop songs and had a front woman, Kay Hanley, with a strong and sweet voice, ever-changing hair color, and tomboyish sex appeal. Named in honor of Hanley's high school pen pal, Letters to Cleo always exuded a down-to-earth personality. When they got their first taste of the big time in 1994—when record labels took them to breakfast meetings in Austin, Texas, promising them big money and stardom—the band members came home and bragged that they'd actually scored a free breakfast.

The year 1994 turned out to be Letters to Cleo's: a successful single, major TV exposure, and more free breakfasts. Hanley had grown up a stone's throw from stardom: her next-door neighbors in Dorchester were the Wahlberg brothers, of Marky Mark and New Kids on the Block fame. But a more profound teenage influence was another neighbor who'd gone to live in an exotic, far-away place—Brookline. "I thought Brookline was full of crazy weirdos, and this family certainly fit the bill. The oldest daughter was always sneaking out to go to the Rat, and that

Kay Hanley onstage with Letters to Cleo. (Photo: Paul Robicheau)

stuck in my head—'You're going to hear all this music that isn't even on the radio; why would anyone want to do that?' But at the same time I found it really fascinating: you could hear music that nobody else knew about."

She got close to the music world in every way she could: first by getting a waitressing job at the Hard Rock Cafe downtown; then by tagging along to see a friend's boyfriend's band, the Mighty Mighty Bosstones, at the Rat. She also joined her Dorchester neighbor Greg McKenna's band, first as a backup singer. Initially called Rebecca Lula, this became Letters to Cleo after a few notable false starts. "We didn't come from money and we all had jobs, so we only could afford to take gigs that would pay—Faneuil Hall bars that made us play three sets a night. So we had to supplement our own songs with covers, some of which were really embarrassing. We did a medley called 'Jane's Funky Groove,' which was 'Jane Says' into 'Groove Is in the Heart' [by Jane's Addiction and Deee-Lite, respectively]. So awful, but that's what it took to entertain people and make our two hundred and fifty dollars."

But their love of heavier Boston bands like the Bosstones and Heretix pulled them in another direction; and hearing Nirvana's primal wails on the radio was the last straw. "That made us say, 'No more covers, no more reggae-tinged funky shit. We are gonna rock.'" The first Cleo fans were hometown friends who came into town from Dorchester; as a result, the band had one of the more polite, clean-cut fan bases in town. "We always felt a little self-conscious about that. Why don't our fans look as cool as other people's fans? But we came to realize that our fans were music nuts; they were the ones who heard our tapes and learned the words to every song." In 1992 the newly formed local label Cherrydisc released the compilation CD *Crush;* Letters to Cleo's "Here & Now"—an infectious tune with a stream-of-syllables chorus—was its biggest local hit. That year the band made it to the semifinals of WBCN's Rumble, alongside Morphine, though both were shut down by the harsher-sounding Big Catholic Guilt.

Oddly, one of the complaints they got in the Rumble wasn't about the music. "One judge didn't like the way I looked," Hanley recalls. "'Put on some lipstick and dress up a bit' was one of the comments we got. But for most of my career I dressed like a boy, and I never thought about it either. I thought the persona I wanted to have was the one I had in real life—the tomboyish, tough bitch. I could never play up the sexiness thing." Some who saw Hanley when her hair was flaming red—or during her short-lived fling with jet-black hair—may well disagree.

In any case, Letters to Cleo was well established as a Boston headliner by the time they went to play the South by Southwest convention —a major music-industry event that brings out top bands and A&R honchos alike—in Austin in the spring of 1993. They packed their amps in the van, showed up ready to rock—and found out their showcase gig had been canceled because of a scheduling glitch. Anyone who did see them in Austin that year would have found them standing forlornly by their van or drowning their sorrows afterward. "We made them feel so bad that they at least gave us passes to the whole week for free," says Hanley.

It took another year before the real payoff came along. In the interim they'd released a full album, the punningly titled *Aurora Gory Alice.* As it was mainly a faithful representation of songs they'd been playing live, it made the local fans happy. Fortunately for the band, one of those fans was Timothy White, the late Boston-rooted editor of the music trade's *Billboard* magazine, who kept up with the local scene. He praised the album on *Billboard's* front page, just in time for the band's return to South by Southwest in 1994. Their manager, Michael Creamer, proceeded to photocopy the review, planted himself in the Four Seasons Hotel, and handed copies out to every high-powered executive in sight. Plenty of free breakfasts ensued.

Giant Records signed them up, re-releasing their independent album with only minor changes (two songs were re-recorded). But it wasn't so much the album that made them famous; it was the video for "Here & Now," which ran over the closing credits of the teen-friendly television show *Melrose Place*. Along with Lou Barlow's soundtrack success, Juliana Hatfield's fashion spreads, and Buffalo Tom's limo, it was a sign that mainstream culture was trying its best to absorb alternative style. The same kind of thrift-store fashion that Hanley had worn in Dorchester was now on a TV show that celebrated downtown Hollywood's young and alienated.

Yet something about Boston bands proved averse to stardom. And if Letters to Cleo had bragged about the breakfasts, they practically apologized to fans and the press for the *Melrose Place* appearance. "All of a sudden, we're inextricably linked to this show. And I can recognize now that it gave us our career. Our record started climbing the charts as a result; and we were on Casey Kasem's American Top 40 for a couple of weeks. But we thought the show was a cheeseball thing, and we didn't want to talk about it. We were embarrassed to have that kind of attention so quickly." Some of that attitude, Hanley admits, was absorbed from Nirvana's famous disdain for the spotlight. "That was definitely part of it, but all the Boston bands we respected felt the same way. You just didn't want to do anything that would be seen as wanting to be a pop star. So whenever we had a photo shoot or made a video, I'd immediately go out the next day and change my hair color. That seemed to get a lot of people upset."

As it turned out, Letters to Cleo's career dipped for a more mundane reason: Giant wanted to release "I See," a song that was popular at early Boston shows, as their follow-up single. But the band was sick of playing "I See" and wanted to get their next album out instead. Unfortunately for them, the band won that battle. The second album (*Wholesale Meats and Fish*) didn't do as well, and fans kept yelling for "I See" at shows. "We refused to play the game, probably to our detriment. My lawyer still brings that one up, as a good example of why you shouldn't ever listen to the artist." The fan base had dwindled by the time the band came out with its third, last, and best album, *Go,* whose cover showed a disturbingly thin Hanley. "By then we'd given up and said, 'Just give us the fancy photographer.' I was fucked up and drinking too much; and it's our happiest record. Go figure—I can't write about being in a dark place when I'm really in one."

Hanley and the guitarist Michael Eisenstein stayed together and made their peace with the industry; they moved to Hollywood and worked on film soundtracks. (That's her voice coming out of an actress's mouth in the movie *Josie and the Pussycats.*) In 2007 the pair was working on Hanley's new solo album, planned to lead off with "Cellars by Starlight." The song celebrates one of the peak moments of Letters to Cleo's career: not the video, the fame, or even the free breakfast, but the first time they got featured in the *Boston Phoenix*'s local music column. You can never tell where your fondest memories will come from.

Scissorfight, Seka: Planet of Ass

So it would seem that everyone making waves in Boston at this point was more or less a pop band; indeed, that was largely the case. When Buffalo Tom, the Lemonheads, and Gigolo Aunts shared a July 1994 bill at Great Woods in Mansfield—a venue usually reserved for established, mainstream stars—it seemed that melody had won the day. That was also true with many club-level bands—most notably the Gravel Pit, a New Haven transplant whose sophisticated songwriting was as much a part of their appeal as their loud rock energy. Their local hit, "Favorite," was one of the catchiest songs on area radio shows in 1998, and their albums had plenty of deeper material for the exploring.

Yet a heavier and nastier sound was also brewing. For years Boston had loved an especially messed-up kind of heavy metal that blended the requisite guitars and adrenaline with a dose of post-hardcore punk, bratty humor, and a few touches of Burma-esque noise. Some of Boston's favorite eighties bands, especially the Bags and Bullet LaVolta, had a foot in metal, and an eighties compilation album called *Suffer This!* brought together a roomful of bands with an especially grisly sound. By the nineties loud and heavy rock was well represented by Stompbox, Slughog (the band that memorably started a fistfight with audience members during their set at the WBCN Rumble), and 6L6. Metalheads were also well aware that Rob Zombie, leader of New York's scum-rock, horror-metal band White Zombie, had been born in Haverhill.

Then there was Scissorfight, a band that initially listed its members as Jarvis, Strongbow, Ironlung, and Fuck You. Their "Planet of Ass" was a gutter anthem that would have made GG Allin proud, and few front people cut as striking a figure onstage as the hulking, bearded Iron-lung—unless it was Linnea Mills of Malachite, an all-female band whose front women wore six shades of eye shadow and growled lyrics such as "Take me to the cemetery! Fuck me in the cemetery!" Malachite was set to record with the star producer Steve Albini, fresh from working with Nirvana, but Mills, who had mixed feelings about the attention she was getting, abruptly disappeared on the eve of the sessions. Some of her bandmates haven't seen her since.

One of the flagship bands for the louder side was Seka, which won the Rumble in 1991. In some ways Seka was the ultimate Boston metal band—raw and fast enough for slightly grown-up hardcore kids, loud and thrashing enough for head bangers, and evincing the snotty humor that Boston bands love. (Not a lot of bands have seen fit to name themselves after porn stars.) The band did have a run of bad luck, however; it was sued by that same porn star just after it signed with Warner Bros. Their new name, Strip Mind, didn't have quite the same ring. And though the Warner's album proved quite respectable (and you can't really fault a song title like "I Wanna Fuck Your Girlfriend"), it didn't come out until after Nirvana had happened nationally, which took the spotlight away from straight-up metal.

There were personnel changes as well, and the new drummer, Sully Erna, clashed with some of the founding members. "We got into fist-fights on the road because he made huge demands," recalls Tim Catz, the group's bassist. "He didn't understand why we didn't have a tour bus, and he wanted personal roadies on his payroll. His feeling was: if you think big, then you will be big." There's no faulting Erna's logic: his next band, Godsmack, was last seen selling a few million albums.

Women of Sodom, Sleep Chamber: These Boots Are Made for Walking

Even in the relatively freewheeling circles of rock and roll, shocking and scandalizing Bostonians can be a ridiculously easy thing to do. But few did it with quite the style of Cynthia von Buhler, a visual artist who spent the mid-nineties leading the subversive, theatrical, and rampantly sexy Women of Sodom. After forty years of Boston rock and roll, it was hard to think of anything that hadn't been done before. But the first time von Buhler put on a nurse's uniform and administered an onstage enema, she had surely found one.

Von Buhler's performances, along with her talents as a visual artist and promoter, made her a media sensation in town; she wound up hanging with rock stars and selling her work to both collectors and celebrities. (Howard Stern bought a painting that she did of him.) In her Boston days she sported a Bettie Page look, with jet-black hair cut in a bob. She would usually dare the journalists who interviewed her to appear in her shows. If you were a guy, you'd come out with a few bruises, but you would be rewarded with an invitation to the yearly Halloween party at her "castle" (actually a wildly redesigned apartment on Ashford Street in Allston). The women who joined the show faced a much easier initiation. "I only made out with girls onstage. Hundreds of them—any girl that got close to me I would make out with." And what did she learn from this experience? "Umm, that kissing girls is nice. Some of the gay magazines got mad at me because I was married and wasn't a lesbian, but we tried to have something for everyone. Even for people who liked animals."

There was already something of a sexual underground within Boston music before von Buhler came along. The arty club Man Ray, in Central Square just across from T.T.'s and around the corner from the Middle East, was home to a goth contingent, elegant vampire types who danced to dark-toned electronic music and tended to flaunt an adventurous sexual taste; you'd see whips and corsets, people of both genders getting chained to various walls and pillars. (More amusingly, you'd also see some of the same vampires eating at the nearby Hi-Fi Pizza after the club had closed.) The local band that fit in most comfortably here was Sleep Chamber—a ritualistic concept band led by the prolific John Zewizz (sometimes spelled ZeWizz), whose songs put forth an unholy mix of "magik" and sexuality. Many of Sleep Chamber's fans were attracted by Zewizz's vision and his uncharacteristically heavy (for Boston) use of electronics. But many others were likely there because Zewizz displayed his fantasies by having women make out with each other at the edge of the stage.

Von Buhler was one of Sleep Chamber's dancers, and she was allowed to design her own performances—one of which featured her as "Subterranean Woman," doing an Indian-style dance while wrapped in tubes with stage blood flowing through them. Yet she broke off from the group early because "it seemed like a lot of the women onstage were worshipping John, and I wanted us to be worshipped instead." Zewizz dreamed up the original concept, the Women of the SS, but since von Buhler wasn't especially keen on the idea of World War II fetishism, it became Women of Sodom instead. "John was serious about the idea of magik and ritual sex; we were more poking fun at it. Whatever was on our minds, we explored. If I had my own sexual fantasies, we'd explore those, or those of the girls in the band. A lot of people thought I was really into S&M, but I was really using it as a way to express ideas. I mean, I must have done everything sexually onstage. But after that, having vanilla sex felt like, Wow, this is really different!"

Though the Women of Sodom had a feminist underpinning, von Buhler admits that breaking taboos also happened to be fun. "It was really more about women being powerful. We didn't mean it to be sexy; it was more about being strong, powerful women. I thought of it less like burlesque than a visual performance, a collage. A lot of it was making fun of things, too. And some of what we did wasn't really sexy at all, like Mother Mary giving birth to Baby Jesus onstage." This was a song that involved von Buhler reaching into the Virgin Mary's vagina—not for real, but the lighting and angles made it seem that way—and producing a handful of Jesus dolls, which were then distributed to the audience as souvenirs. And her Catholic background came out more than once. "We had one girl who waxed a guy's chest hair in the shape of a cross. Another time we found a woman who waxed her vagina, so we smeared peanut butter on it and brought her dog onstage. We used the Nine Inch Nails song 'Animal' for that one."

Von Buhler also managed Splashdown, an electronic pop group that included her husband, Adam Buhler, on guitar and the singer Melissa Kaplan. Signed to Capitol Records and groomed for success, Splashdown's album was produced by Glenn Ballard, who'd helmed Alanis Morissette's smash U.S. debut, *A Jagged Little Pill*. Splashdown's album was both creative and commercial-sounding; yet a last-minute fallout with the label kept it from being released. Of all the Boston bands that got close to national success without making it, Splashdown was among those who came the closest.

Von Buhler meanwhile continued with her performances. *Penthouse* magazine came running in her direction, but the folks there ran the other way once they realized what her act entailed. "They probably thought the enema was a little extreme," von Buhler admits. She ultimately put the Women of Sodom to rest to manage Splashdown. She's now doing visual art full-time in New York, a city that used to upstage Boston when her group was together. "In Boston people were so shocked by our show that they didn't pay attention to the music. Problem with New York was that the audiences were better than us—we had to bring all the leather and corsets we had because the audiences were so dressed up."

The Millennium and Beyond

(2000–)

On New Year's Eve 1999, Boston got ready for the end of the world. This was the night of Y2K hysteria, when the world was about to be struck by . . . well, something bad, anyway. So music fans had no problem about paying far too much to get into their favorite clubs that night. The Middle East had a bill for the ages, with three late-seventies favorites: the Real Kids, Classic Ruins, and Unnatural Axe. If the world was going to get blown up, they figured, maybe it would at least happen during the climax of "All Kindsa Girls" or "They Saved Hitler's Brain." As it turned out, the magic hour came and went without notice; the Real Kids were onstage and John Felice was a few minutes late leading the countdown. Everybody got home in one piece, with a working clock and computer—and probably a working hangover as well.

It's tempting, however, to say that the bad times just hit Boston a few months off schedule. And the holiday that went down in infamy wasn't New Year's Eve, but July 4, 1999—the day when Boston got the news that Mark Sandman, a strong contender for the most admired musician in town, had died onstage in Italy a day earlier. It wasn't the first time Boston had lost a much-loved musician: the death of Paul O'Halloran, the bassist for the Dogmatics, in a motorcycle accident shook up the rock community in 1986; and the deaths of Reddy Teddy's leader, Matthew MacKenzie, Nervous Eaters' drummer, Jeff

Wilkinson, La Peste's drummer, Roger Tripp, and Lou Miami of the Kosmetix had all left a sad mark. But Morphine was on the way to its national breakthrough: their fifth album, *The Night,* an obvious step forward, was only a few weeks away from release. New fans were coming aboard, from the alienated teens who related to the film noir sensibility to the music snobs and leftover Grateful Dead fans who picked up on Morphine's ability to stretch out and jam onstage.

Sandman himself, with his matinee-idol good looks, could be seen hanging around the clubs every night. Sure, at forty-seven he was slightly out of the demographic; but the young girls sighing at Morphine concerts didn't seem to mind. What's more, he was always around—either playing with one of his many bands (aside from Morphine, there was Treat Her Orange, with ex–Treat Her Right and ex–Blood Oranges members, Supergroup, and the Hypnosonics)—or just hanging at the Middle East. But Sandman was never a drug abuser, and Morphine's last local show, only weeks earlier, had been on a sunny afternoon for an all-ages crowd at Cambridge's annual Central Square street fair.

Further, the nature of Sandman's death—of a heart attack before a festival audience—may have been poetic, but it was also especially sad and shocking. As Billy Conway recalls, the gig seemed strange from the start. "What's funny is that we always had a little toast before going onstage; for whatever reason we failed to do it on the night he died. As I recall, the show was going swimmingly; we were having a fantastic time. Then, after a handful of songs, he just collapsed. I've thought a lot about it since then—was there a way of knowing that Mark wasn't feeling well? It never came up, but maybe if we'd all gotten together everyone would have had a piece of information."

The first memorial took place just weeks afterward, with a stage set up outside the Middle East. A pack of local stars turned out. Peter Wolf sang Morphine's "Cure for Pain," and Willie Alexander did the forties standard "Mr. Sandman," during which it wasn't hard to imagine the man looking down at the square he loved. Morphine's remaining members, Conway and Dana Colley, tried out various lineups before solidifying with Laurie Sargent, who'd been the front woman for Face to Face, as the Twinemen. "For a while we called it the Moveable Bubble," Conway explains, "after the emotional bubble we were all in because we needed each other so much—'Where is the bubble going to be tonight?'"

Peter Wolf backstage at Camp Street Studios. (Photo: Jon Strymish)

The corner outside the Middle East has since been officially named Mark Sandman Square; and Hi-N-Dry, the studio he built in Cambridge, remains a hangout for working musicians and has recently launched an in-house record label—so Sandman remains at the forefront of a scene. Says Conway, "If you look at Mark, think about this: not only did he invent his instrument, he wrote the music to go with it; then he scripted the concept to go out there and make it happen. The guy went around the world playing two-string bass. Top that."

Sandman's loss wasn't the only one to hit Boston music around the turn of the millennium. Though best known as a DJ, Michael Linick, better known as Mikey Dee, was part of the scene in just about every way possible: he wrote for the Noise, he worked as a promoter and publicist, he DJ'd on WMFO, and he even played drums in the fractured pop band Butterscott. Most of all, he was a man who lived and breathed local music. Nobody was exempt from his wise-guy sense of humor, but the first notes of a favorite song would invariably send him running up front. If you were also a member of the media, Dee was the kind of guy who'd buttonhole you about the band he loved that you'd given a bad review to—but he'd make sure to buy you a beer first.

So Dee had no shortage of fans and personal friends who were affected when, after routine heart surgery in February 2000, he suffered a stroke that left him paralyzed. Virtually every popular band in town would appear at benefits over the next couple of years; Letters to Cleo played their final show at one, and out of respect they haven't reunited under that name since. Dee would be given videos and tapes of those shows, but when there was one he absolutely couldn't miss, including a reunion of his favorites, the Barnies, at the Linwood, his friends would make sure to get him there in a wheelchair. He was named to the Boston Music Awards Hall of Fame in 2002, and a letter was read that he'd dictated, promising that he'd be back. But it wasn't to be, and Boston went into mourning when he died on July 6, 2003. His weekly radio show continues on WMFO; though many DJ's have hosted it, the show will never be called anything but *On the Town with Mikey Dee*. According to his friend Pete Sutton, bass player for the Willard Grant Conspiracy and Temper, "There was nobody who embodied the spirit of the local scene better. He would always say, 'Go out and see one local band a week. It would do you and the band a helluva lot of good.'"

Another loss that many in town took personally was that of the Rat—and not long afterward, Kenmore Square itself. Nobody denied that the Rat had been faltering for years before the doors shut on November 15, 1997. Julie Farman, Kathei Logue, and Lilli Dennison had long before moved on; Jimmy Ryan's Hoodoo BBQ had been replaced by generic burgers; and the general word was that nobody went there anymore but people over thirty-five and junkies. But, hell, at least that meant somebody was still going. And the old magic still got summoned on occasion. The Bristols maintained their traditional Patriot's Day afternoon shows until 1996, during which you could be blissfully unaware of the marathon runners passing by on the street upstairs.

Cosmetically, the Rat had changed remarkably little during its twenty-year heyday. As Kenmore Square slowly became more streamlined, as the all-night pizza joint Captain Nemo's gave way to the gaudy golden arches of a McDonald's, the Rat held its ground, looking more and more like it was flipping the middle finger at the surrounding gentrification. Jim Harold, its owner, finally took Boston University's buyout offer in 1997, and instead of an all-star send-off he booked the unruly Gang Green—probably the band most likely to incite people to trash the place. Sure enough, everything went out the door during the closing hour—the old Rat sign, chairs and tables, bar pitchers and glasses, bits of the bar itself. And you have to hand it to the intrepid thieves who, once the easily taken mementos were all gone, made a noble effort to steal the cigarette machine.

Also fun while it lasted was Mama Kin, the club Aerosmith owned on Lansdowne Street. Named after one of their songs, the place had a trademark Aerosmith look, all black and silver with red bordello lighting; the wings of their logo were carved into the light fixtures, and song titles were carved into the bar. Aerosmith's members themselves didn't turn up that often; they played the club's opening in 1994 and another time two years later, and Steven Tyler once surprised fans by serving drinks at the bar. In fact, the place had a more alternative booking policy, so plenty of great cult-hero bands passed through before the place closed down in 1999.

One by one, the old clubs bit the dust. The hotel bar over the Rat's old space now charges more for a single drink than the Rat would charge for a life-changing show. The Channel? An office building. Bunratty's? Fern bar. Jonathan Swift's? Audio chain store. Storyville? Pizzeria Uno. Nightstage? Boarded up for more than a decade, apparently with insurmountable back taxes. Even Central Square's gothic art bar, the one-of-a-kind Man Ray, got torn down and left a lot of vampires without a home. And just as some neighborhoods got taken over by chain stores, FM radio started sounding the same in every city. Oedipus and most of his contemporaries are gone from WBCN, which has replaced the politics of the sixties and innovative music programming with humor aimed at adolescents who don't think too much. The latest comedy team, Toucher and Rich, made their debut in 2006; their first show included a long segment about projectile vomiting on strippers.

Godsmack, Staind: Everything Changes

Perhaps appropriately, the two biggest bands to come out of the Boston area during this period—and, in fact, the area's two biggest bands in at least a decade—were among the darkest and heaviest in Boston history. To some extent Godsmack was a remarkable do-it-yourself story. Master-minded by the former Strip Mind drummer (now its front man) Sully Erna, they recorded their first album for a miserly $1,500 and watched it get generous local airplay (especially on Worcester's metal-minded WAAF), get picked up by a major label, and go on to sell three million copies. Yet the elements were exactly the stuff of mainstream rock at the time: sonic overload and a sense of disgust with ex-girlfriends and the world in general. Their hard-rock brethren Staind built their reputation in Springfield and Worcester with a similarly pile-driving brand of metal. But they settled down long enough to write a lovelorn ballad, "It's Been a While," which promptly became a staple of high school proms nationwide. Indeed, it was Worcester audiences—who had grown up watching an endless supply of heavy metal bands roll into the Centrum and the Palladium and listening to WAAF—who first took these bands to heart.

Dropkick Murphys: The Gang's All Here

And once again, revitalization wasn't far away. Hitting big in the new millennium were two bands that could hardly have come from anywhere but Boston. Indeed, you can hardly get more Bostonian than the Dropkick Murphys, who fused Irish music with punk rock. Rick Barton, the band's founding guitarist, was a Rat-era rocker who'd played with the Outlets as a teen in 1980. Nearly two decades later, he was sorting out his life and kicking a drinking habit when some younger guys asked for help with their band.

"I didn't know punk rock still existed," Barton recalls. "And I was surprised that these kids in their mid-twenties wanted to start this little hobby that I'd been practicing for fifteen years. But I told my friend Ken [the bassist Ken Casey] that I'd help him write some music; and the guitar player they had didn't show up, so I was in. It pretty much

The Dropkick Murphys survey Boston. (Photo: Paul Robicheau)

sounded like crap." Still, the Rat was starting a final round of all-ages shows in 1996, and the new band needed something to set them apart. As Barton recalls, the inspiration to add Irish music came from a non-traditional source: the Australian hard rock band AC/DC, whose song "It's a Long Way to the Top" features bagpipes. "Once the Irish thing came in, we started writing more music in three-quarter time. On my part it wasn't conscious at all, but I think Kenny had a plan." By this point it no longer sounded like crap, and when a national punk figure, Lars Frederiksen of Rancid, offered the new band a contract for hundreds of thousands, that sounded good—especially since the band was still poor enough to be collecting the contract from the nearest fax machine, at the local Kinko's.

Barton left to get married (and because "those old personality conflicts sprang up after Ken and I spent too much time together in the van," he admits), but the band's mission of fusing Irish music and punk rock would carry on. What did change was the band's image. The first batch of tunes included rude jokes such as "Pipebomb on Lansdowne" (about the early lineup's low opinion of the Fenway-area clubs) and "Skinhead on the MTA" (in which the Kingston Trio's hero Charlie finally kicks the train conductor's butt). But the Dropkick Murphys were embraced by the city, and the humor grew more inclusive; they now make a tradition of St. Patrick's Day shows—yes, on Lansdowne Street —which sell out hours after the tickets go on sale. And the band had its proudest moment in 2004, when they recorded the old Red Sox anthem "Tessie" in time for that year's World Series; they played at Fenway Park and it became the team's song.

This was perhaps the ultimate vindication for Boston punk: now a rock band was just as much a local institution as the baseball team they celebrated. And two decades after Earth Opera's more sarcastic anthem, the Red Sox really were winning.

Dresden Dolls: Yes, Virginia

"Dig that crazy reverb!" notes Brian Viglione, drummer with the Dresden Dolls (no relation to Joe "the Count" Viglione), his hands tapping a primitive rhythm on his knees. He and his musical partner, Amanda Palmer, a singer and pianist, are taking their first listen to the G-Clefs— who are not only their Boston rock forefathers but also their Roxbury neighbors.

The apartment where the Dresden Dolls live is separated from the G-Clefs' old rehearsal space by roughly half a mile and fifty years of musical history. Palmer and Viglione work out of a slightly tonier part of Roxbury, a couple of stones' throws from Symphony Hall. On the afternoon we visited, the apartment was in a typical state of rock-band disorder. There's a laptop set up for updates to their Web site, piles of homemade CDs by bands they've met or worked with, a few days' worth of plates and wineglasses strewn about. Viglione's hands still have chips of black nail polish from the last gig, and even on an off day, Palmer has painted her trademark curlicues over her eyes; she shaves her eyebrows and repaints them daily. Onstage Palmer wears striped thigh-high stockings, while Viglione's in whiteface and top hat—an odd version of sexiness that somehow works.

The G-Clefs probably never saw a band like this coming. But when we put "Ka-Ding Dong" on the stereo, it's clear how little things have really changed. "We should be making music like this," Palmer says. "What I really like is how groups like this made every song count. I really wonder if in the year 2040, anyone will be listening to the filler songs from a Pearl Jam album and thinking it sounds this good." Adds Viglione, "They've got some Jerry Lee Lewis sound going on in there as well. The guy's got some sex in his stuff, some gravel in his voice. I wonder if people in Boston danced when they heard this stuff, instead of standing there crossing their arms like they do now." As always, the two tend to finish each other's sentences during interviews, an indication of how much time they've spent together since the band was formed.

Taking the blindfold test a little further, I throw on Ultimate Spinach's most crazed piece of psychedelia, "Ballad of the Hip Death Goddess." Since Palmer is a former street performer who's much loved by the vampire-style kids from the modern scene's art and gothic movements, I figure she'd be able to relate. Instead, her carefully penciled eyebrows go up in disbelief, and she does a few jokey interpretive dance moves. Asks Viglione, "You think they were completely serious about this? It sounds just a little too over the top. But if we ever make a movie, this would have to be in the scene where we're driving on some lonely highway. What I'd really love is to see a sock-puppet version of this. There wasn't a lot of tongue-in-cheek rock and roll then, was there?" Adds Palmer, "That's part of the problem, though. You're not supposed to take yourself this seriously now. Everything has to be taken with a giant grain of salt, as if it all could be meant ironically. That's what was great about music in the sixties: you couldn't be retro-ironic when you only had fifteen years' worth of history. What did they have to emulate? Maybe blues guitarists and Elvis. But a band in 2005 has a whole palette of sounds to emulate, so they take what's considered coolest by their peers."

As far as their own peers are concerned, the Dresden Dolls are at once the coolest and least cool band in town. Boston has a long-standing, unwritten law about being too theatrical—looking like a junkie is fine, looking like a mime is frowned upon. In a scene that loves rough-edged garage rock and distrusts a band with a fashion sense, any act with art world connections is a little suspect—especially if they don't even have a guitar. "Boston isn't a sexy city," Palmer notes. "It's a city that prides itself on its coarseness—'I am wearing a winter coat, God damn it!' It's the old Puritan backlash, the opposite of Los Angeles." In other words, a really good place to raise eyebrows.

The Dresden Dolls attract their share of passionate followers while annoying some more traditional ears no end. For that reason alone, they'd be a worthy standard-bearer for the future of rock in Boston.

Dresden Dolls Brian Viglione and Amanda Palmer. (Photo: Lynette Bilello)

But they're also the latest example of an individualist streak that's been here all along. They coined the term *punk rock cabaret* early on; but the sound of Palmer pounding hell out of her keyboard while Viglione churns up mad polyrhythms is more punk than cabaret. Then again, Palmer does have a touch of Marlene Dietrich about her. As a songwriter she's come up with some fairly scathing social satire—"Mandy Goes to Med School" is a suitably creepy song about a back-alley abortion—and she's also written a rather catchy tune about masturbating on a computer chair. "It's actually the chair you were just sitting in," she offers during our interview.

Palmer was already something of a cult figure before she was doing music. Anyone who hung out in Harvard Square at the beginning of the twenty-first century would have seen her as the Eight Foot Bride, a performance piece that she devised and even lived on for a time. She was indeed dressed in a bridal gown and mounted on a high pedestal, never speaking but responding to tips with bits of songs, movement, or other improvs. She got a few hecklers and a stalker or two, along with a number of short but intense connections—pretty much the same things one gets from fronting a rock band.

"For one thing, I learned to be completely focused on the moment, not to be thrown off by what people might be saying. And I learned to be able to look into thousands of people's faces, trying to see what they needed. And I realized that people wanted to be surprised. They wanted to feel that were experiencing a moment that was magic and strange, that they could drop whatever bullshit they were thinking of. Beyond that, everyone seemed to want something different. I had people write some very emotional notes, and there was one woman from Providence—a very normal, working woman in her late thirties—who told me that she'd been on the way to kill herself, and I helped change her mind. Just shows how the smallest things can affect people in the right ways."

As a band, the Dresden Dolls came in through the back door: instead of playing rock clubs, they booked themselves into funkier spaces like the Zeitgeist Gallery, an exhibition and performance space in Inman Square, and Jacques Underground, a transvestite-friendly spot in a dark section of the Theater District. When that didn't work, Palmer threw private parties, performance happenings in their apartment. Thus, the band had an underground following before many rock insiders had heard of them. The goth kids loved them too, even though the Dolls had a nontragic sense of humor. "If you listen to our lyrics, we're not all that morose," Palmer says. "But I understand those teen years where it's all romanticized—'I am obsessed by death and big questions and pain.' Every kid comes up against that, and they may align us with what they want their soundtrack to be."

Bucking another local rock taboo, they also demonstrated a good amount of business sense, running their own operation for the first few years. "Amanda got a reputation for being very business-minded and sort of ruthless," Viglione points out. "People were a little shocked by that, and they perceived the band as having this cutthroat element." She counters:

That's because we never went out for fun. Instead of sitting around at [the hip Allston hangout] the Model Cafe, I was at the computer looking for like-minded bands. We really brought the audience that went to galleries and house parties into the clubs. And really, I knew so little about the scene that I didn't realize Aerosmith was a Boston band until I hit my mid-twenties. From my perspective, we weren't embraced by the rock scene at all. I used to read about bands coming up and thinking there was all this camaraderie around. When we were hanging out in clubs we just felt different. But I was egotistical enough to assume that what we do was interesting enough to find an audience.

Even after they won WBCN's Rumble in 2003, their relation to Boston was still a little uneasy. "I had a pretty sad period for six months after that," Palmer says. "I felt that people actively didn't want to like us. Maybe we just flew in the face of what they expected to be successful."

That too has passed, however. By 2006 the Dresden Dolls had re-leased two albums and a live DVD, opened a high-profile tour for Nine Inch Nails, and been greeted backstage by David Bowie—one of the few experiences that caused Palmer to be starstruck. Palmer also had something of a flamboyant rock-star period, in which she caught two male rock heartthrobs by surprise. First she ran onstage naked at a *Boston Phoenix*–sponsored show at Avalon and kissed the Kaiser Chiefs' singer, Ricky Wilson. She repeated the stunt at the Glastonbury Festival in England, this time with Conor Oberst, leader of Bright Eyes, as her quarry. Neither singer seemed to mind a bit, though the bouncers at the Glastonbury show were less than pleased. "I learned it was okay to have fun," she says. "Really, we were playing these festivals where it was sup-posed to be crazy and wild, and nothing like that was going on. It made me feel the way I felt in college—wildly disappointed. I had to go and stir some shit up."

Indeed, what the Dresden Dolls really want is for creative misfits in other cities to take the hint and get out there. After all, they figure, the Berlin cabaret movement—and punk rock, for that matter—happened during times of political conservatism and social repression; draw your own conclusions about how that relates to Boston in 2007. "You can't escape the fact that there's a war going on and people are dying; and that's symbolic of how youth culture views itself as completely powerless," Palmer says. "You don't need to be explicitly political, but there's an audience for someone who wants to fly a flag for pure, impulsive expression. If that means writing a show tune, you do it. If that means punk rock, do that. I saw that again when we toured with Nine Inch Nails. Every so often they'd get someone yelling, 'You Suck!' at them. And the response would be something like, 'Well, maybe I do suck. But you have faith in yourself and do what you fuckin' do.'"

"If you really look at us, we're a hippie band," Viglione adds. "We're not trying to change the world, just to show people there's an alternative. The hippies were saying that war sucks, poverty sucks, take care of each other, and love your brother. We're not much different from a band in 1969."

A few weeks after our interview, the Dresden Dolls took over the Orpheum Theater to mark the release of their second album. And on this night, they transformed the upscale showcase venue into their own idea of a spectacle. Outside on Hamilton Place—where one usually runs into ticket scalpers, radio promo people, and the occasional guy giving out Jesus pamphlets—they'd instead brought in a crew of fortune tellers and accordion players. Inside, in the theater lobby, there were so many exotically dressed types that it was hard to tell the band's associates from their fans. Instead of the usual bouncers in every corner, there were human "statues" draped across the staircases. The Dresdens played a set that rocked hard and cathartically, but they also had a sword swallower on hand to show his skills before introducing them and a chorus of adolescent girls to back them on the part-mocking, part-serious feel-good anthem "Sing." Boston rock was alive and weird.

Boston Today: A Week in the Life

A random Wednesday night in Boston and Cambridge, fall 2006: Dennis Brennan is holding court at the Lizard Lounge, a dimly lit underground room outside Harvard Square. He's known as a first-division pop songwriter, but on this night Brennan's doing enough deep soul to summon the ghosts of Club 47 from decades past. Sitting in the corner is a local hero, Peter Wolf, who can't stay offstage much longer; during the second set Wolf grabs the mike, takes to the floor, and does his best dance moves while Brennan blows harmonica. The spot is suddenly looking like roadhouse heaven.

The Middle East a few nights later: onstage is Fluttr Effect, a

Father and son local heroes: Jake Brennan
and Dennis Brennan. (Photo: Jon Strymish)

Boston band unlike any that's come before. Instead of bass guitar and organ, there's one exotic woman playing cello and another on electric marimba; the sound gently undulates for a while, before the guitar and drums crash in and all hell breaks loose. Also undulating is the singer, who's working both her vocal range and look (dark clothes, purple hair) for all they're worth. It's a lovely sound, one full of muscle and intrigue.

Considerably less elegant is Darkbuster, a local favorite that played the same room the previous weekend. Lenny Lashley—a singer who once drank a dozen bacon martinis in Las Vegas and came home to brag about it—is leading punk rock's version of a campfire sing-along. It's the same kind of camaraderie that the Geils Band, Mighty Mighty Bosstones, and Dropkick Murphys offered in decades past. And when you hear a song like "Grandma Was a Nazi" or "Balls the Size of Cantaloupes," singing along would be the proper response. Updating the Bosstones' tradition of the annual "Hometown Throwdown," Darkbuster now puts on an annual weeklong event dubbed the "Hometown Throwup."

A few nights later, the Charms are playing at Axis on Lansdowne Street. The sound is classic, wired-up Boston garage rock, but now it's going nationwide: Little Steven Van Zandt, a garage-rock booster better known as Bruce Springsteen's guitarist, has taken them on a national tour (with the reunited New York Dolls) to show what his idea of rock and roll is all about. The singer Ellie Vee knows and loves her Lyres and KISS records; but those bands never looked as good in stockings. "You

Vessela Stoyanova, Valerie Thompson, and Kara Trott of Fluttr Effect.
(Photo: Roy Rubinstein)

Ellie Vee of the Charms onstage.
(Photo: Roy Rubinstein)

think I'm deranged and I am, I am!" she sings, fixing the crowd with a look that's both "come hither" and "don't get too close." It's no wonder that one of Little Steven's associates, Andrew Loog Oldham, has called her the modern Ann-Margaret—and since Oldham used to manage the Rolling Stones, that would carry some weight.

Also happening that fall: another local favorite, the Rudds, headlines at T.T. the Bear's Place. Their front man, John Powhida, has the trashy flash that harks back to Andy Paley and Steven Tyler, but tonight it's different. Since it's Halloween, they're playing a full set of seventies and eighties hits by Hall & Oates, an act more people love than are willing to admit. Is this the future? We can't say. Does it sound great? For sure.

The point isn't that all these bands are around, but that they all played in a random two-week period during a relatively dead time of year. So when you hear someone lamenting that the scene isn't what it used to be—and I can promise that if you spend any time in Boston, you will hear it—it's best not to take it as gospel.

That's not to say things haven't changed; there is indeed less local music on commercial radio and it's easier in any neighborhood to find ten Dunkin' Donuts franchises

John Powhida and Andrea Gillis of the Rudds play the Central Square World's Fair. (Photo: Roy Rubinstein)

than one rock club. But there's still enough here to draw a new crop of musicians every year. "Where I'm from, the idea of getting two hundred people to see your band is pretty much unheard of," notes Brett Rosenberg, who moved here from Albany and stayed a decade before moving to Nashville in April 2007. A crafty and sharp-eyed songwriter, he played guitar in the Rudds and led his own combo, the Brett Rosenberg Problem. "I remember going to O'Brien's in Allston after I moved here. The band before us had a hot blonde with a red dress. Everyone was drinking beers. The Rolling Stones were on the jukebox. My friend Geoff asked me to move his guitar, so I get onstage and everyone's going, 'Woo-hoo!' just because they thought I was in the band. It just seemed like the right place to be."

Indeed, Boston seems to have entered a strange time warp where all the eras are coexisting. At least two-thirds of the musicians in this book—going as far back as the G-Clefs and the Sophomores—performed locally during 2006. The original Remains regrouped a good thirty years after Barry Tashian swore off rock and roll. Aerosmith is on tour again; the Cars had a partial reunion; the Pixies are talking about an album. So are Moving Targets, who regrouped in 2007. Mission of Burma and the Neighborhoods are two of Boston's flagship bands—

again. The nineties favorites Gravel Pit have morphed into the Gentlemen, embodying the local tradition of out-for-kicks rock and roll. (The
Gentlemen's singer, Mike Gent, has another band, the upstate New
York favorites the Figgs, that now plays here so often its been claimed
as a local group.) Willie Alexander, the Real Kids, Lyres, Gang Green,
Classic Ruins, and Unnatural Axe never really went away; nor did the
likes of Asa Brebner, JJ Rassler (whose latest band, the Downbeat 5, is
one of his most popular), Rick Berlin, and Robin Lane. A terrific band
called the Incredible Casuals has played every summer Sunday at the
Beachcomber in Wellfleet for twenty-five years. And the surviving
Morphine members continue to record and play as the much-liked
Twinemen.

 "Hey, we're musicians," says Alexander. "I always looked up to the
jazz guys who kept playing when they got older. Okay, we're older.
And if you lived, you're lucky to keep going." Indeed, the idea of band
reunions no longer seems as shameful as it once did. At a recent reunion show by an out-of-town band, the Prime Movers' guitarist Dick
Tate grabbed me and noted, "Man, it's so sad to see these guys recap-
ture their lost youth." Then he broke into a grin. "So will we see you at
our reunion next week?"

 Central Square still being
such a hot spot, much of the
scene has at least temporarily
moved to the Cambridge side
of the river. Where once there
were "Rat bands," now there
are "Abbey bands"—an array
of rough and garage-ready
bands that cluster around the
Abbey Lounge, an Inman
Square spot that is the latest in
a noble tradition of funky
dives. For those who love their
music raw and catchy, the
bands that frequent this club
(also playing often at T.T. the
Bear's Place and the Middle
East) are the liveliest crew to

Brett Rosenberg onstage.
(Photo: Roy Rubinstein)

Muck & the Mires live in Central Square. (Photo: Roy Rubinstein)

come along in years. Indeed, three decades from now, somebody will likely be getting all warm and fuzzy about the days when you could see the Konks, the Dents, Andrea Gillis, Muck & the Mires, the Downbeat 5, the Coffin Lids, Bang Camaro, Ad Frank, Dirty Ticket, the World's Greatest Sinners, Hooray for Earth, Temper, the Tampoffs, Red Invasion, and the Pug Uglies on a regular basis. Included on that list is everything from sweet pop to scruffy punk to garage rock and soul; I'd recommend seeing them all and discovering who's who.

The next band to make a national breakthrough is anyone's guess. The cute young Click Five had some success in 2005 crossing a Beatles-derived sound with a New Kids on the Block image, and Aberdeen City worked with the same record producer who helmed some of U2's early records. Still more promising is the fact that Humanwine—a surreal circus of a band, with a haunted cabaret sound—now has a major-label deal. Whatever the Puritans saw coming, Holly Brewer—a small, intense singer with a deep voice and copious facial tattoos—surely wasn't it.

What's coming next is more next big things and grizzled vets, artsy types and punks, out-of-nowhere hits and spectacular fizzles—all part of the glorious noise that is the sound of our town. As five Roxbury gentlemen once summed it all up, "Ding! Dong! Ding! Dong! Ka-ding dong, ding dong ding!"

Acknowledgments and Sources

Thanks to Webster Bull for believing in this and to Jon Strymish for kicking it along. To Jill Christiansen, Ann Twombly, and Ron Decker for sharp eyes and expertise. To JJ Rassler, Asa Brebner, and Willie Alexander for being the first to share recollections and to encourage this project. To Clea Simon, a longtime reader and friend. To Perry Adler and Roy Rubinstein for dragging me to shows. To the editors who've published me over the years, especially Jon Garelick, Larry Katz, Matt Ashare, Ken Richardson, Steve Morse, Joel Brown, Ted Drozdowski, Tristram Lozaw, and Greg Reibman. To the local experts who helped me track down interviews, notably Kevin Patey, Jack Warner, T. Max, Johnny Angel, John Bonelli, David Bieber, Erik Lindgren, Paul Lovell, Ed Valauskas, and Gerry Beaudoin. To Oedipus, Amanda Palmer and Brian Viglione, Kristin Hersh and Billy O'-Connell, and Elizabeth Parsons for encouragement when I needed it. To Kay Hanley for immortalizing me in song, Robyn Hitchcock for the dedications, and Dan Zanes for lending me his song title. To Steve Wynn and Pat DiNizio for their help last time around. To Brad Delp, whose generosity was a help to this book and an inspiration to the scene. And to all my Boston rock-and-roll heroes, without whom I would have had to make this whole thing up.

J. Anthony Lukas's *Common Ground: A Turbulent Decade in the Lives of Three American Families* (Vintage, 1986) was my primary source for information on James Brown's Boston Garden concert. Fred Goodman's *The Mansion on the Hill: Dylan, Young, Geffen, Springsteen, and the Head-on Collision of Rock and Commerce* (Vintage, 1998) provided background on Don Law, Ray Riepen, and WBCN, as did David Bieber's *Boston Magazine* article "Rock Solid Radio" (June 1970). Various names, dates, and details were verified on the Web sites New England Music Scrapbook (www.geocities.com/nemsbook/home.htm), www.allmusic.com, and www.dirtywater.com. Steve Trussel's Web site (www.trussel.com) is the definitive archive of articles on the life of Mel Lyman. The *Harvard Crimson*'s July 9, 1963, article on Timothy Leary is archived at www.thecrimson.com/article.aspx?ref=253824. Further background on the Harvard antiwar protests was found at www.bbc.co.uk/dna/h2g2/A715042.

I also used my collection of back issues of the *Boston Phoenix,* the *Noise, Boston Groupie News, Sweet Potato,* and *The Beat* to refresh my memory and rekindle my enthusiasm.

Index